# JayBangs

How Jay Stein, MCA, & Universal
Invented the Modern Theme Park
and Beat Disney at Its Own Game

## Sam Gennawey

**Theme Park Press**
www.ThemeParkPress.com

© 2016 Sam Gennawey

No part of this publication may be reproduced, distributed, or transmitted in any form or by any means, including photocopying, recording, or other electronic or mechanical methods, without the prior written permission of the publisher, except for brief quotations embodied in critical reviews and certain other noncommercial uses permitted by copyright law.

Although every precaution has been taken to verify the accuracy of the information contained herein, no responsibility is assumed for any errors or omissions, and no liability is assumed for damages that may result from the use of this information.

Theme Park Press is not associated with Universal Parks & Resorts.

The views expressed in this book are those of the author and do not necessarily reflect the views of Theme Park Press.

Theme Park Press publishes its books in a variety of print and electronic formats. Some content that appears in one format may not appear in another.

Editors: Leslie Haber & Bob McLain
Layout: Artisanal Text

ISBN 978-1-68390-025-2
Printed in the United States of America

**Theme Park Press | www.ThemeParkPress.com**
Address queries to bob@themeparkpress.com

# Contents

*Foreword* v
*Introduction* ix

   1   Becoming an MCA Man   1
   2   Universal Studios Tour   15
   3   The National Parks   49
   4   On the Hunt   67
   5   Universal Studios Florida: Take One   77
   6   Universal Studios Florida: Take Two   97
   7   Universal Studios Hollywood   171
   8   Cartoon World   181
   9   That's a Wrap   191

*Epilogue* 203
*Appendix* 207
*Acknowledgments* 211
*About the Author* 213
*More Books from Theme Park Press* 215

# Foreword

I received my undergraduate degree from MCA, Jay Stein in particular; my post graduate from Mickey Rudin, a prominent entertainment lawyer; and an advanced degree from Jerry Weintraub. A finer education is unimaginable.

But for Jay Stein and MCA, both Mickey and the presidency of Jerry's Management III and Concerts West and all that followed representing Frank Sinatra, Gregory Peck, Norman Lear, Groucho Marx, the Cary Grant estate, and others, and my running my own entrepreneurial business, would have been impossible. You see, Jay, besides his mentoring, arranged (after my graduation from UCLA and working four years for the Universal Studio Tour) for MCA to pay the tuition for me to go to Georgetown Law School in return for my agreeing to come back to MCA for three years after graduating. It is a rare privilege to be a part of introducing the public to this remarkable man.

In 1965, Mike Ovitz and I were roommates in college; we learned from Herb Steinberg that Universal Studios was hiring college students for summer jobs giving tours of the studio.

Tickets for the tour were $2.50. The tour started from a makeshift facility at the front lot. Cliff Walker was the operations manager and the face of the tour, as far as we were concerned. Cliff lived and breathed outdoor recreation and had his finger on the pulse of managing and understanding young adults. Jules Stein, Lew Wasserman, and Al Dorskind were seen at the tour from time to time, but the operation was an annoyance to the studio. We were forbidden from identifying Cary Grant if we observed him on the lot or from going to an actual filming location.

In time, we were told of plans to expand the tour and open the upper lot, and eventually heard about this "relative" of Jules Stein who was going to be involved with the Tour. This is my first recollection of the name Jay Stein; I guess that was 1967. The upper lot opened, with the stunt show, the make-up show, the Tower of London set, souvenir shops, and food service—nice but certainly not Disney standards.

Guests parked in the new upper lot parking and were directed to kiosks to purchase their tickets before entering the lobby area to board the tram. The tour was a success and attracting near capacity attendance. By this time I was a tour guide foreman who would often double on the turnstile taking tickets. Who was the man in the suit that stood for hours in the lobby just observing and observing what was happening and once in a while whispering in Cliff Walker's ear? This was my first visual introduction to Jay Stein, the new "tower" person responsible for the tour. (The whispering soon stopped). Jay was laser focused and you could practically see the gears of his mind working. While Cliff and Barry Upson were very engaging with all of the employees, Jay followed a careful chain of command, at least at first. You could feel Cliff musing how this "suit" from the tower was going to contribute to his outdoor entertainment domain.

The most important part of the "ticket-taking" job description became the hourly count. Jay, from his new perch in the tower, appeared to be myopically fixated on the count. What the hell difference did it make if the count was one thousand an hour or six hundred—business was good, and people still had to wait too long in line after they passed the turnstile (especially during the summer months). At that time I was not privy to Jay's equal fixation with every other aspect of the tour, its minuet of numbers and margins. Lesson: numbers are critical. Untold additional business gems are revealed in Sam Gennawey's narrative of the MCA/Stein take-no-prisoners winning business acumen.

Jay's "suit/tower style" morphed, somewhat, after he had absorbed all of the operational details of the tour. He would on occasion drop in after the operating day was over to Cliff's office where Cliff and the department heads would participate in a nightly review of the day's and upcoming events with a cocktail, or maybe two. In hindsight, I think it was these off-the-clock but on-the-record gatherings that created the foundation of loyalty and camaraderie with Jay, even when he could be as demanding and speak at decibel levels above OSHA standards.

I became an assistant operations manager of the tour while attending UCLA. The tour was open on the weekend and UCLA was on the quarter system, so I could go to school Tuesday and Thursday and work full-time at the studio the rest of the week and weekends. Jay, Dorskind, and sometimes Wasserman would come up to the tour on weekends and I developed somewhat of a relationship with each of them, in particular, Jay.

At the time I was graduating from UCLA (1969), MCA had just started Landmark Services in Washington, D.C. So not only was MCA going to pay for my law school, but Jay arranged with Tom Mack (a tour guide when I first started and another recipient of Jay's stewardship, now running the operation in Washington) for me to work at Landmark on the weekends.

Upon graduating law school, Jay placed me in an office on the 14$^{th}$ floor around the corner from his palatial office and next to Taft Schreiber's. While I loved the law, Jay had instilled in me a passion for business.

It was now that my relationship with Jay became even closer and that I studied and observed, first hand, his amazing executive prowess. The tour, while very successful, was still in its adolescence. While I had some line responsibility, I attended almost all of Jay's meetings. Jay was a circling lion looking for new opportunities and ways to constantly improve the tour. Most importantly, he was seeking to continually introduce new elements that he could promote and advertise. I was witness to Jay's merciless grilling of the department heads on the numbers and the assumptions. *Why didn't that fucking thing work?* Under no circumstances was Jay going to get positioned with Wasserman or Sheinberg in not being able to answer any question or have proposed or implemented a solution before the question was asked.

Jay's timelines were as demanding as his questioning. There was no moderation to his priorities of items; everything, everything was due yesterday. I recall that Jay's first wife had to have the water running in the bathroom at the time he got home so that he would not have to wait for the water to get hot to wash his hands. (You better not be playing in a slow foursome in front of Jay.)

I worked closely with Jay on the Amphitheatre, Yosemite, the counter-culture plans for the Real Estate, a Tivoli Garden concept for the upper lot, exploring an acquisition of Mammoth, Squaw Valley, developing a theme restaurant based upon the Knights of the Round Table, and many of the other early projects that Sam artfully explores. Lesson: one-of-a-kind attractions with exclusivity and significant barriers to entry will serve you well.

Sam reveals the never-before-known depths of Jay's competitive spirit in making sure the Amphitheatre was a success and that the Greek was going to get the second choice acts for their summer season.

It was during the first year of the Amphitheatre that Jay and I first met Jerry Weintraub, John Denver's manager. Jerry became a friend of Jay's and was a participant in a weekly tennis game at Jules Stein's house in Beverly Hills. We had to sweep the court before we could play, until Jerry got a house with his own court. Sam goes behind-the-scenes of the relationship between Jerry and Jay. Jay was one of the last people to be with Jerry before his sudden death last year.

By 1975, I had worked at MCA for three years and Jerry asked me to come to work for him. I told Jerry that in leaving MCA I really would like to practice law. Jerry arranged an interview with Mickey Rudin, the attorney who represented Jerry and Frank Sinatra. One of my missions while working with Mickey, out of loyalty to MCA and Jay, was convincing Mickey and Frank that Frank should play the Amphitheatre. Frank eventually consented to an engagement and set the Amphitheatre's attendance record.

I was there at the beginning; I was there when Dan Slusser was hired; Tom Williams, Mark and Ron Bension, Terry Winnick, Tony Sauber, but

I never saw Florida, I never saw the development of the multi-million dollar thrill rides. I never saw Jay's realization of his dreams, the result of Jay's magic in engaging the full potential of a cadre of committed ordinary individuals achieving extraordinary results. Sam Gennawey puts you smack in the middle of this amazing journey.

*JayBangs* is the answer to every company that thinks they need MBAs from Ivy League schools, consultants, and market testing. They need a Jay Stein. There is a complete business/show business education to be found in Sam's story of Jay Stein and in Jerry Weintraub's autobiography. Ironically, both of them credit Lew Wasserman.

Robert A. Finkelstein

*Robert A. Finkelstein has known Jay Stein for more than 48 years. He was in the first tour guide class along with Mike Ovitz, Tom Mack, and Jay's second wife, Susan. Finkelstein helped opened Landmark Services and was a key executive in the early years of operating in Yosemite. He is co-chairman of Frank Sinatra Enterprises and the attorney who represents the Frank Sinatra Estate.*

# Introduction

*I am 78 years old, Sid is 80+, Lew is dead, Jules is dead, Drabinsky is in jail, Katzenberg and Spielberg probably don't want to be interviewed; Eisner will probably say I'm lying when he learns what I could show you. You be the judge. I'm determined to get history right. Would you like to interview me and examine my evidence as to what happened? Let me know.*

—Jay Stein

The plot for the Jay Stein story could have been ripped from the typewriter of a Hollywood screenwriter. All the elements are there. An ambitious guy starts out in the mailroom, works hard, claws his way up the ladder, overcomes obstacles and bloodthirsty enemies, to end up a mogul, and then completely revolutionizes an industry. Then he disappears at the top of his game. Years later, he comes back to set the record straight.

Unlike most Hollywood stories, the Jay Stein story is true. Jay was in charge of the Universal Studios theme parks for almost 30 years. He changed the nature of theme parks, including Disney's. Walt Disney may have invented the theme park, but Jay is the real "father" of the modern theme park.

Until Jay developed the Universal Studios tours, and ultimately the Universal parks, most second-tier theme parks were crummy affairs with names slapped on off-the-shelf rides. In Disney's case, there were cute, wholesome attractions, which at best were only mildly scary (in a child-friendly way), along with their versions of something out of real life (or an imagined real life that never actually existed). The Universal parks put visitors in situations that either did not exist in real life or made the experience seem scary or funny, with an adult edge to them; attractions with an attitude.

Jay accomplished it all despite tight budgets and deadlines, often less-than-enthusiastic superiors, and severe external opposition. He insisted on complete involvement (generally from a leadership role) in creation and design, in both the big picture and the smallest details, as well as in advertising and marketing, frequently even coming up with the basic premises of commercials. Jay demanded that his team collaborate, with the best ideas surviving the process. He achieved this through a sometimes cruel, impatient, demanding supervision of subordinates. His management style caused many to leave, but he got the rest to perform beyond their expectations.

*Jay, in his Montecito, California, home, working on this book.*

*Chapter 1*
# Becoming an MCA Man

## Fast Friends

You will not know where you will end up unless you start.

In 1958, Jay Stein was twenty-one, a junior at the University of California at Berkeley, and on his way toward a degree in political science. Considering his chosen path, he could look forward to life as a teacher or work in politics. At the time, neither of those alternatives seemed very appealing, and Jay did what many before him had done. He dropped out of school.

Life goes on, and he had to make a living. With no other ambitions burning in his belly, he enlisted in the California National Guard. He figured the six months of mandatory active duty would give him time to weigh his options. Once he was done, he could move on to the "next thing."

Just a few weeks after dropping out of college, he went off to basic training at Fort Ord, near Monterey Bay, in California.

Bunks were assigned by alphabet and Jay found himself sleeping on the lower bunk below Dennis (Denny) Shryack. Shryack was originally from Duluth, Minnesota, and joined the National Guard as a way to avoid the draft. As a member of the National Guard, both men were obligated for eight years of weekend meetings and two weeks of training every summer.

For Shryack, the arrangement was even better. He had a great job as the head of the mailroom at Revue Studios. Not only would Shryack avoid the draft, but the studio must rehire him after his initial training. He enjoyed his job and was anxious to get back to work. Jay loved hearing Shryack's stories about working in Hollywood. They became fast friends.

As basic training was nearing the end, Jay was still unsure what he wanted to do next. He was becoming increasingly anxious and distracted about his future. Shryack noticed that his friend was troubled and came up with a brilliant idea. Once Jay completed his training, he should apply for a job in the mailroom at the studio. Shryack told Jay he would be delivering mail to some of Hollywood's most influential people and exposed to every studio department. Maybe Jay could find something there that would get him excited.

Moreover, being in the right place at the right time and then being discovered was the Hollywood dream. That was Shryack's motivation. He wanted to be a scriptwriter. Jay was enthusiastic about this job opportunity, and when their active duty ended, Denny made good on his word. Jay began his career as a mail boy in October 1959.

Once he made it through the front door, he decided he would become the most energetic, helpful, and personable mail boy Hollywood had ever seen. Jay would volunteer for any task, and when he was done, Jay would ask what else he could do. He learned these values from his father who always preached that this was a clear path to success. Jay was an ambitious sponge.

## The Mailroom

The Music Corporation of America (MCA) was one of the most influential companies in the entertainment business. Dr. Jules Stein (a practicing ophthalmologist) started MCA in 1924, along with William R. Goodheart Jr. Stein invested $1,000 and began booking dance bands and singers into speakeasies and nightclubs on Chicago's South Side. The firm grossed more than $30,000 in its first year. Stein said he named his company the Music Corporation of America because "RCA [Radio Corporation of America] had started two years before, and I was impressed by the name. So I used MCA."

It was not long before Jules Stein dominated the music market and began to target Hollywood. In 1936, he hired Lew Wasserman, a 23-year-old Cleveland theater usher and former publicity director for a local nightclub. Within two years, Wasserman was promoted to vice president and became Stein's protégé. Stein would describe Wasserman as "the student who surpassed the teacher." Stein and Wasserman signed such luminaries as Henry Fonda, Greta Garbo, Bette Davis, Joan Crawford, Frank Sinatra, and Jack Benny.

Stein built MCA by creating a very distinct corporate culture. He believed that a talent agent was a businessman, not a cigar-chewing promoter. He tended to hire men who were willing to comply with his dicta and his clothing preferences: conservative dark suits, white shirts, and dark blue or gray ties. Lew Wasserman's motto became, "Dress British, Think Yiddish." The first time Jay's father saw Jay's closet he commented that he could have worked in a funeral parlor.

Stein also built a business based on the numbers and the deal. Facts mattered. During the Great Depression, when he was trying to collect money from the owners of the speakeasies where his artists played, Stein would routinely count the soiled napkins. The napkins told him the exact per capita of the venue, thereby giving him an edge in negotiations. This obsessive attention to detail was also a part of the MCA way.

MCA started Revue Productions in 1943 to broadcast radio productions to the troops overseas during the war. While primarily the largest talent agency in the world, it also owned a television production company called Revue Studios. During the 1950s, Revue was responsible for producing and distributing many television classics including *Leave it to Beaver, McHale's Navy, Alfred Hitchcock Presents, General Electric Theater*, and many others.

Jay loved every minute working in the mailroom. Everything that Shryack had told him back in the barracks was dead on. He was meeting famous and influential people, working in a high-stress, high-reward environment, and learning valuable business lessons that would serve him for the rest of his life. Jay had found his calling. He knew this is where careers begin.

He got to know everybody at the studio and made it a point to learn how each one contributed to the success of the place. As he gained seniority, it was not long before he became anxious to move up the corporate ladder. His strategy was to continue to work better, faster, and always ask for more. This approach is how Jay thought he would be noticed.

What Jay did not realize was he was being noticed for the wrong reason. MCA had been moving their key executives from their Beverly Hills office, an elegant building that looked like a European estate and known as the Winter Palace, to the Universal lot. One day, about a week before Christmas, a smartly dressed woman walked into the mailroom and introduced herself as Ruth Cogan. She said she worked for MCA, and this was her first visit to the studio. She was carrying the executives' bonus checks, and she needed a mail boy to direct her to the proper offices. Jay immediately volunteered to assist.

The entertainment giant was not yet a public company and most of the key executives, mostly agents, were paid a mere $100 per week. However, at Christmas time Cogan would deliver their profit-sharing checks based on how well the company was doing. Although Jay had no direct knowledge, he had heard that depending on how well the individual executive performed, the bonus checks were impressively large.

Jay grabbed a golf cart, and they started out on their mission. Cogan asked his name, and when he said Jay Stein, she suddenly shook his hand vigorously while looking directly into his eyes. She had just the hint of a smile on her lips. Jay was surprised and a bit confused.

When they arrived at the first office, all the secretaries recognized Cogan. She announced to the group, "I'd like to introduce Jay Stein, who was kind enough to direct me to your office." The secretaries' faces looked shocked. They all recognized the young man as he had been delivering their mail but when Cogan said his name their jaws dropped. This scenario was repeated in every office they visited. Jay had no clue as to why he kept getting this shocked reaction. When they finished delivering the checks, Cogan thanked Jay and went on her way.

Later that day, on his next mail run, one of the secretaries he just visited asked if he was related to Dr. Jules Stein, founder and chairman of MCA. Jay said no, explaining that he had never met the man or even seen him. Then she asked if he knew who Ruth Cogan was or what she did. Again, Jay said no, only having met her a couple of hours earlier. That was when Jay learned that Cogan was Jules Stein's sister. He also learned that nepotism was not permitted at MCA and to the best of his knowledge, Cogan was the only exception.

One reason she may have been the exception was her incredible stewardship of the retirement fund. Along with MCA comptroller Hal Haas, year in and year out she provided steady returns based on the low-risk investment parameters prescribed by Stein and Wasserman. Wasserman often bragged about the performance of this critical retirement component. He was very proud of this MCA benefit, and always stressed its importance at the management meetings.

From that day forward there was always doubt. People were not sure, and the Ruth Cogan story spread like wildfire almost overnight. Employees continued to believe that Jay and Dr. Stein were somehow related. In fact, Jay would not meet Dr. Stein until six years later. Jay continued to deny the relationship but even after working for the company for 35 years, some people continued to believe he was related to the boss.

Adding to the mystery, years later while he was the head of the Recreation Division, Jay would join Dr. Stein for lunch once a month at his table in the commissary. Jay's bosses, Lew Wasserman and Sidney Sheinberg, had their tables nearby. Within the hallways at MCA, the pecking order of who sat with whom was a major topic of discussion. Jay having exclusive access to their boss made Wasserman and Sheinberg suspicious at first. Jay was the only division president to sit with Dr. Stein regularly. Dr. Stein liked Jay. After the first few lunches, they would press their young executive to reveal the contents of their discussion. "Nothing," Jay replied. Dr. Stein had a passing interest in the Recreation Division, and he used the opportunity to stay connected to that part of the business.

At one of these lunches, Dr. Stein, who was reputed to be a very shrewd investor, gave Jay some sage financial advice. Jay asked what criteria Dr. Stein used when investing in the stock market. Dr. Stein said he was a long time believer in the Dow Theory but offered this supplemental counsel with a trace of a smirk: "Buy low and sell high."

Another new guy at MCA was Sidney Sheinberg. In 1959, while waiting for the results of his California bar examination, Sheinberg joined the legal department of Revue Studios. Sheinberg was a tall, lanky, liberal Texan, caustic and immodest. He was complicated, legally brilliant, and pontifical. Jay was asked to deliver something to Sheinberg, but he had never heard of nor met the man. He located Sheinberg's tiny office in a bungalow that sat nestled among the oak and pine trees on the old front lot.

When Jay entered the room, he found Sheinberg deeply engrossed in something he was reading. Jay interrupted him to confirm if he was, in fact, Sidney Sheinberg. "Yes," Sheinberg barked and started to yell at the messenger for interrupting. Sheinberg's arrogance would be a defining feature in Jay's eyes. As he quickly exited the room, Jay realized he had found a kindred spirit. Sheinberg would be credited for discovering director Steven Spielberg and in June 1973, he became president and CEO of MCA.

## Good Timing

Everything was looking up for Jay until the Writers Guild of America strike of 1960. The strike began on January 16 and lasted twenty weeks and six days. It was the second longest writers' strike in history. At the studio, many employees were laid off. Being the low man in the mailroom, Jay was one of the first to be out of a job. Now what? He was unemployed and could not make his rent or car payments. He had no idea how long this strike was going to last. Shryack warned him that it was going to be a long one.

At this point, Jay was ready to take any job when a high school friend said that he could come work for him in his schmatteh (rags) business. The job entailed riding with a truck driver to all the clothing manufacturers in downtown Los Angeles, picking and sweeping the clothing remnants off the floor and placing them into different piles such as wool or cashmere. Then he had to tie up the piles into large burlap sheets, weigh them, and hand the factory worker a receipt. He was told not to show any strain when holding the scale and confirming the actual weight. The scale may have indicated 30 pounds, but Jay knew the rags weighed much more, as some bags were so heavy he felt he was going to get a hernia. He hated the job, but Jay was paid in cash and was able to provide for himself.

Scriptwriting was another thing Jay tried his hand at while the strike continued. He and Shryack collaborated and wrote and sold two episodes of *M-Squad,* starring Lee Marvin. They had to use fake names to conceal their identity in case they wanted to join the Writers Guild when the strike was settled. Shryack went on to become a successful writer while Jay learned he did not possess the skills necessary to become one himself. His future would lie elsewhere.

Then, consistent with a Hollywood script, Jay learned that luck and timing could affect one's life and one's dreams. The guy that drove the rags truck was a drunk and undependable. One day he showed up an hour late.

Had he been on time, Jay's life would have gone in a far different direction. While Jay was waiting on the driver, Shryack called. The strike had been settled, and if Jay could get to the mailroom immediately, he could get his job back. Shryack had been trying to call the other guys with more seniority, but Jay was the first one to answer the phone. He was able to jump the line. As it turned out, Shryack was only able to rehire four out of the five guys who worked there before the strike. Jay would not have made the cut if he had not acted so quickly.

## Cary Grant and Alfred Hitchcock

Back at his studio job one day, Jay was told to pick up "rush" mail from Cary Grant's office and deliver it to him on a stage where they were shooting *Father Goose* with Leslie Caron. Grant was in a small trailer dressing room on the stage, and his assistant asked, "Are you Jay Stein?" Jay said he was. She instructed him to go right in as Mr. Grant was expecting him.

At first, Jay found this puzzling. When he entered the trailer, there was Grant, his back turned away from the door, resting on a couch. Grant was in his bare feet wearing tattered shorts, a t-shirt, and about a two-week growth of facial hair consistent with the beachcomber character he was portraying.

Without turning around, he said he was glad that Jay finally made it there but that he had not followed instructions. Grant put on reading glasses and began reading some legal document aloud. As he was going on, his back still facing Jay, he was revealing some very personal information. Jay started to feel uncomfortable, so he tried to interrupt the star and let him know that he was just the mail boy. Every time he tried to say, "Mr. Grant I'm the..." Grant would respond, "Just hold on; I'm not finished."

The actor continued reading the document and pointing out errors while Jay kept trying to interrupt. Finally, Grant turned around, and their eyes met. He got to his feet and said, "Who the hell are *you*?" When Jay told him, Grant put his arm around the young man's shoulder and laughed until he began to cough. "I was reading my will to you!" he said. "I thought you were my lawyer. You're the wrong Jay Stein!" He apologized for making Jay feel so uncomfortable and heartily shook his hand. The next day Grant sent Jay a case of wine with an apology note.

Twenty years later, Jay was promoting a Bee Gees concert at Dodger Stadium and was watching the show from owner Peter O'Malley's box, which was packed with VIPs. Jay spotted Grant and went up to him. The actor immediately recognized him and told Jay that he had so much fun telling his Jay Stein story over the years. Jay responded that he had also told that story many times and that it was an encounter he would never forget either.

On another occasion, Jay got a call to rush over to Alfred Hitchcock's bungalow, pick up a package, and to personally hand it to him on Stage 16 where he was filming *Psycho*. At the door was a guard and signs indicating a closed set. No admittance. Jay tried to explain that Mr. Hitchcock was expecting the package, but the guard would have none of it. He told Jay to wait. The guard disappeared behind the soundstage door and then a few minutes later reappeared with instructions that Jay could enter the soundstage but had to be silent and hand the package to Mr. Hitchcock's secretary who would be standing next to the director.

The soundstage was dark. Jay could barely make out the figure of Mr. Hitchcock, seated in a director's chair with his back to the door. As Jay got closer, he began to notice that there were none of the usual stagehands nor the usual cast and crew. The soundstage was virtually empty. The only occupants were Hitchcock, his secretary, and three or four lighting and camera people. In front of the director was a drop-dead gorgeous blonde woman standing in a shower stark naked receiving direction. Now Jay understood why this was a closed set.

Frightened he might interrupt such an intimate moment, he stood there frozen like a deer in the headlights. He remained motionless as the naked model standing in for Janet Leigh began the famous shower scene. For some inexplicable reason, he looked up and there, to his astonishment, he saw every inch of scaffolding crammed with what must have been 100 men—the missing crew! Jay learned later that they were filming the international version of *Psycho* and nudity was permitted. In 1960 American cinema, bare breasts were not acceptable.

Over the years, Jay got to know Alfred Hitchcock. Several times a year Lew Wasserman invited the MCA Group presidents to have lunch in the executive dining room and report on their divisions. Hitchcock owned a lot of MCA stock and once sat next to Jay, who told Hitchcock his mailroom story. Hitchcock innocently smiled and said in his distinctive voice, "Nice breasts."

## Joe Minneci

It did not take long before Jay moved up the corporate ladder. Within six months of returning to the MCA mailroom, he landed a job working for Joe Minneci. Minneci's unique skill was reading a script and costing out to the penny what it would take to build the sets. He was the best in the business and a significant player in the penny-pinching MCA ethos. Minneci had a secret formula that he would not share. He ran his operation out of four tiny offices in a bungalow near the old commissary.

Minneci had three guys working for him. When Jay joined the team, he started his day at 5:30 a.m. to check in the extras. The extras did not go through the main gate where Scotty, the legendary guard of Universal, worked. The extras came through a different entrance and waited in a long hallway. Jay sat at one end of the hall and would pass out hundreds of timecards and direct each extra to makeup, wardrobe, hairdressing, or directly to the back lot or a soundstage.

Jay would then take hundreds of workers' time cards from the previous day and by using an average rate of pay for each category of worker (carpenters, grips, painters, prop men, greens men, electricians, Teamsters, etc.) he could calculate the approximate cost of set construction for that day.

This daily tally gave Minneci enough data to keep set construction costs close to his budgeted amounts, with perhaps some occasional juggling of costs between shows when necessary to stay on budget.

The work would usually last until 9:00 a.m. Jay's next duty was doing everything that a unit production manager or an assistant director did not want to do. MCA's Revue Studios was by far the busiest in Hollywood, at its peak producing 19 hours of prime time television each week. A unit production manager was responsible for overseeing a show's budget, scheduling, below-the-line personnel, and equipment requirements. Many of the unit production managers handled multiple shows.

Jay had to make sure all their requirements such as camera, sound, lighting, transportation, security, meals, "honey wagons," generators, and personnel were met. He was responsible for getting the wagons and period cars as well as any dogs, cats, birds, horses, or exotic animals that were needed. The unit production managers trusted him to make sure their requirements were always properly completed.

One problem: it was a struggle to get time with the unit production managers and heads of production he was trying to serve. He had to verify that there were no production conflicts on the back-lot sets or soundstages. To do so, Jay needed to see the master production boards kept in the two senior production heads' offices. They used big corkboards with pins and different colored flags to track all of the elements necessary for production. It was critical to make sure that a production that was shooting, for example, on Western Street had no other show close enough to interfere.

Frequently, Jay could not gain access to these offices in the afternoon to create the next day's schedule. An extra could make a lot more money if they had a part that included speaking a few words or doing something on camera other than appearing as background. This practice was referred to in the trade as "a piece of business." Office access was blocked until the most attractive (or cooperative) female extras earned their upgraded parts. The production office was a hard-drinking place, and Jay usually could not get in until 8 or 9:00 p.m. Jay recalled that all but one unit production manager he had dealt with had died as a result of alcoholism or lung cancer.

Even with these challenges, Jay loved the job. He was learning how to board a script. Boarding a script is essentially creating the most efficient and economic sequence for filming. It projects the order in which scenes should be shot in the most cost-effective, labor-saving manner. It outlines when and what you shot on location, soundstage, and back lot. It provides for cast, crew, and equipment requirements for each shooting day, including inclement weather alternatives. Jay got his chance to schedule and estimate the cost of all the production elements of an episode of *Leave It to Beaver*.

Jay was gaining a reputation as a hard-working employee who always asked if he could do more. Hustle and attention to detail were paying off. He would often ask a unit production manager to show him what they were doing. He was on a trajectory to become a second assistant director, then a first assistant director, and finally a unit production manager. He could even become the head of production or possibly direct or produce. Anything seemed possible, even though he was only making a flat weekly salary of $90 and was working up to 80 hours a week. Moreover, he was fulfilling his National Guard obligations.

Jay also became responsible for maintaining the permanent star dressing rooms. One day, he could not help overhearing a telephone conversation between Minneci and Taft Schreiber. Schreiber started in 1926 as Jules Stein's messenger boy and rose to become a top executive in the company. Schreiber and Wasserman were rivals, watched each other carefully, and both were fiercely loyal to Jules Stein.

Schreiber told Minneci to move Ronald Reagan out of his permanent dressing room so that James Drury, star of *The Virginian*, could use it. A television show based on Owen Wister's novel *The Virginian* had been Schreiber's idea. Wasserman used to be Reagan's agent and made the deal with General Electric that made the actor a household name.

Minneci handed the task of telling Reagan to Jay. Reagan was being moved from a great dressing room to a dump. Jay suggested it was like going from the Waldorf Astoria to a Motel 6. It was going to be humiliating.

Reagan entered the dressing room only to find Jay. They shook hands and Jay delivered the bad news. Reagan was dumbfounded. He was still a television star and thought that this must be a joke. "Who told you to do this?" Jay replied that he did not know why the move was taking place, but he got the job since nobody else wanted to tell the longtime Universal star. Resigned, Reagan said he understood and did not blame Jay and would contact his agent. Jay found Reagan to be a perfect gentleman. As it turned out, Reagan's television career serving General Electric was ending and this was MCA's way of giving the actor a big hint. Reagan never came back.

Jay worked in a 10-foot by 10-foot windowless office. He got a call from Jerry and Michael, his two best friends from high school in New York. They were planning a visit to southern California, and they wanted to see the studio. Jay was embarrassed to show them his office as he had exaggerated the importance of his job. Before their arrival, Jay went to the main gate and asked Scotty (who knew Jay from his time in the mail room) to direct his friends to the commissary, thereby bypassing his office. His plan was to take them on a walking tour after lunch.

Apparently, when they arrived Scotty was on a break, and they were misdirected to Jules Stein's elegant bungalow office complex. When Jay's friends entered the room they were impressed with the opulence of the furnishings, the two smartly attired secretaries, and Jay's apparent quick rise to success.

They said they were here to see Mr. Stein and were told Mr. Stein was in a meeting, and there was nothing on his schedule showing their names. Michael responded, "That's okay, new guy is expecting us," and without hesitation, they both moved to the conference room doors and pushed them open before Jules' secretary Glenda could stop them. At a large conference table sat a surprised Dr. Stein, Lew Wasserman, Taft Schreiber, and every other high-ranking executive at MCA. For everyone, this was a shockingly terrifying and unforgettable moment. Jay's friends, recognizing they were in the wrong place, sheepishly exited while murmuring profuse apologies.

When they told Jay what happened, he was certain his career was over. He called Glenda to apologize as soon as his friends left and tried to explain how this unfortunate blunder occurred. Although she seemed sympathetic, Jay was still concerned about how Stein (or Wasserman) would react. He was expecting the worst. Although he lived in fear for several weeks expecting a layoff notice, he never heard another word about this unforgettable incident.

## Gordon Forbes

Jay liked working for Joe Minneci. Then one day he got the call to join Gordon Forbes' team. Forbes was the studio manager. He worked for Al Dorskind and was the liaison between production and facilities. It was a critical job. Dorskind was the landlord for Universal City, and the studio was only one tenant. All of the technical departments reported to Forbes.

Forbes was the brother of Malcolm and the uncle of Steve Forbes. The Forbes family was a wealthy, prominent household in New York and publishers of the financial magazine bearing their surname. However, Forbes was the black sheep of the family, and that is how he landed in Hollywood.

Every day Jay would join a group of unit managers for the mandatory three-martini lunch at Sorrentino's in Toluca Lake. He learned to empty his martini by taking a sip, not swallowing, and draining the contents into his water glass.

After lunch, the studio department heads would gather for a half hour to make sure the next day's productions were adequately staffed and equipped. They also made sure there were no conflicts between productions.

Frequently, Jay would find Forbes in his office taking a nap after lunch, and Jay jumped right in and quickly found himself running production meetings. Part of the job meant he had to be cognizant of the nascent Studio Tour and make sure that the trams would not get in the way. In Minneci's office, Jay was usually doing all sorts of tasks. For Forbes, it was much more of an administrative position. Jay was now making $200 a week and became central to the smooth flow of production at the world's largest television studio.

Once again, like the time he spent with Minneci, Jay's last name became an issue while working for Forbes. Around 1963, the eligible young bachelor was dating an outspoken young lady named Marsha with whom he was having a casual but intimate relationship. She called Jay at work, and somehow her request was misdirected to Jules Stein's office. To make matters worse, Stein somehow picked up the call before either of his secretaries did. Marsha, thinking it was Jay answering the phone, poured out a vitriolic tirade laced with profanity. She was angry and humiliated that he had not met her for dinner the previous night without even bothering to call.

When Jay called the next day, she was even angrier. "Don't play innocent with me. I told you yesterday what I was so upset about." A confused Jay asked, "What the hell are you talking about? We never spoke yesterday, and I have been trying to get you on the phone to apologize." Marsha was insistent that she called him at work and that he picked up the phone. All of a sudden, Jay was overcome with apprehension and was speechless. My God, she must have spoken directly with Jules! Now his career was over for sure.

When Jay went to see Glenda, Stein's secretary, to explain what happened, before he could open his mouth she said, "You got yourself into another mess. Dr. Stein told us about the call, and he was not pleased." Jay asked her if he should write an apology note. She said to wait and see if he says anything more about the call. He never did.

Years later, while Jay was the president and general manager of the Universal Studios Tour, he had parked his car in the Black Tower garage and met his boss Al Dorskind while walking toward the elevators. Standing there, also waiting for an elevator, was Dr. Stein and his wife, Doris. Jay could feel his body tense up.

Dorskind said good morning to Dr. Stein and Doris and then asked them if they had ever met the new tour president, Jay Stein. Dr. Stein gave Jay this penetrating stare with full eye contact, then said, "So you're the guy," with just the slightest touch of a smile on his lips. Mrs. Stein looked him up and down quizzically without saying anything. Jay shook his hand and said it was a great pleasure finally to meet him and his wife.

When they exited the elevator, Dorskind turned to Jay and asked, "What did Jules mean, 'So you're the guy?'" Jay replied he was late for a meeting, and he would tell him later; it was nothing important. Jay never did tell him. Jay felt like he had dodged a bullet and all his angst over the years was for naught.

After that, Jay and Dr. Stein had a cordial working relationship until Stein's death in 1981. Jay was an honorary pallbearer at the funeral.

Jay's first encounter with Lew Wasserman came in 1963 while working for Forbes. The partnership between Wasserman and his wife, Edie, was the stuff of Hollywood legend. For her 50$^{th}$ birthday, Wasserman made every effort to impress. The party was a big deal and remains to this day one of the most elaborate and expensive Jay had ever seen.

Wasserman had the largest soundstage on the lot, Stage 12, dressed to look like his hometown of Cleveland circa 1936. True to his nature, he made it clear that *he* wanted to be billed for all costs; not MCA. There were over 700 guests, and each of them considered themselves "A List."

The morning before the party, Wasserman walked into the soundstage unannounced. He began a detailed critique, which included many complimentary remarks along with his expectations. Most of Wasserman's comments were directed at Forbes, and everyone else was following him around, feverishly taking notes.

On an impulse, Wasserman asked Forbes if he had witnessed the balloon drop. When Forbes said he had not, Wasserman asked if he could see how it looked. Forbes looked over to Jay and asked, "Are we ready?" There were thousands of balloons captured in nets hidden in the rafters above the stage. Jay walked over to Virgil Summers, who was in charge of all the studios' technical departments, and asked him if he could make it happen. Summers said it would not be a problem, but it would take some time to collect them and put them back in the nets.

Jay did not want to say no to Forbes, so he told Summers to go ahead. He dispatched a couple of grips who climbed the stairs to the catwalks to get in position to release the balloons. After a short time, Summers hollered up to the grips to see if they were ready. "All set," they responded. Forbes told Wasserman. "Go ahead and drop them!" Wasserman commanded.

Summers shouted, "Drop them on the count of three!" When he reached three, nothing happened. He loudly repeated the number. Again, nothing happened. He tried one more time with the same result. The crew was not sure what was wrong and asked if they could have some time to troubleshoot the problem.

Wasserman, keeping his cool, motioned to all the department heads to move closer to him and described (almost whispering) how important it was to him to have this special birthday for his wife go smoothly. "You all have wives, and you know what it is like to disappoint them, right?" Everyone nodded and murmured "yes" in agreement. Wasserman then went around to every person, looking directly in their eyes, calling each of them by name, and telling them how much he depended on them to make him look good to his wife.

When it came to be Jay's turn, Wasserman looked directly into his eyes and whispered, "Everything is going to work tonight, right, Jay?" For Jay, this was an unforgettable moment. As they had never met before, Jay was flattered and mystified how Wasserman knew his name.

That evening Wasserman arrived early, well before his wife, to make sure everything was in order. Jay watched him as he walked around the giant soundstage peering at the seating arrangements at each table. Suddenly, Wasserman took off his tuxedo jacket, motioned for Forbes and Jay to help him, and frantically began rearranging the tables. He never explained why, but before any guests arrived, the two men were sweating profusely, repositioning tables at his direction. Jay recruited about a dozen tuxedo-clad helpers to lend a hand. Soon after, Wasserman was finally satisfied, and the first guests arrived unaware of the last-minute seating changes. The balloons worked perfectly on cue. The party was a great success, and the Wassermans seemed happy.

Jay learned two valuable lessons from his first encounter with Lew Wasserman. First, when you want to get something done there were two ways to get results: sometimes you whisper, and sometimes you yell. More often than not, higher decibels got results, but not always. Second, Wasserman would tolerate a mistake the first time, but *never* the same mistake made twice. More specifically, do not tell him you are ready when you are not!

# Chapter 2
# Universal Studios Tour

## A Functional Test

By 1957, Revue Studios was pumping out hours of prime time television and the demand forced them to find more studio space. Put in charge of the property search was Albert Dorskind, Vice President of MCA Development Corporation. Dorskind purchased Universal City's 420-acre property for $11 million and then leased it back to Universal for $1 million a year. In essence, buying the cow and paying for it with its milk. By any measure, it was a superb deal, and Dorskind would never let anyone forget it. He was a proud landlord and described the studio property as "one of the biggest real estate developments in the history of the San Fernando Valley."

A year later, Dorskind was combing through the books when he noticed that the commissary was losing $100,000 annually. At MCA, this was not acceptable. The corporate culture was you watched the pennies, and the dollars would take care of themselves. While sitting at the Farmers Market in the Fairfax District of Los Angeles, he noticed that tour buses were unloading hundreds of passengers for lunch. He wondered what would happen if they unloaded the passengers at his commissary instead. He made a deal with the Gray Line tour bus company to allow their guests to visit the lot. He also raised the prices at the commissary by 20 percent. It worked beautifully and the deficit turned into a profit.

Dorskind always wanted to be in control and wondered why he should share anything with the tour bus operator. In 1961, he hired Harrison "Buzz" Price of Economic Research Associates to conduct a feasibility study. Price had worked with Walt Disney on the location search for Disneyland as well as other projects for Disney. What Price found was promising.

On June 17, 1964, the Universal Studios Tour quietly opened to the public. The official grand opening was on July 15. The first general manager was Barry Upson. Upson had worked at the 1962 Seattle World's Fair and was handpicked by Price. Upson and Price had a symbiotic relationship and a strong friendship. Price also understood that Dorskind's real interest was in developing the property in Universal City and not competing with Disney.

When the tour began, Dorskind and Wasserman would not allow any advertising. Upson called the 1964 opening "a functional test to see whether it was a business or not." The quiet venture got a promotional shot in the arm when influential syndicated gossip columnist Hedda Hopper took an early tour and then rushed back to her office and wrote, "For years I've been howling for the studios to do something for millions of tourists who come to our town expecting to see how pictures are made." Their only option was "looking at a bunch of footprints in concrete." She wondered, "It needn't have taken a great brain to know that giving a movie fan a look inside never-never land could be a money-making proposition and also generate good will for an industry that needs it."

By 1967, the Studio Tour was considered a financial success. Upson figured out how to give the public a backstage peek of an authentic Hollywood studio in action and fill the seats of the commissary in the off hours. Wasserman would call down every day to find out how many corn dogs had been sold. No one was sure if he was that interested or if he just wanted everyone to know he was looking.

The Studio Tour was financially successful, but it was causing havoc for Upson. His relationship with Paul Donnelly, who ran production at the studio, was not good. Donnelly was the primary tenant at Universal City, and he was not happy with his landlord. As far as Donnelly was concerned, the tour was a nuisance. He would have been happy if the whole experiment could go away. Since Donnelly could restrict the trams and the guides, he had the ability to make Upson's life a living hell. Donnelly's goal was to squeeze the tour out of the action and then watch the whole thing die.

Like most people, Upson was scared of Dorskind. He frequently came to Forbes' office to ask for help. He knew he needed to add stuff for people to see on the back lot, but no one in Forbes' office, including Jay, cared to help. Upson was in a toxic environment; studio production did not want the tour. Donnelly thought that Dorskind should stick to laundry and real estate and leave production alone. Forbes became the middleman. He was also scared of Dorskind.

Then came Wasserman. Wasserman saw that the tour could easily be the start of something bigger. MCA was already into motion pictures, television, publishing, music, and other activities. Why not see how far they could take this outdoor recreation thing. To see this vision through, Wasserman knew that something had to change. He told Dorskind to fix it. Dorskind decided Upson was not the man. Instead, he needed somebody straight out of the MCA management mold.

# Mr. Dorskind Wants to See You NOW

Jay liked working for Gordon Forbes. He was at the center of the action and had gained enormous responsibilities. As he looked to the future, he saw himself a unit manager, which could lead to becoming a producer. Not bad for a guy just out of the National Guard who had no real career plans before landing his studio gig.

Then came the call from Roberta Ross, Albert Dorskind's secretary. "Dorskind wants to see you *now*." Jay hurried over to Dorskind's office and then was told to wait. He did. For quite awhile. When he was finally ushered into the room, he sat down and faced one of the most powerful men at MCA.

Dorskind was boastful, bald, and had little imagination for the creative side of the business. He was also brilliant. A first-rate businessman and a fine lawyer, he worshiped Wasserman and would do almost anything to please him.

He dressed impeccably and could be charming when he wanted to. However, he had other qualities that were wasteful and debilitating to those people reporting to him. For instance, you could almost never make an appointment with him as his secretary was trained to say his schedule was full but she would call whenever there is an opening. You never knew when the call was going to come. When it did come, you were told, "Mr. Dorskind wants to see you NOW." And then, when you got there, you were always told to please wait; he was on a call. Often people waited hours to get in. Finally, his secretary would say, "Okay, he's off the phone; you can go in now."

When you entered his imposing office, Dorskind was always reading something with his feet up on the desk or shuffling papers. He would never look up and acknowledge you for several minutes, as if you were not there. Then, when he finally looked up he said, "Yes?" He always appeared bored no matter the topic or who you were.

When he was ready, you had to talk fast because you knew a continuous volley of calls, which were all conducted on his speakerphone so you could see how important he was, would interrupt the conversation. The vast majority of these calls were trivial, family oriented, and inconsequential. Often, before you were finished, Dorskind would stand up and say he had to go and that you should get on his calendar again as soon as there was an opening.

Once Jay sat down, Dorskind said, "I have been looking at you." Naturally, Jay became concerned. Then came the bombshell. "I want to offer you the chance of a lifetime," Dorskind said. "I want you to run the Studio Tour. You will become a president of your own division." Flattered and confused, Jay asked if he could think about it. Dorskind agreed on the condition that he wanted an answer the next day.

On the way out, Dorskind stopped Jay and dropped another bombshell. "Tony Fredricks also wants you to work for him." Fredricks was the head of labor relations. Now Jay was left with the choice of keeping his current job, working in labor relations, or running the tour. For Jay, this was all too much.

What to do? Jay determined quickly that the labor relations job was not a good fit. He felt he was already on track to do something big and changing jobs would be like starting over. In his current job, he had spent countless hours trying to keep the tour out of the way of production and now he was expected to become its greatest advocate?

At that point, the entire division consisted of two trams and a Quonset hut. Jay had no idea why he was picked but figured his biggest asset was he could get things done. He had no concept of the tour's potential but the chance to become a president of a division at MCA, at the age of 26, had strong appeal.

Jay asked his father for advice. His father was a traveling salesman for a big company. His response was succinct. "If the boss asks you to do something and you turn it down you may never get asked again." Good advice. He suggested his son take the job, which is what Jay did. He started right away.

Little did Dorskind know that he put a man in charge whose ambitions were as great as Walt Disney's. Jay would become a transformational figure at Universal and for the entire theme park industry. Over the years, he built the Studio Tour into the equivalent of a box office smash each and every year without risk or reinvestment. When the time came, he began the shift from the industrial tour into creating the only real competitor to the Disney theme parks.

## Veterans Day

On Veterans Day 1967, Jay was to learn a valuable lesson: MCA was a gladiator's training ground. On that day, Dorskind decided to take him on a walk through the upper-lot Tour Center to make sure his new general manager knew what was expected of him. To make the walk even more uncomfortable, Dorskind brought along Upson just a few days after he had been fired.

Upson was about to start a new job at the architectural firm of Smith and Williams. Jay would use the company for many of the early projects at Universal City. Upson's demonstration of patience, loyalty, and commitment would impress Jay, and in later years, Upson returned to head the Planning and Development team. Over the next couple of decades, Upson had his hand in the development of every North American Universal park.

Throughout the walk, Dorskind pointed out all of the things that he disliked and wanted to be changed. Some of the deficiencies included sloppy uniforms, poor maintenance, and the trash. While Jay was busy taking notes, he noticed that Dorskind's demeanor changed as the walk progressed. Dorskind began talking loud enough to be overheard by the guests. He screamed, "You see that? I never want to see that again." Jay was embarrassed and confused. However, he kept taking notes.

At first, Jay thought that Dorskind was turning his anger and frustration toward him as if he was responsible and the cause of his displeasure. Then he looked up only to see Dorskind smiling and winking at Barry as if to say "you no longer have to put with this verbal abuse anymore." Upson was visibly uncomfortable, and many employees heard Dorskind's tirade. That was the day that Jay learned that his boss was an incredibly demanding bully.

"There would be no tour if they did not put me in charge," Jay said. The only reason the tour succeeded was that the production bosses liked Jay, and they wanted to see him succeed. He came from their ranks. Barry Upson never worked at the studio. He was an outside person recommended by a consultant (Harrison Price) and hired by Dorskind. He never stood a chance. Jay was the perfect guy for the job. He was an MCA man.

Running the tour was not without consequences. An ambitious Michael Ovitz was angling for the job. He had been one of the first tour guides hired. Disappointed, Ovitz left and went to 20th Century Fox to start a tour there. Warner Bros. also got into the act and created a tour of their studio. Neither of those lasted long.

Many years later, when Jay was looking for a partner to build Universal Studios Florida, Ovitz told everyone in a meeting, "Jay gave me a lesson in competition. He beat us into submission." Sheinberg turned to Jay and asked, "You did that?" Jay smiled, "If you don't have the horse don't get into the race."

## Lessons from Cliff Walker

Jay had no idea what he was doing when he took over the tour. Fortunately, Cliff Walker took him under his wing. Walker was working at Freedomland in New York when he got a call from Barry Upson. The two had worked together at the Seattle World's Fair. Upson arranged for Walker to take Dorskind on a tour of the theme park just before the opening of the Studio Tour. Several weeks later, Upson called Walker and offered him the job of operations manager.

Right after he started, Lew Wasserman told Walker that if the tour made money and carried its weight, it stays. If it loses money, it would be closed down. Walker was responsible for all of the scheduling, training, and much more. He was an ex-merchant marine that nobody wanted to cross. In fact, everybody worshipped him. He was all about the guests. His focus was on creating an experience that would exceed the guests' expectations while he turned them upside down to get every nickel. He was responsible for everything experiential from a physical standpoint. Signature Walker policies included clean restrooms, directional signs, and ease of access.

Walker taught Jay that the only way to manage people was to lead by example and talk to *everyone*. Do not sit in your office. If you want to be good at anything, go out in the park, learn it from the ground up, and take no shortcuts. Jay was inspired and worked at every single job on the tour during his first 72 days. Jay spent many hours in the Information Booth and Guest Relations and tried to learn everything he could about visitors' expectations, their complaints, and their needs. It was an incredible learning experience.

Walker explained that the guides were the stars in a new show in show business; the outdoor thematic show. The guides were told that their role "deals with our audience in a sensitive person-to-person relationship. Here in our tour program, we meet our audience face to face. In truth, they are our personal guests." To the guides, who had aspirations of an acting career, they were performing in a play, and some number of them went on to "show biz" greatness.

Walker's attention to detail was legendary. As he walked through the park, he picked up trash and noticed things that needed repair or enhancements. The park workers could tell who was a real, credible boss, and who was not. The key was whether they picked up trash or just stepped over it.

Each day Walker would send a tour employee along the tram route to pick up litter. An issue developed about which union—tour union or lower lot studio union—should be used for this task. After intense negotiations, litter was defined as leaves, branches, and the like, and they would be removed by the lower lot union. Trash was set as wrappers and paper cups. Those would be picked up by tour staff.

Every morning Walker would drive through the back lot with Ed Huntington to check out the animations. When something did break down, Jay was relentless in having Walker get it fixed. Bigger problems received greater levels of relentlessness. Despite this pressure, Walker was very subtle and very effective with how he handled personnel issues and how he handled pressure, rarely passing it on.

## Ark Park

By 1970, it was evident to everyone at MCA that the Studio Tour was a hit. Jay wanted to upgrade the facility to reflect its stature as a world-class tourist destination. It was not easy, but he convinced Wasserman and Dorskind to invest $2 million for a new entry and improved infrastructure on the hilltop, showing them how it would result in more profits. Jay also argued that it would be unsafe to have lines of people winding through the parking lot. Dorskind was hesitant, but he understood risk management and signed off on the idea.

Jay hired Smith and Williams (where Barry Upson now worked) to design a distinctive, colorful entrance plaza. The facility was flexible enough to act as the gateway to the tour during the day and then be converted into a young adult nightclub for 500 people at night. The most prominent new landmark was a giant flagpole.

One of the early struggles for the tour was coming up with things for children to do. Jay expanded the little Ma & Pa Kettle Petting Zoo into the Ark Park. The Mt. Ararat petting zoo contained more than 200 animals and birds, representing 30 species. It was complete with goat ladders and obstacle courses. Next-door was Noah's Nursery and the Noah's Love Inn playhouse for children and animals. The petting zoo had a separate admission of 25¢ for non-tour guests. He described it as unspectacular, but it had some appeal to kids and their parents.

According to Ron Bension, former parking lot sweeper and Jay's future successor, one of the orneriest human beings on the face of the planet was Lee Naud. Naud ran the Ark Park with a scowl and walked the park with his giant Russian wolfhound. He wanted to make the attraction more "exotic" by adding lions and tigers, but Cliff Walker would only approve a few monitor lizards. These six-foot long lizards ate whole chickens. With great fanfare the lizards arrived, and Naud was as proud as a peacock. They were placed in their new home, which resembled a giant doghouse. Naud figured it was just a matter of time before the crowds would flock to the petting zoo area to see the beasts.

Unfortunately, the temperature that first evening dropped significantly. The next morning, when it was time to feed them their chickens, Naud discovered that the lizards were almost frozen. Bension described them as stiff as boards and not moving. Naud began to panic as only he could, thinking that the death of the lizards was no less a catastrophe than the sinking of the *Titanic*. An exotic pet veterinarian was called, and the lizards were slowly thawed out. They were returned to the doghouse—now outfitted with a new heating lamp—to live out their miserable, lethargic lives. Bension said they were useless and dangerous. More importantly, the crowds never came.

More problems arose. It was not uncommon to see the petting zoo staff wearing pith helmets and chasing the monkeys who had escaped their island by jumping over the pond. Then there was a *mean* turkey named General Lee. He was kept in an area just outside the petting zoo. Bension described him as too nasty to allow out. He would try to bite everyone and had a particular hatred for Naud's right-hand man, Hank. Every time the turkey saw Hank, he would go on the attack. The duel provided the staff many moments of entertainment. One Friday after Thanksgiving, someone discovered that General Lee was missing. The case was never solved, but everyone including Bension knew Hank had his Thanksgiving dinner.

Another constant problem were Guinea hens who would walk through the theme park and interrupt the shows. The staff had had enough. A supervisor named Greg Curtis gathered up the "Keystone Cops," including Mike Taylor, Pete Mundel, Felix Mussenden, and Ron Bension. The posse went to costuming and dressed up in either cowboy or safari outfits.

They decided that the best and most humane solution would be to shoot the Guinea hens with tranquilizer darts. Bension said, "We filled darts up with enough sedative to take down an elephant." The group spotted their first victim and nailed it with the dart gun. Expecting it to hit the ground immediately, they were all shocked when it flew away, red dart and all. Now they were worried that if they did not find the bird wearing a dart, they would be fired.

They loaded another dart and went on the hunt. They thought they had cornered the same hen and fired a second dart. Alas, it was a different bird, but the dart had the same effect. None. Now they were getting anxious and decided they needed more firepower than a dart gun. Bension went home and grabbed his .22 rifle. Mundel was lining up a shot when someone in the group yelled, "Wait!" They realized if they missed the hen they would be shooting directly into the Black Tower. That would not be good. Mundel slammed the butt of the rifle down, and it fired into the air.

Frustrated, Curtis could not understand why the dart gun was not working. He filled up another dart, loaded the gun, and with everybody standing around, fired it into a wood stump. The dart ricocheted right into his boot with the tranquilizer dripping down the outside of his boot. On to Plan B. They grabbed a bunch of nets and caught the birds that way.

One of the animals, a Clydesdale horse, was a gentle giant during the day but a roamer at night. He had escaped from his enclosure on several occasions before being recaptured on the lower lot and led obediently back to the Ark Park. Very early one morning, Jay got a call from the animal handler. The horse had escaped again, and had apparently eaten something. He told Jay a large crane had been ordered to lift the poor animal into a truck so it could be rushed to a horse veterinarian. Nobody could explain why the horse became so horribly bloated and why it was rapidly expanding in girth. Despite all good intent, the unwitting Clydesdale was strapped to the crane and took flight in his last moments. The explosion occurred during the flight.

Sadly, one of the fan favorites, Elma, the giant pig, was getting old, and they had to put her down. Bension took her to the butcher. They had a BBQ in her honor.

## Let's Go Right Now

When the Studio Tour opened in 1964, Albert Dorskind refused to let Barry Upson advertise. Wasserman hired Herb Steinberg to head up the marketing department for the tour. Steinberg got the job because of his connections, public relations shrewdness, and his extensive background in dealing with celebrities and politicians. Steinberg could handle the press or big-name talent better than anyone in the industry. He was old-school, hardworking, and loyal to Wasserman and his wife, Edie. Anytime Wasserman had an event or party at his home; Steinberg handled the details. Jay described Steinberg as "the quintessential majordomo." The article Hedda Hopper wrote shortly after the tour opened certainly helped. Steinberg was responsible for that article. It would be the first of many articles that praised the tour.

Attendance reached one million visitors by 1967. Dorskind and Wasserman hailed it as a significant achievement. The tour was a nice little business that could operate without interrupting production, help promote Universal's movies and television shows, and make a modest profit. They were all happy, and Dorskind looked like a genius.

Maintaining attendance became the order of the day. That was achieved by targeting tourists already vacationing in southern California. Newspaper and magazine advertising, aggressive brochure distribution in hotels, airports, tourist attractions, and any place that had a brochure rack were in the arsenal of tools Jay had available. The tour also ran radio commercials and had billboards scattered throughout southern California locales. Jay also initiated an aggressive and comprehensive group sales effort that was highly efficient and represented approximately 25% of the business.

Jay did have an early job scare. He was given an office on the 14$^{th}$ floor of the MCA tower. It was about the size of a cubicle, but it was a corner office and close to Wasserman. One day, Taft Schreiber walked in with a well-dressed man named Jim Hall. Hall was at MCA for about a year as their government affairs officer. Even though he knew nothing about banks, Schreiber had him placed on the board of directors for Columbia Savings. He would show up for board meetings and talk mysteriously about things happening that he was not authorized to speak of. Fellow board members started referring to him as "Mr. Secrets."

Schreiber told Jay that he was bringing him on board to oversee what Jay was doing. Jay was not happy. He asked, "What do you mean?" In his mind, he was thinking, "You are not going to bring in some dumb bastard to run my business." He told Schreiber that he did not need supervision and suggested that if this was a problem, they should see Wasserman. Jim Hall never returned.

Dorskind was happy with one million annual visitors, but Jay knew the tour had more potential. He just needed to *experiment*. Resting on one's laurels does not create a success strategy. He wanted to grow attendance. He began by reading visitor complaint letters. Many wrote to say that the back lot appeared empty and sterile when there was no filming visible. This input inspired Jay to "bring to life" areas of the back lot which looked non-threatening by putting visitors in surprise situations that deliver an element of danger.

These back-lot animated vignettes could become the centerpiece of a television advertising campaign that, if properly filmed and directed, would make exciting and memorable commercials of visitors having fun. What more perfect medium than television to highlight a tourist attraction based on the production of television programs.

Dorskind disagreed. He opposed showing what a studio does behind the scenes in television advertising. He was adamant that if the public saw how the tour did things there would be no reason to visit. He believed the commercials could hurt the box office take for Universal's films. Additionally, Disneyland did not advertise on television locally, so why should Universal? Thus, the beginning of a two-year struggle between the division heads began.

Jay knew they were about to kill the golden goose. He was amazed that Dorskind could not see what effect television would have upon viewers. Commercials would stimulate business more than all their other efforts combined. After all, Walt Disney had featured backstage peeks at his productions and into Disneyland for years during his prime-time shows with great success.

This point was non-negotiable as far as Dorskind was concerned, and he became even stronger in his conviction anytime Jay wanted to discuss it. When Jay showed him storyboards prepared by the Carson Roberts Agency, he remained unconvinced. It reached a point where Dorskind would lecture Jay, challenging him about who was in charge and demanded him never to bring the matter up again. He said, "You're not going to give this tour away."

Dorskind selected him and gave him the opportunity to run a fledgling business, but his inflexibility was capping growth. If Jay could not convince

Dorskind to change his mind, then they would never get to realize the growth potential Jay *knew* was there. Jay had a decision to make about his future. A big decision.

He decided to confront Dorskind one more time and put his job on the line. He demanded that he be allowed to experiment with television advertising, or he was going directly to Wasserman and explain the situation. Dorskind glared at Jay in disbelief and angrily blurted out, "Let's go right now."

The men took the stairs to the 15th floor, and Dorskind asked Wasserman's secretary if there was anyone in his office. When she replied no, he knocked on the door and walked in with Jay following. Wasserman looked up and said, "What the hell do you guys want? You seem angry, Al. What's the matter?" Still standing, Dorskind began his tirade describing how Jay was going to destroy the tour and the studio's movie box office by giving away our secrets, by showing what we offer, and how we do things. "Jay wanted this confrontation, so here we are." Silence. Then Jay explained that he had been trying to convince Dorskind to let him experiment with television ads for over two years and was unable to get his approval. Therefore, in desperation Jay wanted to make his arguments directly to Wasserman. He said, "I don't believe we've even scratched the surface in realizing our growth potential and I will prove it to you if you give me the go-ahead to run some TV commercials."

Much to Jay's surprise and delight, Wasserman took his side without any further questions. He told Dorskind he thought the arguments were persuasive, and he saw nothing wrong with seeing if TV could move the attendance needle. He saw little downside risk.

Another battle arose over operations. When Jay started, the tour only ran five days a week. Dorskind told Jay that nobody would want to visit a vacant back lot on the weekends, so why have it open. For an entire year, Jay fought with Dorskind. Dorskind was fearful, conservative, and succeeded by focusing on small bets. He thought the additional cost of two more days would be prohibitive to the bottom line. Jay argued that his new advertising campaign would attract more locals who could not come during the work week but only on weekends. He was frustrated and worried he would never get Dorskind to change his mind. Now, with his newfound power, Jay decided to open the gates seven days a week. Disneyland did not get around to year-round operations for another fifteen years.

These confrontations changed Jay's attitude and career. MCA was a gladiator school. Wasserman would take division presidents and put them in a room together to argue about how much money they needed. You were required to fight for what you believed in. More importantly, you were allowed to make your point more than once. Clearly, Wasserman loved the spectacle of it all, but also respected the passion with which each division head argued his case.

Wasserman admired tenacity, conviction, commitment, and the willingness to get your nose bloodied for what you thought was good for business. If you failed, he let you know it; yet, admirably, Wasserman would allow his executives to fail more than once during their careers at MCA. Learning from those mistakes was essential if the executives were to survive and thrive. As a result, the projects they completed were the better for it.

Although nothing was declared officially, Jay gradually began to go directly to Wasserman for approvals. Dorskind did little to interfere with his efforts to grow attendance. From that day forward, they would become fierce competitors fighting over how best to develop the Universal City property.

## Captain Numbers

Once Jay began reporting to Wasserman, the Recreation Division hit full stride. They were able to get approvals and direction on a fast-track basis. Wasserman knew how to cut to the chase. In fact, meetings with Wasserman did not last long, and if you were well prepared and anticipated the questions he would ask, you could be out the door in 15 minutes.

Jay was not a numbers guy. For many meetings with Wasserman, Jay had the benefit of financial council and preparation from CFO Bernie Fisher, better known as Captain Numbers. Although Fisher was an engineer, Jay benefited from his most valued quality of being able to transform complex financial information into understandable English. He helped him evaluate complex acquisitions, identify strengths and weaknesses, and highlight this information in words as well as numbers. When you presented anything to Wasserman, he would always put you to the test. Fisher gave Jay the financial back up to satisfy most of Wasserman's probing questions.

Sometimes Fisher could be horrible to deal with. Nevertheless, to survive in Wasserman's world, you had better know your math, or your proposal would be killed. The mantra at MCA was "How good of a deal can you make?" How did the numbers work? Wasserman was known to make his point rounding the numbers up and down to strengthen his argument for or against something. If you did not call him on it right there, his numbers became the facts.

Fisher always had the guts to argue with Wasserman and not accept his "hedging" of the numbers, but sometimes Wasserman would round up (or down) a figure to make a point and Fisher, rather than let that go, would correct Wasserman when it was entirely unnecessary to do so. Jay would have to get Fisher to quiet down.

With only the most rudimentary of computer assistance, Fisher created spreadsheets for the then-proposed Florida project that satisfied Wasserman's financially oriented questions about risk, payback, and return on investment. The spreadsheets were revised to reflect changing attendance estimates, per-capita spending, and interest rate changes. Everything was guess work this far out, and the numbers were all within reason.

During this period, Jay felt it was a privilege working for Wasserman. Wasserman was at the top of his game, and he got the best out of his young executive. He was a no-nonsense boss who always demanded your best and Jay always found him to be fair and even *forgiving*...as long as you never repeated a mistake. His compliments were rare, his tirades of anger were legendary, but when he was convinced you were on the right track, his support and encouragement made you feel like you could walk through a brick wall. Moreover, Jay, as a boss, put to use what he learned from Wasserman. Deal with everyone as an individual and try to motivate them by appealing to their unique personality characteristics. Many people were motivated, without yelling, by appealing to their intellect, their pride, their competitiveness, or sometimes a final warning. Jay's reputation was a screamer and tough in the Wasserman mold, but with many subordinates, he got results that they did not think possible.

## An Injection of Excitement

In 1968, new rules from the Screen Actors Guild barred visitors from the soundstages where 75% of production took place. Furthermore, production was often being shot on location more frequently. Worse yet, MCA's share of the television market had diminished from the heights of the early 1960s.

As Jay read complaint letters from guests, an overwhelming number of them referenced the back lot as feeling tired, empty, rundown, and not what they had expected. They complained that the sets were falling down. On the other hand, and on the rare days that visitors were able to observe an actual production on the back lot, the complaint letters trickled down to very few. The tour needed an injection of excitement.

Jay knew there was strong potential for them to bring the static back lot to life with an infusion of action. Without these innovations, he would struggle to get repeat business; the lifeblood of the theme park industry. Jay's keen instincts about what had to change is how he saved the Studio Tour.

Jay and Virgil Summers began by wandering around the back lot looking for ways to pump some life into the existing set streets. Jay had gotten to know Summers well when Jay had been the assistant studio manager running the daily production meetings. Summers was the head of all technical departments at the studio.

As they wandered, they came up with a list of possible concepts that would put the guests sitting in the trams safely in "peril" for a couple of minutes. Terry Winnick, one of the first tour guides, joined Jay and Summers in the discussions. They let their imaginations run wild. The list included fire, wind, rain and thunder, snow, rock slides, a flash flood, lightning, the parting of the Red Sea, ship battles, explosions, an avalanche, a runaway train, a collapsing bridge, and earthquakes. This list became the blueprint for many years to come.

The producers and directors that Jay got to know while working in production provided yet another rich source of ideas for kicking the tour into high gear. One of his favorites was Jennings Lang. Lang was a successful MCA talent agent turned producer and the man behind such hits as *Airport*, *Earthquake*, *The Front Page*, *High Plains Drifter*, *The Sting*, and *Play Misty for Me*. Jay used to deliver mail to his office.

Lang recognized the symbiotic relationship between the tour and feature films. Even before *Airport* and *Earthquake* went into production, Jay and Lang were talking about potential attractions. Jay got access to the dailies and was given scripts in advance to formulate ideas on how to create attractions based on these films. It was a real win-win as Lang benefited by millions of guest impressions months before the release of his films in theatres.

In 1968, the Flash Flood set opened and was the first special-effects demonstration. 20,000 gallons of water would rush 200 feet down a narrow Mexican village street and threaten to engulf the tram. The force of the water would uproot an old tree and knock it down, threatening the last car of the tram.

When the Flash Flood set first opened, it did not work. Early on, the technicians struggled to get the water levels right. It was a maintenance nightmare. Terry Winnick said, "It would leak, spill; the water would overflow." Reportedly, a group of dignitaries, including actor John Wayne, got an early peek and walked away soaked.

Another water-based attraction that created problems was the Parting of the Red Sea, which opened in 1973. The attraction incorporated a gag that would be used frequently on the Studio Tour; as the tram passed by Park Lake, it comes across an obstacle. The guide and driver have two choices; they pick the wrong one (as they always would), and mayhem ensues.

In this case, the tram approaches the bridge used in *Sweet Charity*, which is obviously too small for the tram. The tram cannot back up, so the only thing people can hope for is a miracle. The miracle comes in the form of a 600-foot long, 15-foot wide, 5-foot deep trough that drains 40,000 gallons of water in less than 3 minutes. On occasion, the tram would get caught in the Red Sea and John Lake, the tour general manager, had to come to the rescue with new clothes from the shops, putting visitors up for a night in the hotel, or other freebies that cost Universal very little. The experience was fun and memorable. When word got out, the turnstiles *really* started clicking.

## It's Just the Opposite

Now that Jay had the go-ahead to advertise on television, he asked the advertising agency to submit some scripts. He was very disappointed. The company suggested that the commercial focus on the workings of the attractions. Jay disagreed. If you just treated it as a ride, there is a coldness. The commercial is a continuation of the film. See the movie. Then ride the movie. The ads should show people having fun. He wanted to show people smiling and laughing. To convey his vision, he drew stick figures and let his team at it. He required at least six different alternatives. He challenged the marketers to show him how to do what he wanted or to show him a better way. He never thought of it as art. He took great pride with these 30-second commercials. The ads won numerous Belding Awards from the prestigious Los Angeles Advertising Club.

Jay knew he was on to something when he convinced famed director Alfred Hitchcock to star in his ads. Vice President of Public Relations Herb Steinberg made the appointment for Jay to pitch the director to appear in a television commercial for the tour. Remember, in earlier days Jay thought his future was in television production so he knew how to spin a story. Hitchcock loved the idea. The commercial was shot in one take. Attendance grew beyond Jay's expectations. Life was good.

A couple of years later, the marketing team turned to Kent McCord and Martin Milner for a new commercial. McCord and Milner starred in the popular television police drama *Adam 12*. The story line was simple: the two cops would drive their cruiser around the back lot reacting to the Collapsing Bridge, the Flash Flood, and the Runaway Train. When they arrived at the Red Sea, Charlton Heston was there in person to part the waters. Heston raised his arms, looked to the heavens, uttered his plea, and the sea parted as planned. The *Adam 12* car, with both actors, made some scripted observations from their squad car and proceeded to drive through the parting sea.

At the halfway point, something very frightening happened. The water weir closed prematurely, and the sea began to "refill" before the car could make it out. Everyone started screaming for McCord and Milner to get out of their vehicle and climb to the roof of the car. The actors were young and agile. They got out with a few seconds to spare, wet and smiling. They were good sports and shot the scene again. This time, the sea cooperated.

Charlton Heston was a big supporter of the Studio Tour. He was a friend of Herb Steinberg. He gained a reputation as one who would never say no and could always be counted on to appear when needed. Heston always appeared gratis. He was the epitome of a classic Hollywood star who did all he could to promote his industry. Jay felt Heston was one of a kind.

The television spots worked like magic. As attendance climbed, Jay's relationship with Wasserman also blossomed; Wasserman was now a believer and allowed, in fact, *encouraged* expansion. This success was no surprise to Jay. "At first, some MCA executives were concerned that revealing the secrets of movie making would hurt the films' box office," he said. "It's just the opposite. People are stimulated to see more movies." Shortly after that, Jay became a corporate vice president of parent company MCA, one of the youngest ever to achieve that.

Now that he was armed with his advertising weapon of choice, it was time to liven up the dead back lot and produce some attractions that would create excitement in television commercials. The priority was to animate the back lot to create a reliable and repeatable experience. The mantra became, "If it doesn't make a great commercial, don't build it."

With success came visibility. In 1973, Lew Wasserman invited Jay over to his Palm Springs home to watch the Notre Dame football game and have dinner. The party was Jay's first time at Wasserman's desert home, and he was excited and nervous. Wasserman comes out of his wine cellar with an incredibly rare and expensive magnum of 1942 Dom Perignon champagne, given to him by Alfred Hitchcock, and asks Jay to open it. Dutifully, Jay pops the cork and takes a taste. It tastes like vinegar. The bottle had gone bad. Without hesitation, Wasserman comes back with *another* bottle. Jay pops the cork. He takes a taste. Once again, the bubbly was past its prime. Wasserman brings in bottle number three. Jay is beginning to sweat. *Was it him?* Off comes the cork. Another dud. Not to be dissuaded, Wasserman brought out a *fourth* bottle. This time, he had a winner. Throughout the experience, and terribly uncomfortable, Jay felt each bad bottle was like telling Wasserman he had an ugly child.

## The Universal Amphitheatre

For decades, the Universal Amphitheatre was *the* premier location to see popular music in the Los Angeles region. How this unusual and legendary venue got its start was yet another brainchild of Jay's.

In 1970, the very popular Western stunt show moved into a new amphitheatre. The facility could seat 1,500 guests with another 1,500 able to rest on concrete risers. Stage elements were placed on railroad tracks so that they could be moved easily.

It dawned on Jay that the theatre could be repurposed to attract more locals, especially at night in the summer. The tour was a hit during the day, but it mostly attracted non-local tourists. Jay was confident he could bring in more locals. He knew he could convince Wasserman to let him build a concert venue to rival the iconic Greek Theatre. He began *small*. Well before the Universal Amphitheatre and City Walk opened, Jay presented "The World's Longest, Cheapest, Peanut, Beer, Hot Dog, Wine, Outdoor Film Festival!"

The experiment was simple. To attract young people, the forerunner of the Universal Amphitheatre offered continuous screenings of films featuring the Marx Brothers, W.C. Fields, Dracula, the Wolfman, and a variety of others. They sold hot dogs, beer, and wine. Terry Winnick suggested they also provide an unlimited supply of free peanuts, placed in several watering troughs. A large portable screen was put in front of the sets used in the live-action stunt show and a small enclosure was built for the projector. They heavily advertised the two-night event on the radio.

On the first night, the crowds were so large that they had to turn people away. Despite the size of the group, they were well behaved and mellow. The next day word spread quickly that the first night was a great success. Then Jay got a message from Taft Schreiber. Schreiber wanted to bring Groucho Marx to the event to show the veteran comedian that young people knew who he was and that he was loved. Jay was excited to meet Groucho. When Groucho arrived, he walked with a cane, wore a beret, and was very frail. They brought him a chair and he watched as the amphitheatre filled with 1,700 enthusiastic young people and another 2,000 or more seated or reclining anywhere they could find room.

About ten minutes into the program, a girl in the audience stood up and threw a handful of peanuts playfully at someone seated behind her; within seconds, peanuts were flying in every direction like swarming locusts. It was frightening, and Jay was completely helpless to stop it. The entire audience was participating. Then, just as suddenly as it started, it stopped. Groucho, always the comedian, said, "This is how I started in show business, the audience throwing anything they could find at me." Roaring laughter and applause. The successful event allowed Jay to demonstrate he could draw night crowds and it fortified his argument to build the Universal Amphitheatre, but Wasserman was still not convinced.

It took one more night event, called the Mardi Gras de Mexico, to fully demonstrate the feasibility of drawing crowds after dark. The event was built around 50 Mexican artisans, food vendors, and mariachi bands, singers, and was highlighted by a spectacular closing act, the Voladores of Papantla (the Dance of the Flyers). The ritualistic act consisted of human fliers climbing and then jumping from the top of a 60-foot pole with ropes tied to their waists descending in circles until they reached the ground.

Following the acrobats was a finale where a bare-breasted maiden was supposed to be sacrificed. Unfortunately, what was supposed to be a family-friendly event went wrong when the bare-breasted sacrificial maiden was being carried to out to the audience to meet her fate. Although she had been told to cover her breasts, no one told her to wear panties. Jules Stein, who had a front-row seat, was far from thrilled with the crotch view, and that was the last of Mardi Gras de Mexico. Nevertheless, it did convince Wasserman to give Jay the green light for the amphitheatre.

Jay knew nothing about the concert business. He just knew that he had an excellent venue available in the center of Los Angeles, right off a major freeway, with easy close parking that, with the right programming, might bring some extra food, beverage, and parking revenue. Jay turned to his good friend, Ned Tanen. Tanen suggested Jay speak with Doug Weston of the world-famous Troubadour nightclub in West Hollywood. Weston told Jay that he could not compete with the Greek Theatre and declined to help with the amphitheatre. Next came legendary concert promoter Bill Graham, who was also not interested. It seemed clear to Jay that they both declined because they were fearful of the other local competition. Jay once again turned to Tanen, but he could not help.

However, Tanen *did* have another idea. It was *Jesus Christ Superstar* that put the Universal Amphitheatre on the map. The Andrew Lloyd-Webber musical came to Universal City on June 28, 1972, for a six-week run. The show was a smashing success, both critically and financially. The show was extended another five weeks until the weather got too cold. Noise complaints from the neighbors plagued Jay's office. There was even a complaint from actor Jonathan Winters, who lived nearby. Jay sent Terry Winnick to the actor's home and when he arrived Winters pulled out a tape recorder and played a portion of the musical. Winnick was impressed and asked if he recorded that at the amphitheatre. Winters said no. The recording was made from his backyard.

With that success, Jay decided to return to the rock music concept. Since nobody was willing to help, he decided to book the bands himself. That is how Flash Cadillac and the Continental Kids became the first rock band to play the Universal Amphitheatre.

Jay was so naïve about the concert business, he was unaware of just how loud a rock band can be. While rehearsing, Jay told the band they had to turn down the volume. Of course, during the concert they did no such thing. In fact, they were louder than they had been during the sound check. Jay thought they were a disaster, and the neighbors went crazy. But the audience loved it. Recognizing that booking bands was not his strong suit, he recruited, with Ned Tanen's help, Ralphy Etkes to make the most of the early big-name bookings before hiring professional booker Larry Vallon.

Now that MCA was in the concert business, Jay was determined to build the greatest outdoor performance venue in Los Angeles. He wanted to compete with the Greek Theatre. To beat the legendary concert spot, Jay needed a theatre with the *best* sound system, the *best* sightlines, and *more bathrooms* than any other concert venue in the world. For the 1973 season, Jay spent $400,000 to expand the seating to 5,200 seats and add special sound walls to muffle the noise and reduce complaints from the neighbors.

On June 2, 1973, the Grateful Dead kicked off a 12-week season of concerts. Other acts included the Carpenters, John Denver, and Tom Jones. However, it was Bette Midler who made the Universal Amphitheatre *the* premier showcase in Los Angeles. Her sold-out seven-night engagement grossed more than $250,000. From that point forward, everybody wanted to perform at the Universal Amphitheatre.

Jay knew that booking Bette Midler away from the Greek would legitimize his theatre. In order to book her, extreme measures were taken. Word got back to Jay and Tanen that Aaron Russo, Midler's manager, was ready to make a deal contingent upon Russo being given a Rolls Royce Silver Cloud—for himself. The automobile gift was *not* part of the contract. Jay said yes. Somehow, someway, soon Russo was driving a shiny new Rolls.

In 1980, the venue was enclosed at a cost of $20 million. The venue was never a huge moneymaker due to the structure of the deals with the artists. As Jay would say, MCA was in it for the "popcorn, parking, beer, and prestige." After many years, and to commemorate the newly redesigned theatre, Jay decided to reward Tanen's loyalty by secretly having a full-size statue cast of him. Only Sheinberg and Wasserman were in on the secret. Inscribed on the pedestal were the words: "The Father of the Amphitheatre."

At the opening night of the newly covered amphitheatre, while Jay kept Tanen busy, several hundred invited employees were driven to the amphitheatre by the trams. When Jay and Tanen arrived, they found a full house. What nobody knew was that Jay had Ray Berwick, Universal's world-famous animal trainer, train a pigeon to land on, and take a shit on, the statue of Tanen's sculpted head as soon as it was revealed. Everything worked flawlessly, and Tanen loved it. It was a memorable moment, an unforgettable thank you, and a reminder to stay humble when you work for MCA.

A few years later, Jay lost control of the amphitheatre to legendary music manager Irving Azoff. Azoff was hired to head the troubled MCA music division. As part of the deal, he got to run the amphitheatre. Jay and Azoff were good friends, and they played tennis together, but Jay did not learn of the change until after it was done. He was not mad at Azoff but was furious with Sheinberg for not discussing it with him first. Ultimately, Sheinberg was right. The theatre had become a distraction and Jay was actually relieved.

With the success of the Universal Amphitheatre under his belt, Jay was ready to move on to bigger things. His drive had not slowed down one bit. What if Universal City became the live music capital of Los Angeles? That would be a huge draw. A big fan of research, Jay learned that there was a ready audience of baby boomers in a demographic bubble caught between teenagers and young adults.

The attraction? Rockplex, a 2.5-acre counter-culture entertainment complex that would provide a diverse variety of top quality entertainment at fair prices in pleasant surroundings. At the heart of the project would be the newly expanded Universal Amphitheatre. Two new 400-seat nightclubs based on famous Hollywood hot spots would join it. The Troubadour was the inspiration for the folk music club while the Whisky-a-Go-Go would be the model for a high-energy rock club. Moreover, this project would not interfere with studio operations or the tour and would maximize the parking revenue from nightly entertainment.

Another component would include one of the earliest and largest multiplex motion picture theatres in the United States. The four-screen facility would have theatres with seating for 650, 300, 300, and 200 guests. One benefit of smaller theatres was the ability to turn away people on occasion instead of having big empty houses.

With so many diversions available, Rockplex would soak up the crowds. Just in case, the ever-cautious Lew Wasserman wanted to ensure that the theatres be designed to allow flexibility so that they could be converted quickly into convention meeting space or live performances if the movie theatres did not succeed.

Connecting the theatres together would be an outdoor entertainment plaza area with an overhead grid. Integrated within this "people place" would be two 250-seat restaurants. Films projected on the buildings and a light show wired into the grid would energize the space. Jay wanted to create an authentic destination, just like the tour.

Jay was excited by the prospects until he ran into Albert Dorskind. Dorskind was not a fan of the project. He wanted to reserve the land for shopping malls, hotels, and office buildings. He commissioned a study conducted by his go-to feasibility study guy, Harrison "Buzz" Price of Economic Research Associates (ERA). That study suggested the Rockplex facility contemplated by Jay would be an economical home run. The projections indicated that the facility could draw as many as 2 million additional visitors per year to Universal City

No matter, Dorskind killed Rockplex. He still controlled real estate development and had Wasserman's support in that area. Ironically, while the project did not move forward at the time, many of the elements would materialize two decades later with the opening of CityWalk. On December

6, 2011, Universal announced that the amphitheatre would be closing and demolished to make room for the Harry Potter expansion in the theme park. It officially closed on September 6, 2013.

## Ron Benison

In 1970, Marc Bension hired his brother Ron and started him as a housekeeper/sweeper. One day, Marc spotted Ron goofing around, pulled him aside, and said, "I got you this job, and if you keep screwing around, I'll make sure you lose it." This lecture had a real impact upon Ron Bension, and he knew he had to do better. Like Jay, he became a super employee. Bension was always raising his hand for extra work. Just as Jay learned his working and management style from Wasserman, Bension learned his from Jay.

One of Ron Bension's early assignments was hosing down the amphitheatre after shows. He loved the job. It gave him a chance to see every big-name act in the business, including David Bowie, Elton John, and Frank Sinatra. When the shows ended, he got to clean up all of the drug paraphernalia, underwear, and money left under the seats. Four decades later, Bension would go on to run the House of Blues and said that this experience "set me up well for my current job, especially when asked what do I know about the music business."

Eighteen months after being hired, Bension moved up to tour guide. Training was simple. His boss, Denise, told him to ride along with the tram tours and learn what the guides did. Bension had to cut his last class in high school and go to the studio, ride the tram, and memorize the spiel. He took the tour four times that first week and two more the next week. He never read the tour guide manual or the script that they gave him. Instead, he used a technique he used while learning his haftarah as a child, studying for his bar mitzvah.

Two weeks later, while Bension was cleaning up the stunt show arena, he noticed Denise standing at the top of the amphitheatre grandstands. She told him that he was ready to join the hallowed ranks of the tour guides even though he had not been formally trained. It did not matter; Denise needed tour guides *now*. Bension quickly ran to wardrobe, grabbed a uniform that was at least four sizes too big, and speedily arrived at the dispatch where he was immediately placed on a full tram.

He repeated Denise's spiel word for word and things were going well. Then, when they got to the soundstages and Lucille Ball's dressing room, things started going horribly wrong. As Bension was telling his 100 guests to "look around and see all the prop trucks and set trucks driving around" he looked up and noticed that there was nothing. It was Saturday, and he had only been on the tour during the week. There was no film activity, no trucks, *nothing*. He froze. Denise got up and took the microphone and finished the Lucy section. While they walked to the soundstage, Denise asked Bension if he was okay to continue. Bension said yes and three hours later his first day as a tour guide was over. He worked on and off part-time, finally working his way up to a full-time guide. Always a go-getter, within a few months he was promoted to dispatcher. By 1972, he had moved up to supervisor. One day he was wearing a uniform and the next day he was dressed in a tie. He was game for anything. He even clocked in two 100-hour weeks during this time.

As the park was fast becoming more successful, the management team was trying to keep pace. In 1976, a tram had jackknifed on Fire House Hill, a steep road that separated the upper and lower lots by a 12% downhill grade. Inside of Jay's office there must have been 15 people, all on a witch hunt to find someone to blame.

Jay turned to Dan Slusser, his new labor relations guy, who had recently returned from Yosemite after righting that ship (see Chapter 3). "You want to weigh in on this?" Jay asked. Slusser noted that the incident was only an hour-and-a-half old, and it was hard for him to believe that they had enough information to reach a conclusion at that time. Jay told him to get on this and to get back to him in the morning. Slusser suggested that he would get back to Jay when he knew something. Fair enough. Jay agreed.

After two-and-a-half days of investigation, there was little or no real evidence that anyone was directly at fault. If there was an area of blame, it was the lack of training the drivers received. However, it was evident to Slusser that the tour managers, notably John Lake, were clueless as to what was going on in their transportation department. The tram drivers were taking direction from Teamsters on the lower lot. They were poorly trained by people with limited experience. In addition, fellow teamsters were scheduling their hours without regard for overtime costs.

Things dramatically changed due to Slusser's investigations. Lake needed help, and the hunt began for a new operations manager. It was decided that it should be someone from the inside, as Lake was still new to operations. After much brainstorming, it was determined that Ron Bension, a park supervisor, might fit the bill. Many had doubts. The biggest concern was about his maturity and whether he could supervise his fellow employees, those he worked with for so many years. Therefore, conditions were placed on him. Bension was told that if he were ever going to go any further, he would have to go back to school and get his degree. He said he would and, after three years, achieved his proudest personal achievement and graduated.

That was the beginning of a great operations team consisting of John Lake, Ron Bension, and Dan Slusser. Their priority was the transportation.

The drivers and mechanics were working under a labor agreement that applied to studio production employees, not a theme park. Bension took control of the scheduling and training.

Bension was given a station wagon to check out the back-lot animation just as Cliff Walker had done. One day, he was driving along the top of a hill when it was being graded to make it flatter. Suddenly, the station wagon rolled over. Bension crawled out of the car, called the tram garage, and had it turned upright. At the time, it was very scary.

It was not long before Bension replaced Cliff Walker as the full-time operations manager. Bension unexpectedly requested the opportunity to learn every front-line role within the park. A training program was created that allowed him to spend up to a week in every operating department, from maintenance to accounting, group sales, food service and retail, human resources, and wardrobe. He even performed as Frankenstein one day.

In his new job, Bension was in constant contact with Jay and Wasserman. Wasserman would call on the weekends about the counts and breakdowns and per caps. Jay would get his "numbers" in the morning, and if something were wrong, the phone would be handed to Bension.

From Bension's perspective, the attention to detail and tenacity of both Jay and Wasserman was at times ridiculous. He would spend hours chasing down minutia or being screamed at by Jay. Then Wasserman would call asking why the per capita at the hot dog stand was down 5 cents from the day before. Crazy as it was, it taught Bension to be meticulous, to know his numbers, jump on problems, develop contingency plans, and raise his level of inquisition.

Another duty was to spend time with Wasserman on weekends when he would bring his grandchildren up to the park. At those times, Wasserman was always graceful and always "on."

Marc Bension also became a top executive at Universal. He started in the Recreation Division, moved over to MCA Concerts in 1986, and then left to become chief operating officer at Ticketmaster.

## How to Design an Attraction

The early tour demonstrations were okay, but their reliability was poor. Due to their training, the studio technicians were capable of making any illusion happen *at least* once for the cameras. That was all right for film-making, but that did not cut it when the gag had to be repeated every two minutes on the tour. Jay assigned Virgil Summers and Terry Winnick to find solutions.

They began by getting outside help. By not building up a large creative staff like Walt Disney's Imagineering division, Jay felt he could better manage unnecessary overhead. Moreover, consultants were highly motivated to deliver on time and budget, or face his wrath.

The first new tour addition in 1974 was the Rockslide. The concept made for a compelling commercial. The Oliver & William Elevator Company developed a system that would allow Styrofoam "boulders" to roll down a hill, drop into a trough, be compacted, and then be carted back up the hill. Terry Winnick said, "It was the first independent use of a design and engineering group that was not related to the studio construction department." Disney used to send spies over to figure out how the attraction worked. Unfortunately, the reality did not match the fiction, and the boulders quickly disintegrated.

More successful was the addition of the Collapsing Bridge in 1974. The guide would tell visitors that the tram was going to take a detour over a rickety old bridge. Just as the tram crossed, the bridge would start to shake and drop slightly. An early fan favorite, the attraction remains today in its original location, though it is rarely used. The attraction showed that the tour had a potential to surprise visitors with bearable thrills, and they seemed to like it. The bridge was a far more sophisticated and convincing demonstration than the fake boulders. Most importantly, the press ate it up with *The Los Angeles Times* calling it "one of the most exciting special effects ever created."

Terry Winnick came up with the idea while he was digging a trench in front of his house in Northridge during a downpour in 1973. He quickly rushed into the house and told his wife about the gag. She liked it and told him to draw up a few sketches. He showed them to Jay, who said, "This is great. It has all the elements. It was movie making. It was fun." As usual, Winnick and Virgil Summers had just a few months to put it together.

In the early days, two guests were traveling together from India. One was a doctor. As the tram started to shake on the bridge, the two visitors believed the storyline and thought they were in danger. They jumped over the tram railing, fortunately landing on the bridge and not falling over the edge. The doctor fell on his camera, which was hanging around his neck and though injured slightly, he was too embarrassed to raise any claim.

Oddly, over the years Jay would tinker with the drop on the Collapsing Bridge to make it more realistic. It had to have a certain number of "G's." For many who worked with Jay, they found this humorous but typical of Jay's obsession over details.

Opened in 1975, the Runaway Train promised to run over a tram every two minutes. While driving past Denver Street, the tram would approach a railroad crossing. For some unknown reason, the tram would stop with the center car over the tracks. Off in the distance, the loud chug of a steam train and its distinctive whistle could be heard, and the warning light next to the tram would wave frantically. Then the visitors would see it. Bearing down on the tram at 7 miles per hour would be a 9-ton locomotive. Fortunately, the train would stop inches from the tram.

While checking out the Runaway Train, Ron Bension watched as the train came closer and closer, actually ramming the side of his station wagon. The shock absorber brake mechanism had failed and the only thing that stopped the train was the dead-stop emergency block. The boys at the tram garage and maintenance had a good time for years with that one. He had recently flipped over the same station wagon. On his 20th anniversary, Bension was presented with a photograph of the legendary vehicle.

Also in 1975, the Doomed Glacier Expedition (sourced from the movie *Eiger Sanction*) debuted, placing the tram inside of a tunnel with a spinning wall giving the impression that the tram was tumbling from a snow covered peak out of control. It was a simple yet effective illusion and another strong addition to the tour.

Reactions to the tour trams varied. Cliff Walker recalled that Frank McGrath (the cook on the *Wagon Train* series) frequently came down to the ticket booth on his electric cart, which was dressed up to look like a covered wagon, and visited with waiting guests. The actors from *McHale's Navy* would often walk out to talk with guests. Comedic actor Marty Feldman used to jump on the trams. Director John Landis occasionally would stop the tram in front of his bungalow and have the guests disembark and then video tape them singing happy birthday to various studio executives. Landis was such a fan of the tour he also directed the television commercial for the *The Wild Wild Wild West Stunt Show*.

Some actors were not so happy. Once, Shirley MacLaine mooned a tram full of stunned guests while smoking a cigar. Jim Drury from *The Virginian* threatened to walk off the set if another tram pointed him out. Richard Boone, star of *Have Gun Will Travel*, made the same threat but after a couple of afternoon drinks, he would step out of his trailer and wave to the trams.

So how do you create memorable attractions with limited resources and keep the turnstiles spinning to ever-increasing numbers? It took Jay years to figure out his formula, but once he did it served him well for over three decades.

It all began with the right movie or television property to exploit. That was the most important ingredient. He spent a lot of time working his network of producers and directors to see what was happening. Not only was he looking for shows produced by Universal but all around Hollywood for ideas. Later on, Sid Sheinberg, who was made president of MCA in 1973, was another rich source of leads and would often hunt down the right people (studio heads or principal actor or directors) for something Jay was interested in and make a deal.

For many years, the Studio Tour did not pay to use the intellectual properties. What Jay did was to promise lots of exposure. Fortunately, many perceptive producers were smart enough to take Jay up on his offer when he came calling. Sometimes the producers would contact him. Not all box office hits or highly rated television shows translated well into an attraction. Jay knew what motivated his audience. It was not a cheap laugh. It had to do with the story. He learned this by hiding and watching guests. Whatever the source, the tour needed a constant stream of new and relevant properties to attract visitors.

The next ingredient was the script or a rough cut of the show. Jay had a knack for generating concepts based on what would be promotable. He had an uncanny ability to create a television commercial in his mind and then work backward to create an attraction that would fulfill his objective. Jay never deviated from this premise.

With the right property on hand and some ideas on how to promote it, he would call a meeting with the Planning & Development (P&D) team. This was Jay's favorite part of the job. With his small staff gathered, he described his concept, starting from the advertising pitch. Then came a discussion on how it might work. At the forefront of the discussion was how the new attraction would contribute to the overall entertainment value of the tour, a top priority.

During these meetings, Jay would have a habit of calling on people randomly. He did this to keep his staff on their toes and to rattle them. It worked to get some good ideas from those who might not usually speak up.

After about two weeks, Jay would gather his team again, and they would pitch their best ideas. These were not necessarily friendly, supportive meetings. Whoever was making the pitch had to believe in their idea and defend it. Jay felt this process would flesh out the best components, coming from all participants, until he was satisfied that he had a potential winner. This was a two-way discussion with much give and take, and he was more concerned about the best ideas and not worried about who suggested them. Jay took pride in fostering a collaborative environment. Consistent with the MCA ethos, the tour is the star and the people behind the star should remain in the background.

From there, P&D would go on to work on the preliminary design, storyboards, and high-quality color renderings, and to conceive budget alternatives and sometimes build a scale model. At the top of the list was the maximum number of "JayBangs" they could attain. Jay defined a "JayBang" as an audience reaction to some physical activity. It was that moment when the guest would be stunned, shocked, surprised, emotionally moved, dropped, splashed with water, or blasted with air, heat, or cold. They were ranked one through ten on an imaginary scale. Jay wanted *fear* or some version of fear or surprise to be part of every attraction. His creative staff would learn to write the JayBangs right on the cover of the scripts. Get the right number of JayBangs and your project moves forward. Do not get that number right and you would get a note with NGE (not good enough) written on the cover letter. Jay was not shy about marking up scripts with every four-letter word available. Frequent comments included: Where's the bang? You call this a ride? Do you want them to go to sleep? You call this creativitiy? Keep working, this sucks! This is not what I asked for! You're taking the easy way out! This doesn't cut it!

It often took many rounds, but once Jay was satisfied he would gather the team and they would prepare a highly rehearsed presentation for Wasserman and later, Sid Sheinberg. Jay would start the presentation, provide some background, and then turn the meeting over to his team to deliver a polished, enthusiastically presented script. Frequently, the man in charge of the pitch was Barry Upson. Upson returned to the tour in 1978 after running an architectural firm and then the San Diego Wild Animal Park. One day, Jay asked Upson, "Do you want to come back and see if you can get it right the second time?" Jay admired and respected Upson. He was well organized, realistic, less emotional, and would tell him when he was wrong. Upson would become the head of the tour's creative department, known as Planning and Development, or P&D.

Upson would describe what the visitors would see and experience and then one of the small team of show producers (Phil Hettema, Bob Ward, Terry Winnick, Peter Alexander) would deliver a frantically gesticulated full presentation, often using verbal sound effects and props to enhance the pitch and sell the show. They were magnificent, and even when they were interrupted, they could restart their presentations seamlessly. They were professionals.

Knowing that Sheinberg and Wasserman would challenge the P&D team, Jay prepared for battle by anticipating and preparing for questions. Jay relied on his small team of creative and talented people at these presentations. However, if something unanticipated came up, it was Jay's job to step in immediately. He never let a member of P&D meet with Wasserman or Sheinberg alone. Jay knew they would not stand a chance. If the pitch worked, you got the green light right away. When it did not work, it was time to go back to the drawing board or move on to the next project. At MCA, there was no ambiguity after the meeting.

With the tour adding new attractions every year, it was time to freshen up the makeup show. This show had been an integral part of the Universal experience from the beginning. It had to absorb the large crowds descending on the tour, so a new 1,500-seat amphitheatre was built for a show that could run up to 10 times a day.

Jay had a special affection for the Universal monsters and thought they could be exploited for the tour. He knew they were well known and revered. He asked Terry Winnick to provide some preliminary show concepts for a live show based on those characters that would use live actors, smoke, and mirror effects, some mechanical assists, and flying bats. The show was called The Land of a Thousand Faces.

Winnick approached Nick Marcelino, head of makeup at the studio, and asked him to find someone who could create a new show. Marcelino recommended makeup artist, magician, and musician Verne Langdon. Langdon had worked on *Hello Dolly!* (1969) and the five *Planet of the Apes* films. His most recent work was running the Ringling Brothers Clown College. Winnick was familiar with Langdon and, as a long-time member of the Magic Castle, he had seen Langdon perform. Winnick had his man.

For the show climax, Jay envisioned bats flying over the audience members' heads, but that was deemed too dangerous. Therefore, Winnick hired Ray Berwick to train a flock of little green parrots who would be painted black using a special dye. After three months of training, it was time for a final run-through. At the proper moment, the cage door was lifted, and all of the parrots flew toward the stage, took a hard left, and flew out of the arena, never to be seen again. Berwick started over using pigeons.

Other than the updates to the Western stunt show, this was Jay's first attempt at a live theatre performance. Even after extensive tweaking the show never lived up to his expectations. The good news was that the marketing campaign was more successful than the show. Attendance did increase, and Jay's confidence that he knew how to sell tickets had increased as well.

Wasserman and Sheinberg thought that the audience reacted to the show favorably, but guest surveys proved otherwise. Jay admitted the show was a B-, at best. For the MCA team, this was unacceptable, and a few months later Sheinberg suggested Jay take a look at *Conan the Barbarian* starring a hot new actor named Arnold Schwarzenegger.

With the Conan, the Barbarian live-action stunt spectacular, the Universal Studio Tour re-invented the theme park show. The Castle Dracula show that replaced the Land of a Thousand Faces makeup show was running out of gas. Jay wanted an update and told Peter Alexander about *Conan the Barbarian* (1982), starring one of Sheinberg's friends, bodybuilder Arnold Schwarzenegger. Jay told Alexander to develop a show around the property.

To find the right person to draft a treatment, Alexander turned to his Rolodex and called Disney Imagineer Rolly Crump for help. Crump listened but declined to work on the project. It was live entertainment, and he said that was not his thing. However, he did know somebody who would be perfect for the job, and recommended Gary Goddard.

Goddard had worked at Walt Disney Imagineering. He was the youngest person ever hired at the design company. After a few years, he left Disney and became a successful consultant, developing projects on his own. Barry Upson made the introduction and Goddard got the job. Over the years, Jay felt they had good chemistry and always enjoyed working with Goddard. He was a genuine talent and a straight shooter. Jay was a tough sell, and more often than not, Goddard prevailed. He was an excellent showman and one of the few who finished their jobs on schedule with shows that worked. Not always an A+, but it got done. He had a sense of humor and was not intimated by Jay. Barry Upson and Peter Alexander were always angry that Goddard took credit for everything, including elements of a show or attraction he had nothing to do with. However, Jay found him to be first among equals and always regretted not bringing him on board full time.

Goddard was already a big fan of the Conan stories and fully understood the mythology. What he proposed to do was to capture the spirit of the film by using an unprecedented array of live special effects. Jay was hesitant at first but finally relented. Goddard convinced Jay that he could do something spectacular, combining a realistic (not so much) animated fire-breathing dragon, lasers, and modest explosions with live actors in a theatre setting. He worked up a storyline supported by multiple action renderings and Jay approved his concepts.

The next step was to get Sheinberg on board. A meeting was set up in Goddard's office. Everyone knew this was going to take a lot of money, more than had ever been invested in a show before. Goddard did his magic with a brilliant presentation. Jay thought Goddard was one the most talented people in the business and that he had a multi-dimensional grasp on how to use technology. He was a story guy, and Jay liked their collaborations.

Sheinberg signed off. The show opened in 1983 and ran for ten years. Jay felt the show was a B- on his entertainment scale. The fights looked like they were in slow motion. The show never got the audience reaction or the guest ratings they had set as their goal. The best moment was one the public never saw. At the casting session for the female part, every stuntwoman in Hollywood showed up. There were more than 50 stunning Amazon-type women in skimpy attire, and the crew and theme park executives had a lot of fun. Still, the show created an entirely new genre of theme park special effects shows. Moreover, due to a very ingenious advertising campaign, the show brought visitors through the gates. Success again.

Gary Goddard worked on rides based on *Jurassic Park*, *Spider-Man*, *The Terminator*, and many others. He created a checklist—never shared with his client—for winning jobs from Universal:

## The Ten Commandments (Plus 1) for Writing a Universal Studios Attraction

1. Thou shalt honor the rule of the JayBangs, and keep them wholly burned into thy brain ever and always—and never shalt thou stray from them or thou wilst face the withering scorn and bellowing angry rage of hell itself.

2. Thou shalt cut to the chase, for truly there is nothing to be gained by the writing of long dialogue scenes which causeth the audience to become bored and frustrated and which may causeth them to leaveth the park early. For is it not written that we must take every penny from each guest beforeth they depart the hallowed grounds? Therefore, cut to the chase without mercy that thou might retain thy job.

3. Thou shalt not kill—unless thee devises the most grisly and spectacular death that shall bring the masses to their feet in spontaneous cries of ecstasy and pleasure.

4. As surely as the rains fall from heaven, so too shalt thou ensure that creatures with huge pointed teeth or razor sharp fangs find favor in your script. And blessed be he who will see that such creatures shall drip venom or blood as often as possible, for truly such writing will be praised from the rooftops of the high black tower.

5. Honor the well-timed explosion and spread them as you would seeds for the fall harvest; for hath it not been written in stone that a Universal show with no explosion is like the still-born calf who will never see the light of day? Therefore, be generous in thy use of pyrotechnics, knowing that explosions are to our attractions as manna from heaven is to the parched and starved.

6. Thou shalt cut to the chase AGAIN—and AGAIN—and yet AGAIN! For should your writing ever slow down the action—even for a moment—then surely you will be damned and you shall be as with the plague and thou shalt be written up and reprimanded and sent away to labor in the fields of crowd control or churro sales.

7. Never shall thee attempt to pen the so-called "message" into your writing—for indeed you will be cursed from the highest office of the black tower, as a message hath no place in a Universal attraction. Let your pen instead seek absolution through the use of the holy trinity of Universal attractions; explosions, floods, and fires. And, if addition thou canst devise a staged pestilence of raining toads, or of windborne locusts, or of rivers of blood, or other horrific spectacles, then surely there is a place for you at the coveted lunch table of Sid or Jay.

8. Thou shalt not covet thy neighbor's attraction budget, for surely it is known that the Magic Kingdom has a treasury like no other. Therefore, thou shalt labor to create massive and spectacular attractions with budgets that are but a fraction of the Kingdom's, and yea though you walk through the bleak and dark valley of cheaper/better/faster—thou whilst find a way to succeed or thou shalt dwell forever in the land of cruise ship shows.

9. And be not like the foolish writer who crieth out in anguish that he must create something with heart and soul, unless of course the heart is being ripped out of some creature, or stabbed through with a long, sharp, ice pick, even whilst the soul is being tortured with great spikes or burned at the stake.

10. Thou shalt be as patient as Job as you are beckoned to rewrite and rewrite and to rewrite once more—yea, though thee are called upon to write one thousand times, never shalt thou complain nor refuse, for truly the rewrite is to Universal as gold is to Midas. And worry not that notes thou art given are moronic or without intelligence, but instead find thee a way to make it work and most surely thou shalt inherit a blessed parking spot near the front of the lot and be granted an annual pass to the park.

And the most important commandment:

11. Thou shalt always, always, always tell a great tale. Therefore, with all of the prior commandments in mind, be sure that thine writing hangs these elements on a great story with a beginning, a middle, and an end (and another end, and yet another end for maximum effect!). And let your tale be told in a manner that wilst excite, surprise, and delight the masses, and always in a manner that puts each person in the midst of the action, for indeed the passive "sit and watch and skip and wave show" hath no place in the land of Universal.

If your writing can meet these 10 and 1 commandments, then surely you will find favor in the Kingdom of Universal.

## We're Gonna Need a Bigger Boat

Only a handful of motion pictures changed the business. One of those films was Steven Spielberg's *Jaws*. The film was released in 1975 and went on to define the concept of the summer blockbuster.

Well before the release of the movie, Jay had noticed an opportunity for the Studio Tour while looking at the studio's film and television slate. What could be better than having a shark attack the tram? He asked Virgil Summers if it were possible. On paper, his designs look good. However, similar to the mechanical shark used in the production of the movie, the Studio Tour shark also did not work very well. Summers was used to building incredible effects that operated perfectly...once. Special effects for the Studio Tour had to function properly every two minutes all day long. The studio personnel did not have the background or experience to make a shark that could work repeatedly and realistically.

Terry Winnick and Jim Kessler fixed the problem by fabricating an entirely new shark that jumped out of the water at a steeper angle. Winnick also was responsible for finding the right design and engineering experts to figure out a way of making sharkskin that would not tear.

For the two weeks after the attraction opened, Jay spent hours hidden in the set of buildings of Amity Village observing audience reactions and making notes on what might be done to elicit more appropriate and dramatic responses for the guests. The show finally worked, but Jay was not satisfied. It was not getting the audience reactions he was expecting.

Jay tweaked the timing, added bigger teeth, more blood, loud water explosions, better distractions, more surprises, and sudden drops in the waterfront dock the tram was on. He also improved the training of the guides to get the results he was looking for.

One day Sheinberg brought Spielberg down to observe the audience's reaction from Jay's hidden vantage points. The young director was just becoming a household name. Spielberg was not involved with the attraction, and Jay was unaware of what Sheinberg may have told him before the visit. Spielberg was pleased with what he saw.

It was a crucial moment. Two years earlier Spielberg himself was overwhelmed with mechanical shark problems on the movie. The production schedule was not being met, and the costs were spiraling out of control. If not for Sheinberg, Spielberg likely would not have been able to complete the film. At Universal, Spielberg did provide several helpful and constructive suggestions, but seemed cautious about suggesting too much because of the mechanical shark failures he had experienced in the picture.

What impressed Jay most about the director was his ability to take a mechanical shark that did not work as anticipated and show only the parts that partially worked. Spielberg created a psychological thriller by combining great editing, music, excellent acting, and brilliant direction. The film became one of the most fruitful and frightening movies ever made. Audiences *believed* in the shark; movie attendance and ticket sales reached new records...and people going swimming in the oceans reached new lows.

Jay found a winning strategy. He established the doctrine that Universal needed to reinvest to grow and compete. He believed that keeping the tour fresh with new demonstrations, highlighted by great television commercials, would draw a crowd, and he was right.

With success came more problems. The tour was approaching capacity. The trams were running full. During the peak months, the trams were dispatched every two minutes, yet wait times consistently hovered above two hours. The hilltop Tour Entertainment Center was overflowing with guests, and the shows were scheduled back to back. They were turning people away at the front gate because the park experience was suffering from overcrowding.

One solution would have been to expand the Entertainment Center, providing more space, and more shows, to absorb the people, but that would have taken a lot of capital and would have used land still claimed by Al Dorskind for real estate development, or by the studio for production. Therefore, between Wasserman and Dorskind, it was not possible.

The only solution left was to increase tram capacity, thereby keeping more people on the tram rides so that there would be less in the Entertainment Center—sort of like a juggler adding some balls and keeping them all in the air.

One way to increase capacity, in the abstract, was to add more trams, but that was logistically impossible as they could only dispatch trams roughly every 2 minutes. All of the tram-related attractions were in 2-minute cycles, and the course the trams had to follow already was full of trams about 2 minutes apart. The tram "circuit" was full and more 90-seat trams would not help.

Their first attempt to solve the capacity problem was in 1976 when they added a fourth car to each tram. That helped, increasing the number of people in trams by roughly one-third, to 120 seats. They also developed more shows to "eat up" people in the Entertainment Center.

However, attendance kept growing, and the four-car trams made by Minibus were just not powerful enough on hot days to pull themselves up some of the steep hills.

As a result, they bought a fleet of bigger, more powerful trams from Winnebago. With the new Winnebago Super Trams, capacity was increased from 120 to 175 with no increase in labor costs, by continuing to operate with one driver and one guide per tram. It was like printing extra money.

On the hunt for another addition to the park in 1977, Jay noticed a new CBS television program on the production schedule called *The Incredible Hulk*, based on the Marvel Comics character. Jay found his promotion for the summer of 1978.

When the television show finally debuted, it was an instant hit, and the tour was ready. He had Upson and Winnick build a unique breakaway brick wall inside of the Land of a Thousand Faces show for $30,000. A guy in green paint would break through the wall and then run out of the theatre. The first Hulk was bodybuilder Jake Steinfeld, who would go on to fame as "Body by Jake."

No other attraction gave the park more bang for the buck than the Hulk. It was an incredible return on investment. The television commercial did its job, as did the balance of the supportive and complimentary media. The Hulk served as the prime example of how an attraction could translate well into an exciting television commercial.

Another benefit was how its success demonstrated to television production executives that exposure on the tour helped keep their ratings high. Everyone wanted to take a picture with the Hulk. It was a win-win for all involved. The gag was so effective that it was credited with an additional 100,000 visitors, bringing attendance up to 3.3 million in 1978.

# Chapter 3
# The National Parks

## Landmark Services

Once Jay had the keys to the Studio Tour, he immediately began looking for opportunities to grow the division. One business was not enough. As a handicap, he had no record of accomplishment and thus was given very modest budgets for expansion.

In January 1968, Al Dorskind summoned Jay and told him to go to Montreal immediately. Dorskind wanted to purchase the gigantic geodesic dome that housed the USA Pavilion at Expo 67. Richard Buckminster Fuller's dome measured 250 feet in diameter and was made of steel and acrylic cells. He told Jay that they could helicopter the structure back to Universal City. Jay thought this was probably the most impractical idea he had ever heard. Coming from anyone else, Jay would have thought it was a joke, but he was new on the job, and when his boss told him to do something, he knew the only answer was *yes*.

Before he went to Montreal, Jay met in his office with Bud Dardeen, president of Minibus. Minibus was in dire financial condition, and it was not long before Jay convinced Wasserman to buy the company. At the time, no one else was willing to tool up to make a stylized bus (called the Glamor Trams) like the one Minibus did for the tour. When MCA sold the company years later, they made a profit.

While in a meeting with Dardeen, Jay's secretary came in to report on his travel arrangements to Montreal. When Dardeen learned of Jay's plans, he asked a favor. The National Park Service (NPS) was considering interpretive tours of the Federal Mall in Washington, D.C. They wanted to use similar trams as the ones used at Universal City. Could Jay extend his trip, travel to Washington and meet with the director of the NPS and tell them how well the Minibus trams performed? Dardeen had hoped that Jay's endorsement might help make the sale.

Jay was in Montreal when Dardeen called with some exciting news. He found out that the NPS was drafting a prospectus asking companies to submit bids to provide tour guides, vehicles, and interpretive expertise for exclusive rights to provide sightseeing services on the Federal Mall in Washington, D.C.

Jay saw an opening and decided to extend his trip an extra day. However, he needed to work on his current "mission impossible." Not wanting to risk a phone call to Dorskind to deliver the bad news on the impracticality of flying the USA Pavilion to Universal City and then tell him he was running off to Washington in pursuit of a different opportunity, Jay hired the hotel secretary and dictated a detailed memorandum explaining his intent. Then he instructed the front desk to fax it to Dorskind only *after* they confirmed that Jay was in the air.

The meeting was a success. Jay had sold the NPS on MCA's capabilities to provide all-weather, articulated trams, hire and train tour guides, and work with the NPS on approved narration. He promised that the tour would operate every day, that MCA would keep fares low, and that they would properly maintain the vehicles to the highest standards. The NPS told him that they would have to go out to bid but asked if he could draft the specifications for the trams used in the contract bidding process.

Tom Mack and Jay collaborated on a prospectus. Tom Mack was the first tour guide hired by Barry Upson in 1964, and the first black tour guide at Universal. At a time when Disneyland restricted black employees to backstage or performer roles, Mack was the face of the Studio Tour. He set the standard and was named the tour's personnel director a year later.

Six companies bid on the concession contract. All the bidders were well connected in Washington. Some were major transportation companies, and most thought that MCA, as Westerners, had little chance of being awarded the bid. They were wrong. The NPS ordered twelve trams, then contracted with MCA to hire and train guides and drivers, hire a management and office staff, and rent office facilities and a maintenance garage. Landmark Services, Inc. was born. The public would know the service as Tourmobile.

Mack was ready to go. He had fully staffed and trained the employees, purchased the trams and other equipment, furnished the offices, and was all set to operate. On the day before the tours were to officially open to the public, the NPS was served with an injunction obtained by local sightseeing companies preventing MCA from operating. At question was whether the NPS had the legal right to award an exclusive contract to provide interpretive transportation services on the Federal Mall.

The delay took two years as the case worked its way through the courts and made it all the way to the United States Supreme Court, which ruled in the NPS' favor. MCA did more than "stand by" the NPS in the Supreme Court case—its law firm carried the "laboring oar" throughout the proceedings. As a result, no one else could collect fares and transport passengers for sightseeing purposes around the Mall except MCA.

From there, Jay and Mack secured contracts to expand the tour to Arlington National Cemetery and to operate a themed restaurant and the gift shop at Mt. Vernon. Landmark would become the largest sightseeing company in the world.

When Jay returned to Universal City, Al Dorskind called him into his office. He was livid that Jay would fly to Washington, D.C. without his permission, and he ordered Jay never to waste MCA's money on "unworthy pursuits." Shortly after this episode, Dorskind demanded that Jay wear a buzzer (this was before cell phones) and when he heard it buzz he was required to call him immediately. Jay refused. Their future battles would only get worse.

## A Piece of Heaven

For MCA and Jay, the Washington, D.C. contract was turning out to be a smash hit. However, this was Hollywood, and you are only as good as your last picture's box office returns. What about a sequel?

Jay's first inclination was to take it right to the market leader and go head-to-head with Disney. However, Wasserman was hesitant. He was friendly with the folks at Disney, and he did not want to dedicate the amount of capital it would take to become a serious contender. After all, Wasserman was opposed to the purchase of Universal City at first, and when they were walking the lot for the first time told Albert Dorskind, "Real estate in the motion picture business is a liability. Too much overhead." So, Jay refocused his energies toward acquisitions.

In 1973, while Jay was in Washington, D.C. for a meeting with NPS officials, the regional director asked him if he was aware that the concession in Yosemite National Park was in the process of being sold. The bids were due in two weeks, and there were already five other large companies looking into to acquiring the Yosemite Park and Curry Company (YP&Co.), the operators of the concessions within the park. The director suggested if MCA were interested, they had to act quickly.

Jay had developed a close relationship with the NPS. They liked how MCA was not reluctant to put up the capital to run a good business. Once he learned that United States Natural Resources (a public company) was planning to sell the Yosemite concession, Jay phoned John Del Favaro, president of USNR, and met with him two days later in Menlo Park. Jay did not know much about the company and did not have the time to do the usual due diligence. He was flying blind. In fact, he did not even have the permission from his bosses to bid on anything, nor did they know he was even taking the meeting.

During the meeting, Jay asked Del Favaro what it would take to buy his business. Timing is everything, and Del Favaro told Jay that he was getting tired of negotiating. Therefore, he blurted out that he wanted a firm bid of $14 million with no contingencies. Jay stood up, offered his hand, said they had a deal, and promised a check by the end of the week. Del Favaro smiled, told Jay he liked his straightforward style, and shook his hand.

Jay went straight to Sid Sheinberg's office upon his return. He told him the story about how this one-of-a-kind gem and prestigious acquisition was such a good deal. MCA would have 20 years left in the concession agreement to get a decent return, and the operating fee to the government was very reasonable. He also mentioned he needed a check by the end of the week.

Sheinberg looked at Jay incredulously. Only a few months earlier, Sheinberg was made the president of MCA, and this would be his first acquisition. Fortunately for Jay, Sheinberg grasped the potential and suggested they talk with Lew Wasserman. In typical Wasserman fashion, he asked a few hard questions and told Sheinberg to go ahead if he liked the deal. Then he turned to Jay and asked what would he have done if he had said "no." Jay's response was simple. He knew that they were both too smart to pass on such a unique one-of-a-kind opportunity. Just like that, MCA was in the hospitality business.

At 1,200 square miles, Yosemite National Park was enormous, roughly the size of Rhode Island. Contrast that with Walt Disney World, which was only 43 square miles. MCA would operate four hotels including the revered Ahwahnee, the Yosemite Lodge, Curry Village, the Wawona, and six high-country camps. Overall, they would be operating sleeping facilities able to accommodate 5,000 guests per night. They also ran Badger Pass, the first downhill skiing facility built in California. Jay joked that MCA would be responsible for everything in the park except the post office and the hospital. He was not far off. Yosemite became the most profitable concession in the national park system.

## Sierra!

Just about the same time MCA took over the Yosemite concession, President Richard M. Nixon appointed Ron Walker to become the new director of the NPS. Walker was a political appointee with no experience in either the national parks or the environmental movement. He was a businessman who wanted to improve the operations of the highly bureaucratic agency. The new director created a lot of concern amongst government employees nationwide.

Environmental groups also became alarmed. They were becoming increasingly concerned that "movie companies" with no environmental credentials were taking over major national parks. Walt Disney Productions was embroiled in controversy over their plans to build a ski resort at

Mineral King in the Sierra Nevada Mountains around that time. Mineral King was a pristine alpine valley just east of Three Rivers where the NPS had solicited bids for a ski resort. Disney won the right to develop the valley, but the project was subject to a lawsuit by the Sierra Club, which made it all the way to the United States Supreme Court. Although Disney prevailed at the Supreme Court, additional environmental burdens made the project economically unfeasible.

Adding to the suspicion was Ron Walker's idea for a television show. The park official approached MCA and suggested they produce a television series based on the NPS. He described his vision as something like the then-popular *FBI* series. Walker wanted to show how they enforce federal law, protect the environment, serve park visitors, and effect wilderness rescues. His hope was that the show would put the agency in a favorable light with the public. MCA agreed to produce a series called *Sierra* and put Jack Webb (*Dragnet*) in charge.

Filmed in Yosemite during the summer and fall of 1974 with the full approval and assistance of the NPS, the production crew members took up some rooms during peak season, reducing those that were available to the public. Even during the best of times, the demand for rooms outstripped the supply. The filming created temporary roadblocks and limited access to areas of the park. Jay's recreation division was not involved in the television production in any way, but the inconveniences to guests indeed reflected upon MCA.

For many of the environmental groups, the most incendiary was the time the production crew was filming a scene where the actors portraying rangers were trying to save a climber (stuntman) hanging from a rope high on a granite wall. The production crews posed the ranger-actors (the series' stars) in front of a rock wall at ground level and wanted to portray them as being high up, climbing with ropes. The ground level wall was a different color than the long shot of the stuntmen high up. Therefore, they painted the rock. They painted it under the supervision and with the approval of the NPS ranger who was supervising their activities. The production crew used water-soluble paint, which after the scene was shot, they immediately washed off, leaving no trace, no harm, or change to the rock.

It was too late. Environmental groups claimed that MCA did not think the park was "pretty enough" so they "painted the rocks." Newspaper headlines read, "MCA thinks they can improve on nature." The NPS never came to MCA's defense, never acknowledged that they had supervised the painting, and never pointed out that everything was returned to its original condition.

Jay had speculated that many of these groups saw these transgressions as an opportunity to cause public outrage, thereby raising contributions for them to "save" the national parks and to achieve their elitist goals to reduce or eliminate the man-made structures in the parks. All of this noise for a show that debuted on NBC in September 1974 and was cancelled by the end of the year. Still, as with any television program, whether successful or not, millions of people saw the NPS presented in a favorable light.

## The Mayor of Yosemite Valley

Once MCA took over, they immediately began to make capital investments to modernize and rehab the facilities. One of the first items was the replacement of cabins that were destroyed by a flood. The NPS asked the previous concessionaire to complete the project, but they lacked the capital. MCA was ready to go but was told by the NPS to wait until a new master plan was completed.

As a key stakeholder, MCA participated in the master plan process. As a partner, Jay treated the NPS management as if they had more sophistication and business sense then they did. When a frustrated Jay would point out the impracticality of some of their proposals, they would become insulted. Park officials claimed that MCA had created an atmosphere that was overbearing and demanding. Jay was one of the "suit-and-tie" people from Los Angeles.

From the start, Jay realized that Yosemite National Park was being loved to death. By the mid-1970s, overcrowding was frequent in certain popular and easily accessible areas. MCA had proposed that capacity (as determined by the NPS) be limited in those areas. Park rangers would be given the flexibility to close them off as necessary. Jay argued that the park visitor would have benefited from better service and greater opportunity to enjoy the natural aspects of Yosemite, in an environmentally sound manner. NPS officials spinelessly rejected the idea.

After numerous public hearings and a master plan effort that had been in the works for almost 20 years, the NPS could not find the courage to overcome the fear of public or political complaints. Jay felt there was no conceivable excuse for not completing a master plan after 20 years of effort. That is incompetence, pure and straightforward, and incompetence was the central issue of this whole saga. Worst of all, no one in the NPS was held accountable for its failure. Environmental groups came out strongly against the plan during the public comment period.

The environmental activists' vision was a "park [that] can be enjoyed on its own terms" and not based on man-made or unnatural structures. They recommended that structures within Yosemite Valley either be reduced or removed entirely. In their mass fundraising mailings, they urged followers to prevent the park from being "destroyed" and "commercialized."

The Sierra Club even went so far as to suggest that the historic Ahwahnee Hotel was inappropriate in a national park and should either be removed or turned into a visitor's center.

Jay did not agree. He knew they were more concerned about protecting their bureaucracy and that the Sierra Club, Friends of the Earth, and other groups were elitist and exclusionary. He said that the NPS always took the easy way out by kicking the can down the road and starting another in a never-ending series of perpetual master plans. It kept them employed and their most vocal critics happy because it promoted fund raising efforts.

MCA had invested large sums of money in restoring and updating the facilities. Jay was proud of MCA's stewardship of Yosemite. His team implemented a sound public policy that enhanced the visitor experience while protecting the very thing they came to see. Nevertheless, things were getting worse.

Because of his views and attitude in meetings, Jay and his team alienated Regional Director Howard Chapman and Park Superintendent Les Arnberger. More importantly, MCA found itself in deeper trouble with rank-and-file NPS personnel. Many of the employees had close ties to the environmental groups with whom they told their version of MCA's actions. The environmental groups used MCA to build membership and to stir up support from friendly congressmen. Their claim was that MCA was pressuring the NPS to develop and deface the beautiful Yosemite National Park and turn it into an amusement park with no regard to environmental sensibilities. For Jay, nothing could be further from the truth, and he was angry. Jay's brusque, argumentative, business-like manner, as well as that of some of his Los Angeles associates, certainly presented a challenge that the NPS had never experienced and did not like.

Instead of directly confronting the government officials, Jay bowed out and put Ed Hardy in charge—he was the man in Yosemite, running the company and dealing directly with the NPS. MCA Recreation Comptroller Don Stevens recommended Hardy, who came from the Los Angeles Athletic Club an organization that operated a downtown "gentlemen's" club, the Riviera Country Club in Pacific Palisades, and a marina in Newport Beach. Hardy had the right background. As an athletic young man growing up in northern California, he frequently went backpacking in Yosemite. He knew and loved the park.

Hardy had the credentials and the temperament that Jay was looking for. His approach was much more low-key and folksy than Jay or Jay's Los Angeles associates. After a short time in the park, he knew most of his employees by name and frequently went out of his way to greet and talk sincerely with the lowest of workers. Hardy was an able, tough, and fair negotiator, with a built-in environmental sense, and unlike the Los

Angeles group (and MCA executives in general at the time), he dressed casually instead of in suits and ties. Hardy liked the spotlight; he liked shaking hands, liked talking to people, and was an accomplished politician. Quite accurately, people referred to him as the mayor of Yosemite Valley.

Hardy's team instituted a weekend duty officer program that required senior managers to be in all the facilities throughout the weekend and to write a report on their observations. Their notes would be reviewed the following Tuesday and follow-up action taken, be it compliments or corrective action. That program was later adopted by the Universal theme parks. For the folks over at the NPS, Hardy was a vast improvement, but it was too late. The damage was done.

## "Give 'em Hell"

Jay's battles with the United States House of Representatives were formidable and exhausting. In July 1975, two congressional committees began hearings on the Yosemite Master Plan and MCA activities as a concessionaire. Neither of the committees had direct supervision over the national parks but their chairpersons, Jack Brooks of Texas and John Dingell of Michigan, both Democrats, were powerful men with strong political motivations broader than protecting the park. Brooks chaired the Government Operations Committee and represented an area with major oil producers. Dingell represented the major automobile manufacturers.

Both decided this would be their chance to win some points by acting as if they were concerned with the environment. Both of them had big polluters in their districts. Jay noted they were delighted to have an issue they could exploit so that they could show their credentials and saw MCA as a perfect target for environmentalists and the pseudo-environmentalists to attack.

Shortly before the hearing, Dingell, ever the publicity hound, was making public statements about the ways MCA was destroying Yosemite. He claimed that they were "stomping it flat" and made other statements that were either outright lies or highly misleading. Dingell made these allegations in statements to the media, and the issue got an enormous amount of publicity.

In preparation for the hearing, MCA hired former Democratic Party Chairman Robert S. Strauss and William Ruckelshaus. Ruckelshaus was the first head of the Environmental Protection Agency (EPA). President Richard Nixon had fired him while he was the number two person in the Justice Department for refusing to fire the Watergate Special Prosecutor Archibald Cox as part of the "Saturday Night Massacre."

Jay and Tony Sauber worked for months preparing a long, aggressive position paper defending their actions and placing the blame where they felt it belonged: on the hidden agenda of the environmentalists and the NPS. This brief, they thought, would be Jay's written testimony and would finally set the record straight.

Before the hearings, they met with Ruckelshaus and his partner Henry Diamond. It was a revelation. Jay and Sauber came "armed for bear" and assumed that the legal team either would make no changes or would make it even tougher. Instead, they essentially threw it out and said that it would defeat their purpose and demonstrate that they were, in fact, too aggressive in dealing with the NPS.

Ruckelshaus strongly felt advice was that MCA's position should be that of a "cooperative concessionaire." They should publicly state that they would do whatever the NPS told them to do. If the NPS asked MCA to build or remove facilities or activities, then that is what would happen. It was NPS' park, and MCA was there to serve them and the public. After some argument, Jay reluctantly agreed.

To get him to agree, Jay was reminded that MCA had a "reasonable opportunity to make a profit" by statute (then called Public Law 89-249) and they had certain statutory financial interests ("possessory interests") in all of the structures. Therefore, any decreases could require payment from the NPS. Considering that the NPS was notoriously under-funded, it would not have the money to pay off the possessory interest. Nevertheless, the strategy for the hearings was to state MCA's desire to abide by the wishes of the NPS. Ruckelshaus, along with his partner Henry Diamond, drafted a statement that took the conciliatory approach.

Sauber also devised a plan to work with the environmental groups and speak directly to other user groups. He realized that the general public might have stronger feelings about maintaining the facilities and activities in Yosemite than the environmental groups. He contacted organizations such as AARP, the Auto Club, recreational vehicle organizations, horse riding groups, and travel organizations. His hope was that they would ultimately put considerable pressure on the NPS (and congressmen) in the opposite direction from the environmental groups.

Once the hearing began, Dingell and Brooks loaded the agenda with environmental advocates who spoke critically of MCA's stewardship. After hours of testimony, it was MCA's turn.

Jay walked to the table, took a seat, and prepared to read a summary of his accurate written statement. Then, Dingell pushed back his chair, leaned into the microphone, told the committee that he had to be somewhere else, said, "Give 'em hell, Jack," and excused himself. Dingell left the questioning to his staff. Jay was angry and frustrated that he never got the chance to respond directly to Dingell, rebutting the things he had said. All he could do was submit his written testimony for the record.

The incident reinforced what he had suspected all along. Neither of these two congressmen had any interest in protecting Yosemite. They knew how to play the game, and their only objective was to make nice to their environmental critics at MCA's expense.

Ironically, years later, MCA's Political Action Committee donated money to Dingell, and Jay had to participate.

## The MCA Executive Training Camp

Yosemite would become the training ground for many future MCA executives.

In 1974, a young labor attorney working in the MCA Legal Department named Tony Sauber boarded the same elevator as another young lawyer working for Jay, Bob Finkelstein. Finkelstein mentioned that the Teamsters and another union were attempting to organize the employees of the MCA subsidiary in Yosemite. MCA had hired an outside law firm to handle the matter, but Finkelstein was not happy. He handed Sauber some of the campaign materials to be distributed to the employees. The arguments read like a legal brief. Sauber realized that these types of arguments would not be absorbed by nor convince the rank-and-file Yosemite workers. Sauber found himself in the right place and at a specific moment that caused his life to take a dramatic and unexpected turn. Sauber would soon become an integral part of the growth of MCA and its recreation division.

Sauber was a longtime member of the Sierra Club and used that experience to draft anti-union propaganda asking employees to reject the unions by emphasizing the then-rampant, well-known, corruption of the Teamsters, and how they and the other unions would despoil the pristine atmosphere of the park.

After drafting the materials, he sent them directly to Jay with a cover note to the effect that these might help in the Yosemite campaign. Then Sauber got a call from Mary Wheeler, Jay's secretary. "Mr. Stein wants to see you in his office." Jay had a well-deserved reputation as a screamer/yeller, who despite his young age (at this point about his mid-30's) could easily intimidate both older executives and underlings.

Therefore, with some trepidation, he went to see Jay. His discomfort was not helped when he walked in. Jay did not look up from the papers he was reading. After a "beat," he said to Sauber, "Did you write this shit?" The 33-year old-attorney answered yes, and then Jay asked if he could write some more, which Sauber promptly did. That was the beginning of Sauber's 26-year career working for Jay and his successors in the Recreation Division.

Over the years, Sauber would rise to the position of executive vice president, Business, and Legal Affairs, and would perform or supervise all of the legal work for the division, as well as negotiating numerous deals and legal settlements, including acquiring third-party rights in creative properties used in theme parks.

He would also become Jay's speech/memo writer, his legal and diplomacy counselor, an honest, even-tempered, sensitive, loyal, team player, and most importantly his friend and conscience. Sauber drafted most of Jay's memos. He would take notes and come back with a first draft so that Jay could "sink his teeth into them." Jay relied on memos to Wasserman, Sheinberg, and Spielberg to explain what he wanted to do. To make the presentation verbally would invite an opportunity to find one negative thing to focus on and then the meeting would be as good as over.

Sauber also kept the Recreation Division out of trouble. He was never a sycophant. Everyone respected him and that respect was earned. Sauber felt that, as a lawyer or executive, he was, at best, a B+ player. He did not have the detailed mind or patience to negotiate or draft highly complex contracts. On the other hand, Sauber could formulate complex agreements in relatively simple terms ("deal memos"). He was excellent at things like soliciting public groups to get involved in arguing for "fair use" of Yosemite National Park and securing the rights and making the deals for various properties Universal wanted to use in their theme parks. His contributions were performed mostly under the radar and cannot be overstated.

Dan Slusser also got his start at Yosemite and become a key figure at MCA. Slusser was working for 20th Century Fox as director of Labor Relations when Gary Hughes, the vice president of Industrial Relations for MCA, started asking Slusser for advice on union avoidance techniques. It was not long before Hughes asked Slusser to join MCA and "go to Yosemite." Slusser was flattered but declined.

The MCA team was relentless. Slusser recalled that during the next month somebody would ask if he was coming on board to help resolve their labor issues at least 50 times. On one occasion during negotiations, Lew Wasserman asked him if he had visited Yosemite. Slusser said, "Good God, I didn't know where Yosemite was or what it was, I was a recently transported New Jersey guy." Eventually, he visited Yosemite and was treated like a king by Ed Hardy. At one point, the two drunken men walked right into the Yosemite Falls after dinner.

After his visit, he talked with his wife about the opportunity. She was not very enthusiastic but agreed to take a trip and visit the park. They stayed in a suite at the historic Ahwahnee Hotel and were treated like royalty. Slusser was told if he accepted the offer he would get a nine-room house on the Ahwahnee Meadow, rent-free. In fact, everything was free.

After leaving that week and seriously considering moving to Yosemite, they were told that domestic pets could not stay in a national park. Slusser's family had a dog, and that was the end of the conversation. Hughes kept at it until he came up with a letter permitting Slusser to bring the dog. With that issue resolved, his next step was to meet with Jay. They had lunch at the studio commissary and engaged in small talk. Finally, Slusser asked Jay if he had any questions. Jay said, "No. I'm told you walk on water, and I'm aware that Lew likes you. If he likes you, I'm going to love you." The union vote would be in 20 days.

Initially, Jay put Sauber in charge of the union elections in Yosemite. When Dan Slusser came to work for MCA, he took over with Sauber assisting him. A former Teamster, Slusser started by gaining the trust of the union's executive board. After all, he was a friend of their president, Frank Fitzsimmons. Then Slusser arrived in Yosemite late on the night of June 15, 1974, the same day as his last day at 20$^{th}$ Century Fox. He was in his new office at 8:00 a.m. the following morning.

The first order of business was meeting with Hardy's direct reports and getting a briefing on the state of the organizing efforts. After the meeting, it was easy for Slusser to see why the Teamsters were there. He took control and told the management team to avoid conversations with the employees about the negotiations. Slusser then began a campaign to meet with employees of every unit including those who worked at the Ahwahnee Hotel, the Yosemite Lodge, Curry Village, Wawona Hotel, Deagens, and the Stables. He invited their lead organizer, Vicki Saporta, to attend and Slusser promised that there would be no restrictions on attendance, other than trying to have a civil conversation. During those meetings, he told Ed Hardy and his number two guy, L.L. Branscum, to attend but they could not talk nor answer questions. As it would turn out, Slusser had more problems with a defensive Hardy and Branscum at the meetings than with the employees.

After that, with the assistance of Tony Sauber, Bob Finkelstein, and John Crofut, they created and distributed white papers for the employees, telling them what they could expect if the union prevailed. Slusser's largest headache came from the string of lawyers from MCA's law firm who were dumped into the process. Good, corporate-type lawyers, but clueless about union organizing efforts. Everyone in the recreation group kept saying "these are Wasserman's people, and you will have to work with them."

Slusser wanted Hollywood labor lawyer Howard Fabrick. Without anyone knowing, he called Wasserman. Wasserman said Slusser was getting one more attorney the next day, a young man by the name of Steve Kroft. Wasserman told him if he was not happy with Kroft he could do whatever he wanted. It was his show. Time was getting short, and Kroft was willing to work hard and was bright. Therefore, Slusser made the best of it.

Kroft, Sauber, and Crofut came up with "Yosemite Sam" as MCA's no-union mascot. The team got little sleep. The election was held in early July, and the voting process went on for a few days because of the immense size of the park. On July 7, 1974, to the surprise of everyone, including Lew Wasserman, a staunch supporter of unions, MCA prevailed when employees voted to reject union representation. It was Slusser's 36th birthday, and this was the perfect gift.

Then the hard part started. Yosemite management returned to their old behavior. Branscum and others returned to their previous style, berating employees in front of their peers, making rules up as they went along because they could.

Slusser organized the Employee Council, established a formal grievance process, and took key managers to the meetings, so they could see what their actions were creating. Hardy made incredible positive strides. Bill Germany, who ran Curry Village, was a blessing. Slusser worked with the management team to streamline the organization and hired Mike Gehan as CFO and Steve Lew to run the hotel division. He also increased the responsibilities of a bright, fast learner named Tom Williams.

About 14 months after MCA's victory over the Teamsters, a new union organizing group showed up. S.E.I.U. (Service Employees International Union) were experts at organizing minimum-wage employees. Their organizers were bright, well-educated, and had much in common with the employees of YP&Co.

After repeating many of the earlier campaign programs and with the help of many loyal employees, it came down to a very tight race as to weather the union would prevail. Before the vote count, with the aid of Steve Kroft, MCA bombarded the NLRB (National Labor Relations Board) with ballot challenges. They used every possible challenge. They succeeded in tying up close to 100 ballots.

The election outcome was in doubt, as counting the challenged ballots would be the only way to determine the result of the election. The NLRB heard arguments from the union, and from Kroft and Slusser, as to why a ballot should be counted or not counted. Slusser was certain he knew what the challenged ballots would say, and it was not good for MCA.

Trying to snatch some victory from defeat, Slusser reached out to a friend who knew Tim Toomey, the president of S.E.I.U., and set up a time to meet with him. The meeting took place in Los Angeles, and Slusser offered him a choice: the union could be in negotiations for an agreement with YP&Co in less than a month, or they could be counting challenged ballots for the next three months while MCA prepared charges with the NLRB and push the matter into the 9th Circuit Court. If at the end of this 10–12-month process the Union did prevail, they would never get a dues withholding provision in their agreement. These employees are never going to go on strike so a union can take money out of their checks. Slusser told him to think about what it would take to collect dues from seasonal employees.

Toomey asked, "What do you need?" Slusser replied, "Not much." Slusser offered a 6% increase spread over three years, a 90-day probationary period for all new employees, all new hires would be paid minimum wage for their first 30 days of employment, and any seasonal employee who did not complete his or her seasonal agreement would not be rehired. He also took the subject of employee housing off the table. The two men shook hands and were at the bargaining table in less than three weeks.

Slusser returned his attention to the ongoing problems of the Yosemite management team. There was more drinking going on then there should have been, and he had to admit that for a while, he was part of it. Some of it spilled over into the operations.

One day he received a call from the superintendent of the NPS, Les Arnberger. He wanted to meet. Slusser met him at his house. Arnberger voiced concern about Hardy and some of the things Hardy was doing without input from the NPS. Slusser met with Hardy and convinced him to try to involve the NPS senior management and make them his partner. Slusser continued to meet with Arnberger and tried to be a buffer. Things did get a little better, but not as good as they should have been.

From Slusser's first day in Yosemite, he had trepidations about his long-range relationship with MCA. Fox executive Dennis Stafill had sent Bill Immerman, his executive vice president, to the park to offer Slusser the position of vice president of Industrial Relations.

For a while, he was on the fence. Jay continued to scream at Hardy, Branscum, and others on a regular basis, but never at him. There were stories of Wasserman screaming at MCA employees, something (at that time) he had never seen. Slusser did see it later in his career, but it was never leveled at him. What he found amazing was that Jay got results. He motivated some people with his screaming—not all of his staff but a large number. Instead of leaving for Fox, Slusser remained with MCA and was relocated to the studio as vice president of Industrial Relations for the Recreation Division.

Slusser was the only Recreation division executive that Jay was comfortable with in a meeting alone with Sheinberg or Wasserman. Slusser helped convince the top men that Jay was on the right track. He kept Jay out of trouble or got him out of trouble when he did not listen. Slusser was an outstanding negotiator and Jay had complete confidence in his guidance and abilities. He was an honest, straight talker, and Jay continued to value his wisdom and friendship.

Steve Lew also began his career at Yosemite. He interviewed sometime in mid-1975 and got the job being in charge of all of the lodging facilities. At the interview, Lew briefly met Jay, and his first impression was that his future boss was feared, fearless, and an intense executive. Over time, he would learn that Jay was fiscally astute, gave clear direction, and could be very demanding. Lew noticed that Jay knew how to ask the right questions and to "drill down" on an issue.

Sauber always claimed that Jay had a "bullshit detector." He could be talking to a consultant who was an expert in some technical field, and by asking a few questions find out how firmly the person believed what they were saying. At times, this management style could be overbearing. Jay always required fiscal and personal discipline. Jay refused to take no for an answer unless he was convinced the alternative was better. Lew had learned the lessons well. He would go on to run both the Florida theme park and the California park at different times. Jay thought Lew was a loyal soldier and a fine executive. He was detail-and profit-oriented, and no one worked harder than Lew.

The Recreation Division top management typically met weekly in groups. When Jay attended or led a meeting, he sat at the head of the table. He wanted what he wanted when he wanted it. He was very detail-oriented and grasped the fiscal implications. Lew found Jay to be a good listener. The respect and loyalty Jay received was earned, and he treated people in the same manner. The old saying, "If you can't stand the heat, get out of the kitchen," applied to Jay. As a result, most management people who left the division did so on their own.

Jay learned that the proof of a good executive was the ability to fire your best friend. Jay was not known as a person who fired people. In fact, during Jay's tenure, he only fired two employees. One of those was Cliff Walker, and though they parted ways professionally, they remain close friends.

## Spitting Mad

Not long after the Yosemite battle, still in 1974, Tony Sauber discovered first hand what others had experienced at the hands of Lew Wasserman. Sauber, still in the MCA Corporate Legal Department, was working on a grievance from the Musicians Guild. The Recreation Division had a contract with performers who were to appear in an afternoon concert at the location of the original stunt show (which later became the site of the Universal Amphitheatre). When tickets did not sell, the Universal promoters cancelled the concert and declined to pay the musicians, since they had not yet signed their contracts.

The grievance was about to enter arbitration. Sauber was arguing what might be an unfair position but perhaps legally correct. That was his job. That is when he got a call to come up to Wasserman's office *right away*.

Wasserman knew who Sauber was from previous jobs and was calm and "chatty" when the attorney hesitantly walked into his office. Then

Wasserman handed him a letter from the attorney for one of the performers. Sauber read the letter and then started to explain the legal position he was taking when Wasserman interrupted him and was told to look at a framed certificate on the wall near his door. It was an award from the Musicians Guild naming Wasserman "Honorary Member Number 1."

Then he asked Sauber, *still* in a calm voice, "Tony, how much money is involved in your case?" Of course, Wasserman knew the answer was $7,500. Then he asked, "Do you have any idea how much money this company saves every year on music production costs for our movies based on waivers we get from the Musicians Guild?" Sauber had no idea, and Wasserman revealed a number in the multiple millions of dollars.

Then, no more Mr. Nice Guy, Wasserman stood up, started screaming, saliva literally dripping from his mouth, waving his arms, and unhooking his watch and throwing it down on his desk. Saying, in essence, whom did Sauber think he was to jeopardize millions of dollars just to save $7,500? It was a long, long tirade.

As Sauber recalled, he was sitting in a chair in front of Wasserman's desk and truly had an out-of-body experience: he saw a shadow of himself stepping out of his body and standing to the side watching Wasserman scream, wave his arms, and go berserk while he sat there. His only thought was this was the wealthiest, most prominent man he would ever know in his life, a close associate of many presidents, and he is taking the time to yell at Sauber, one on one. Wasserman ordered Sauber to pay them the money, and if he ever did anything that stupid again, he would be fired. Sauber sent a check off that night.

## Goodbye Yosemite

Yosemite was a hit for MCA. It had contributed more than $75 million to the bottom line. In 1986, Jay told his team, "All of this is a credit to your management abilities, your innovative spirit, and your abilities to deal successfully with your highly regulated environment. Except for the contemplated October visit with my family, if it takes my benign neglect to induce you to such heights, I promise to continue to curb my natural instincts." He added, "You have done a great job!" Then he went off to work on the Florida project.

He decided to put Ron Bension in charge of Yosemite to watch over Ed Hardy. Bension had never been to Yosemite before and arranged for a visit without telling Hardy. What a revelation.

Unfortunately, Jay's "benign neglect" had its impact. Benison found much about the way the concessions were run to be disappointing. About a month later, Jay asked Bension about his trip. He was anxious to hear about his protégé's experience. It had been three years since Jay's last visit to Yosemite because of Florida. The stories Bension told him shocked him. Jay knew that Bension could right the ship and told him to fix this "steaming turd," but Bension never really got the chance.

The end of MCA's involvement with Yosemite began in January 1990. Prompted by the surprise sale of MCA to the Japanese conglomerate Matsushita Industrial Electric Co. (at the time the 12th largest company in the world), Secretary of the Interior Manuel Lujan Jr. and NPS Director James Ridenour decided to score political points by claiming that the Yosemite concession should stay with an American company instead of one owned by a Japanese corporation. Yosemite was the most profitable of all national park concessions, and now, by their thinking, MCA was a Japanese corporation.

MCA proposed spinning off YP&Co, placing the company in escrow, to be then sold to an American buyer within a year. Lujan refused approval of the escrow agreement, forcing YP&Co to remain in Japanese hands. Then he began a campaign of Japanese bashing. Lujan wanted to drive down the price of the Yosemite operation so the government itself could get it at a lower price. He told the press how terrible it was that a foreign company was now running the businesses in one of America's oldest, most beautiful national parks. Others jumped on board and there was a fair amount of publicity.

The careful management at Matsushita overestimated the impact of Lujan's public statements and decided that they did not want to "take the heat." Since the Yosemite concessions were such a small piece of the total MCA purchase, they felt the company should be sold quickly, and they could move on.

Jay disagreed and vigorously fought the sale. However, Wasserman did as his new bosses told him and YP&Co was sold. Jay played no part in the transaction. Instead, MCA's general counsel, Bob Hadl, and George Smith, corporate vice president in charge of taxes, were put in charge of negotiating a transfer of ownership. Ultimately, MCA found and negotiated a sale for $61.5 million to Delaware North Company, a Buffalo, New York, organization that ran sports stadium food concessions.

The deal was concluded in September 1990, but under the terms negotiated, the transfer of ownership was not to be effective until September 1993.

Delaware North's payment to MCA included interest on the sale price set three years earlier so that Delaware North could claim they got a good price (the 1990 price) and MCA could claim the compensation they got was the price including three years of relatively high interest (and the interim earnings).

Jay was proud of MCA's role in Yosemite. They provided adequate funding to keep the equipment and facilities in excellent condition. Jay knew his team was one of the best operators in the entire national park system. MCA made history with their in-park transportation system, their recycling efforts, and the bear-proof dumpsters long before other national parks.

To enhance the visitor experience, MCA operated a free-to-the-public shuttle service providing transportation to virtually everywhere in Yosemite Valley. The parking lots appeared full, but that was because once people reached their overnight destination, they did not need their cars to enjoy any of the valley's sights and experiences. Thousands of cars were replaced with a handful of free, open-air, propane-powered, quiet trams. Now visitors could take in all the valley's beauty. The trams ran continuously and frequently, with much less pollution than the thousands of gasoline cars that would otherwise be driving around. As a result, traffic jams in the valley were eliminated. This operation took a huge capital investment and considerable management time but was provided for only a reimbursement of costs.

Bears were a nuisance and could pose a danger to visitors in the valley. They were attracted to the garbage in trash cans and dumpsters. Hardy came up with a solution. He designed a trash receptacle that even the smartest bear could not open. His solution was less extreme and far more humane than how the NPS in Yosemite tried to deal with the bear problem. The NPS would just secretly shoot the bears and dump their bodies in a remote canyon. Jay noted the hypocrisy of those who were more offended by painting a rock with water-soluble paint that was quickly removed than the far more egregious action of shooting bears. To this day, most of the general public never knew about the shootings.

MCA also instituted the first-ever bottle/can deposit program. When anyone bought a drink from the grocery store in the valley or other outlets, he or she paid a 5-cent deposit, and the can or bottle was individually stamped. Such a program effectively eliminated can/bottle litter in the park since individuals, particularly children, would pick up the discards and turn them in for the reward. These types of programs have now become nationwide. Jay and his team were once again ahead of their time.

## Chapter 4
# On the Hunt

## The Grand Tour

After winning the labor dispute in Yosemite, Jay was feeling confident yet frustrated. He felt he knew enough to get him anywhere he wanted to *go*. He was not intimidated by anyone. It was time to build a park or buy *something*.

During August 1974, he grabbed Tony Sauber and Bernie Fisher and they went on a trip to look at the concession operations in several national parks to consider whether MCA should attempt to purchase any of them.

Their first stop was Glacier National Park, where Don Hummel, the owner of the concession operations, showed them all of his facilities over a three-day period. Hummel expressed interest in selling. Then they went to Yellowstone where they looked around on their own for a few days. Mt. Rushmore and Greenbrier also got looked over.

Ultimately, Jay decided not to pursue any of those businesses. Unlike Yosemite and Washington, D.C., they were in remote locations and had very limited seasons—at best from Memorial Day to Labor Day. The facilities would require an unjustifiable investment to bring them up to MCA quality standards and it would cost even more to "winterize" them.

The next road trip took place during November 1974 when a group of five from the Recreation Division went to look at an amusement park in New Jersey called Great Adventure. At the time, the park was in foreclosure and a bank MCA dealt with approached the entertainment giant about purchasing their interest.

Warner LeRoy operated the park. He was the son of famous movie director Mervyn LeRoy and was named after Jack Warner. He was also a prominent restaurateur in New York. The park was colorful and attractive, in a beautiful woodsy setting, but was overbuilt with too much money put into making it elegant. LeRoy had great taste but no sense of budget.

After a couple of days showing the group around the park, he took them to lunch at one of his restaurants, the ultra-trendy Maxwell's Plum—he also owned the equally trendy Tavern on the Green. LeRoy was cordial to the men from MCA during the visit but once he learned that they were considering buying the park and putting in their management he talked to his father, who called Lew Wasserman to get them to back off. LeRoy wanted to continue to run the park. He initially thought they would just put up some money to get it back on its feet.

Next on the itinerary was an early 1975 trip to Orlando, Florida. Jay and Sauber looked at the Disney operations carefully, as well as a handful of second-rate theme/amusement parks in the area. They had a meeting with an executive of Sea World, ostensibly and partially to discuss the Orlando market for MCA's potential entry, but also so Jay could evaluate the overall company.

Jay looked at some ski operations, including Mammoth Mountain. The owner, Dave McCoy, was interested in selling the peripheral businesses (hotels, restaurants, shops, etc.), but wanted to keep the ski lifts and mountains for himself and his children. In the early 1960s, Walt Disney had offered to purchase everything and an agreement had been drawn up, but the family withdrew at the last moment over the ski lift and mountains issue.

Mammoth would have delivered synergies with Yosemite. It was nearby, and counter-cyclical, so that many employees and executives in Yosemite could supervise it during Yosemite's slower winter months.

Jay and McCoy talked over the years, and the ski activities were, in fact, a very successful asset, which expanded significantly over time. McCoy benefited from a very liberal management attitude from the National Forest Service, which had a much more "user" friendly mandate than the NPS. They allowed McCoy to expand to several adjacent mountains. In 2005, McCoy sold his stake in Mammoth Mountain to the Starwood Capital Group for $365 million. Jay also looked at several ski areas in Colorado and Utah, which also turned out to have significant growth, but again they could never make a deal.

## Sea World

For Jay, Sea World was the perfect acquisition. He loved everything about the place. He was always fascinated by the ocean and as a young man made many visits to Marineland of the Pacific, the forerunner of Sea World. He was a lifelong fisherman and a catch-and-release advocate before it was given a name.

The Sea World story begins to take shape in 1976 after the Yosemite acquisition. The tour was doing well, Yosemite was a prestigious and profitable acquisition, and Sid Sheinberg was supportive and enthusiastic when Jay proposed they visit the San Diego park. Jay made arrangements to fly down with their wives and show Sheinberg why he was so excited about Sea World and what a good fit it would be.

The night before the trip, Jay and his wife were invited to dinner at the Sheinberg's home in Beverly Hills. The other dinner guests were Jack Webb and Darren McGavin and their wives. Jay had never observed Sheinberg so relaxed and confident. He was a congenial host, and when they sat down for dinner, he handed everyone shot glasses and began pouring Aquavit (a Swedish vodka). The shot glasses had a ball-shaped bottom so you could not put them down without draining your glass. Jay thought it was a fun night, but he was so intoxicated he never remembered driving home. He paid the price the next morning with a screaming hangover. They barely made their flight to San Diego.

Dave DeMott, one of the founders of Sea World, met them. DeMott was cordial but appeared to Jay a little nervous and suspicious. Sheinberg seemed delighted by everything they were seeing, and Jay could tell that Sheinberg was aware of the potential of combining the two companies and that Sea World would be complementary to the Studio Tour.

Jay tried every argument he could think of to show DeMott what MCA could bring to the table to assist them in achieving their goals more quickly, but to no avail. Then DeMott suggested that Sheinberg's wife, Lorraine, might enjoy the opportunity of being "kissed" by Shamu in the killer whale show. Jay was not anticipating this. Lorraine agreed, and Jay's heart was in his stomach until the stunt was over. They were seated in the front row and they all walked away soaked. Lorraine was a good sport and the negotiation hopes were still alive.

Nevertheless, every time Jay suggested the benefits of a possible merger he was politely rebuffed. Sea World wanted to remain independent, and DeMott was firm in his conviction that they could finance their growth and saw no benefit from merging the two companies.

Shortly after their visit to Sea World, Jay began to formulate a hostile takeover strategy. A breakfast meeting was set up at the Beverly Hills Hotel with Felix Rohatyn, the legendary investment banker from Lazard Freres, with Wasserman, Sheinberg, and Jay attending. They planned to accumulate 8% of Sea World stock and make a hostile bid for the balance of their shares at $22 per share at a time when the stock was selling for $17, making the total value of the offer $35 million. At the time, Jay remembered thinking that this was a ridiculously low offer for a company with so much potential to grow, but he was happy to have gotten this far into the process, so he said nothing. He had no experience in this area and felt sure they would be willing to bid more if circumstances warranted. There was no discussion on how high MCA would be prepared to go if another bidder appeared. Jay was confident that MCA would at least be willing to make a counter offer.

Finally, after years of searching for the textbook acquisition, Sea World, the most attractive theme park Jay had analyzed, was almost within his grasp. Most importantly, he had Sheinberg and Wasserman on board.

The night before the offer was to go public, Jay could barely sleep. Jay had dozens of ideas on how to improve their visitor's experience, even without a killer whale show. He was excited and eager to take the next step. Not long after he did fall asleep, he was awakened by the telephone around 5:30 a.m. The voice on the other end of the line said, "We have been outbid by Harcourt Brace Jovanovic." Confused and shocked, Jay blurted out, "What the fuck is a Harcourt Brace Son of a Bitch, who the hell are they? What are they? I never heard of them."

Sea World had found a white knight in Harcourt Brace Jovanovic (HBJ), a publishing company who had made a higher offer to fight off the merger. Jay showered and rushed to the studio where a counter strategy meeting was to be held in the MCA boardroom. The room was filled with all the key executives who were involved in the merger offer. What he thought was going to be a productive counter-bid strategy meeting did not last long.

Wasserman declared, "We have been outbid by someone who knows nothing about the theme park business. Does anyone have a different view?" Total silence. After a pause, Jay said, "Lew, we low balled our bid, I think we need to come back with a higher bid. The Harcourt Brace offer of $65 million was still weak in my opinion. You cannot build one park for that price, and they already have two, with one more being built, and several more planned." Then, once again total silence.

Jay continued to press his arguments further until Wasserman started to scream, "Just because one of our executives is emotional I am not going to get into a bidding war and be made to look like a fool and pay more than the company is worth." Jay bravely made one additional attempt urging Wasserman to make at least one counter bid, but he refused. Jay was devastated.

Years later, Wasserman met with William Jovanovich, HBJ company head, for lunch at LeSerre, a fancy French restaurant near the studios, to discuss a possible combination. Wasserman came back after the lunch and told Jay that he could never deal with Jovanovich—who had a full bottle of whiskey on his table that he kept drinking from, and never took off this big hat during lunch.

Several years after MCA's failed takeover attempt Wasserman told Jay, "We should have bought Sea World." This statement was as close to an apology as Jay ever got from Wasserman. He admitted he made a mistake. Jay got another unlikely apology from Hal Haas, MCA's comptroller, a few months before his death. Haas told Jay he should have said something in the Sea World meeting. He said, "You were right; we should have made a higher bid."

As fate would have it, MCA got another chance to bid on Sea World in August 1989. HBJ got into financial trouble and decided to put Sea World on the market. This time, MCA put in a more realistic bid of $900 million. It was still not enough. Anheuser-Busch acquired Sea World for $1.1 billion.

# Cedar Point, Odeque, MGM, Knotts, Colonial Williamsburg

Lew Wasserman always had a soft spot for his hometown of Cleveland, Ohio. Cleveland was where he got his start, and it was where MCA started with their band business. He *was* Cleveland. That is the main reason he was interested in purchasing Cedar Point, an Ohio amusement park. Owning the amusement park would be a sentimental move that would also make money. MCA treasurer Harold Haas said, "It is a business with which we're familiar. We see Cedar Point as a good investment."

To facilitate the transaction, Wasserman sent Jay and Sheinberg to North Eleuthera in the Bahamas to meet with Cedar Point owner Robert L. Munger Jr. They chartered a plane, which immediately flew into bad weather. When they first met Munger, he was drunk. Negotiations began, but did not seem to be going anywhere. In December 1979, MCA made a bid of $11.47 million. The Cedar Point board rejected it. When gas prices and interest rates shot up, Wasserman's taste for Cedar Point subsided. Ultimately, the investment bankers assisting MCA purchased Cedar Point. Once again, MCA's low-ball bid strategy failed.

Another opportunity appeared in 1984. Odeque, a Japanese railroad and department store conglomerate contacted MCA with an offer to provide land and partner with Universal to build a theme park a short distance from Tokyo. Sid Sheinberg put Biff Gale in charge of the project. Gale was a recent hire with international business experience. His previous employers included Studebaker and Ampex, both companies that went bankrupt. As the only attorney in the Recreation Division, Tony Sauber was assigned to work with Gale.

Gale and Sauber made three two-week trips to Japan in March, May, and July 1984. Members of Jay's P&D (Planning & Development) team joined them on the first trip to examine the property. Although Gale was optimistic a deal could be struck, Sauber was not so sure. He felt something was not right from the start. More importantly, as the only divisional lawyer, it was tough being away from the office and generally out of touch for so long.

What impressed Sauber most about Gale was his ability to take any conversation and turn it into a discussion about himself and his accomplishments in life. He was a friendly person with interesting stories, but as far as Sauber could tell, he only knew how to talk about himself. Sauber felt he had the skills of a great chess master. No matter what subject you open a conversation with, within three exchanges he could turn the issue to himself and keep it there.

Ultimately, Odeque walked away. In fact, they never intended to make a deal. The deal did not fall apart due to any intransigent deal term. Instead, Sauber learned that they were using a potential deal with MCA as leverage with a local municipality who wanted the land utilized for another purpose. When they got the best deal possible, they told MCA the city was insisting the land be used for this other purpose.

Because of his experience with technology and international business, Gale served on the joint venture board with Pioneer for MCA's ill-fated Laser Disc project. The MCA team thought they could solve the problem by bringing in IBM, but MCA simply did not have any business being in the consumer electronics manufacturing business. Gale was let go in August 1984.

The NPS asked Jay to look at Colonial Williamsburg. He quickly determined that the way it was structured—multiple individuals costumed and acting as colonial artisans and shopkeepers in an artfully authentic recreation of 16$^{th}$ century life—would be cumbersome and complicated by having to deal with dozens of individual private contractors.

In 1990, yet another theme park opportunity crossed Jay's desk. Lew Wasserman had set up a meeting with Kirk Kerkorian, MGM's owner, and his lieutenant, Fred Benninger. MGM had already made an incredibly bad deal with Disney for the rights to use their iconic brand for the park in Florida.

Now Kerkorian was determined to build his theme park on property adjacent to his casino in Las Vegas. For Kerkorian, this was a bold move and consistent with the city's effort at the time to rebrand itself as a family-friendly resort destination. What would happen if Universal and MGM became partners in Las Vegas?

Jay was immediately suspicious that this would be no more than a courtesy meeting. He knew that the MCA culture would be an obstacle in dealing with a casino operator. A few years earlier, Jay had approached Wasserman and Sheinberg about doing a deal with Bill Harrah. Harrah was the legendary owner of casino resorts in Lake Tahoe and Reno. During that meeting, Wasserman showed no enthusiasm for the deal and told Jay that Jules Stein never wanted to be associated with gambling interests. To emphasize the point, he pushed his nose to the side as if it were broken and said we do not want to be in business with guys like that. Jay got the message.

However, the idea of a new park with a viable partner got Jay's creative juices flowing, and before hearing the MGM pitch, he started to ponder the viability of an enclosed, climate-controlled park. At the lunch meeting in the MCA executive dining room, Kerkorian and Benninger revealed their plans to build a movie theme park adjacent to the MGM Grand Hotel.

Jay started to ask questions. How much land did MGM set aside for this project, how many attractions would be open to the weather, and what was the budget? He learned that they only had 55 acres, most of the attractions would be outdoors, and the budget was set at a paltry $200 million.

When Jay heard those answers, he realized that a deal was unlikely. However, he knew if MCA could make the right deal, it might be an opportunity to challenge Disney's relationship with MGM. There were other benefits for MCA. Jay had a crack design team that had just finished one theme park. He figured they could work fast to save money and it would only take four months to complete the conceptual design.

More importantly, he would gain a strategic advantage in his battle with Disney. At lunch, discussion focused on an MGM-Universal park. If a deal could be made, MGM would have one park with Disney on the East Coast and Universal on the West Coast. As part of the deal, Universal would also gain the rights to collaborate with MGM developing hotels worldwide, including Florida.

Nonetheless, Wasserman was even more skeptical and doubted that it would be profitable enough for MCA. However, he did have one suggestion. Although he knew he did not want to do a stand-alone park deal, Wasserman cleverly suggested that maybe MGM could give MCA a small incremental share of the gaming revenues. The meeting ended shortly after that and on a cordial basis.

MGM would go on to build their park. They tried to emulate a movie studio with themed areas representing New York, Asia, a French street, a Salem waterfront, New Orleans, Olde England, and the Wild West. Featured characters included Betty Boop and King Looey. The park opened on December 18, 1993. Over the years of lagging attendance, the park suffered from cutbacks and its space began to be used for other purposes. It finally closed to the public on September 4, 2000.

MCA's next target, in 1993, was Knott's Berry Farm. The park was in trouble, and the vultures were circling. Attendance had decreased from 4 million in 1976 to 3.4 million in 1992. Bension took a look and found that Disney, Warner Bros., and Sony had already started to kick the tires and Paramount had already taken steps to acquire the property.

In a March 1993 memo to Jay, Bension assessment of Knott's was that it "tried to be too many things—multiple, inconsistent themes." He added, "What they did was not carried out well." The Knott family had stopped investing and lacked the financial commitment to make it a first-class park. They let their franchise deteriorate and were no longer even marginally competitive. Moreover, they cut back on marketing and let Magic

Mountain become dominant in the thrill ride market. The only positive aspect Bension could find was that the park was well maintained.

Bension estimated that it would cost MCA at least $100 million to upgrade the park. He thought that many of the rides and infrastructures could be recycled. Looking to the future, he felt they had four primary options: they could enhance the Western theme, create a new theme, convert the facility into a thrill park, or create a family park like Williamsburg. A fifth option was to scrap the 15 acres of parking clean and build a second gate right in Disney's neighborhood. After all, Bension felt the regulatory hurdles would be far less onerous in Buena Park than Universal City. Jay felt that given MCA's financial strength and their creative theming abilities, they could have become a reliable non-movie theme park alternative and a profitable enterprise.

The biggest hurdle would be MCA's leadership. At the time, Jay knew that MCA would not last long in a bidding war, especially after what happened with Sea World. Strategically, Jay felt that it would have been in Disney's best interests to try to outbid MCA. There was no way that they would let a major competitor gain a foothold in Orange County. Jay figured that a Universal park would have affected Disney's attendance significantly, and that threat would take the price to astronomical levels.

Looking back, Jay was glad that MCA bowed out to concentrate on expanding in Florida. There, he had land to optimize growth and give them the credibility to export their park franchise all over the world. At Knott's, MCA would not have been able to build a second gate or multiple hotels. Moreover, the financial demands required to make Knott's fully competitive with Disney would have altered or delayed his Florida plans.

## Destination Dining

In 1979, Jay decided that MCA should enter the destination dining business. Victoria Station had built a facility near the tour entrance, and it was a huge success. Next time, Jay vowed that MCA would own the restaurant and keep all the profits. Themed restaurants were becoming a popular trend and Universal City was the perfect location for such a venue. Jay wanted his place right at the tour entrance.

He got the idea from a photo of an old rural building housing a business of some kind in the Old West, with the Whomphopper name on a shingle over the door. Capitalizing on the country-western craze created by the film *Urban Cowboy* (1980), he asked Terry Winnick to come up with a concept. One day, while watching television, Winnick saw a commercial by Cal Worthington, the legendary southern Californian car salesman. The light went on.

Like a theme park attraction, the restaurant had an elaborate back story. Linked to the history of the local area, C.L. Womphopper began to sell new and used horse-drawn wagons on the site in 1851. That is why the restaurant became known as Whomphopper's Wagon Works.

It was run by a costumed, mustached character named C.J Whomphopper, who was the forerunner of the fast-talking, over-the-top television auto pitchmen. All the waiters would be costumed as mustached con-men wagon salesmen; the menu would be a humorous parody of car sales lingo, and there would be old broken-down wagons all over with signs in front intended to be humorous. There would be good ribs and Western dancing at night to music performed by Jim Gibson, a favorite country western group. They even used Jay's recipe for the chili, even though they lost money on every bowl because the ingredients were too expensive!

To set the right tone, Tony Sauber hired comedy writer Milt Rosen, whose television writing dated back to the classic variety shows on TV in the 1950s. He had also done a lot of ghostwriting for celebrities, such as Milton Berle and later Arnold Schwarzenegger. He cranked out a huge volume of material.

Gary Meyer did the concept drawings, and architect Lynn Paxton was hired due to her experience with other themed restaurants. Jay was able to get authentic time-worn timbers from Idaho, Oregon, and Washington. Winnick searched the back lot for every old wagon he could find.

The 13,000 square foot facility had five different decors and nine distinct rooms. Each room was themed to reflect a different aspect of the wagon business. Actor Ron Schneider was hired to portray C.L. Whomphopper. He described one room as an "elegant private booth for our Hollywood clientele and a gilded VIP cage, representing Womphopper's former accounting department." Disney's Imagineers were so impressed that many of them became weekly lunch customers. It took only six months to complete the project at a cost of $3 million.

The restaurant opened around Labor Day 1980. For a few years, it was very popular, and, with over 500 seats, one of the highest grossing eateries in Los Angeles. Then the bloom faded on country-western music and dancing. To maintain the same level of profits MCA had earned in the good days, they tried raising the prices and cutting back on food costs. Then the market dried up. The restaurant was closed by 1990 and leased to a new operator.

*Chapter 5*
# Universal Studios Florida: Take One

## Putting a Stake in the Ground

It did not take Jay long after getting the job running the tour in 1967 to look at areas for potential expansion. He hired the Stanford Research Institute (SRI) to look at Miami, New Orleans, and Atlanta. Miami was already the center for television production within Florida, so it made sense to start there. After a visit looking for opportunities, Jay found none.

Then he left Miami and visited Cypress Gardens in central Florida. While talking with owner Dick Pope, Pope turned to introduce an associate by saying, "I want you to meet my head nigger." After this, Jay decided a deal for Cypress Gardens might not work, and learned that Pope was not interested in selling. Although Jay left Florida empty handed, he realized that the state was the future of the Recreation Division.

In the early 1960s, Walt Disney had purchased 27,443-acres in central Florida to build a demonstration city and a vacation resort. The anchor of the project would be an East Coast Disneyland.

What worked in Los Angeles could certainly work in Florida. In 1969, Jay began to work on the design of a facility similar to what MCA had at Universal City. He and Terry Winnick collaborated on ideas in his living room. However, they decided to start by building up the Hollywood Tour, so Jay put his Florida project on the back burner.

Cut to November 1977. When real estate agent Allan Keen picked up the phone, little did he know that he was going to be drafted as a secret agent in the battle between MCA and Disney. On the line was Bill Bieberbach, a former college roommate and close friend. Bieberbach began his career working at Walt Disney World as a financial analyst, and now he was working for Nelson Schwab, executive vice president at Taft Broadcasting Co. Bieberbach wanted to enlist Keen to be their exclusive real estate broker for some property in Florida.

Bieberbach told Keen what they were looking for and why they wanted the land. Keen scribbled on a yellow pad that they wanted a "thrill-ride" park and "in the womb of Disney." His new clients wanted to fall somewhere along Interstate 4, from US 27 in Polk County to Lake Mary Boulevard in Seminole County. There were approximately 25 potential interchanges within the study area.

In early 1978, Schwab and two men described as potential "investors" visited Keen. The investors were Jay and Al Dorskind. Also at the meeting was Richard R. Swann, of Swann & Haddock. Schwab asked Keen to recommend a local legal team, and he suggested Swann because he had many connections and understood the local politics.

Keen and Swann had no idea who the men were. After a brief meeting, Keen and Swann took them up in a helicopter to give them a birds-eye view of the frontage along Interstate 4. They had identified five sites that met the criteria first outlined by Bieberbach.

That evening, the four of them had dinner at La Belle Verre on Park Avenue in downtown Winter Park. Keen was doing his best trying to promote Orlando as a place to do business, mentioning all the great things happening in the area. During the pitch, Keen mentioned a recent *Orlando Sentinel* article suggesting that some of the movie studios were thinking of coming to the area to make films.

When Jay heard this, he leaned over to Keen and asked, "What are you talking about? What exactly did you read? What exactly did it say?" Keen was taken aback and intimidated by Jay's reaction. Jay told him to research exactly where this information came from and to report to him immediately. He then said, "This could be one of the most important things that you do for us." Despite extensive research, Keen could not locate the article.

A week later, Bieberbach called and asked, "How did your meeting with Universal go?" Keen said at that moment, "The rockets went off, and I immediately figured out why Jay was so upset that night and whom I was dealing with." Keen later learned that MCA and Taft had created a partnership to look for land in Florida and Bieberbach was acting as the "front" man. Two weeks after that, Keen was officially informed that his client was MCA/Universal Studios.

The land acquisition strategy was to contract with three separate landowners at the same time, for acreage south and west of an area between Orlando and Walt Disney World. However, Jay and Dorskind were not satisfied with the first five locations. The initial three sites included the Westworld Site (located on the property where Sea World is today), the Marriott World Site (then called the Barley Site), and a third site owned by Major Realty.

Fortuitously, several days before the MCA visit, Swann's partner, Ed Haddock, brought to his attention that he had been representing a client who had had the Major property under contract, but the client had dropped the contract. Haddock thought it might be an ideal property for Universal. Swann told Haddock to make sure he got a release from the client in case the Major property became relevant to Universal Studios Florida (USF).

Haddock mentioned it to Keen, who liked the property but said it did not meet the parameters that he had been instructed to look for. When Jay and Dorskind stated that they wanted to look at more properties, Haddock mentioned the Major site and produced the information related to it.

There was a discussion about the property. Dorskind noted that the Major site reminded him of the Universal Studio site in Los Angeles, and he wanted to look at it. Jay, Dorskind, and Keen hopped back in the car to look at the Major property. When Jay came back to the real estate offices, there was an air of excitement. Jay and Dorskind thought it might be an easy sell to Lew Wasserman (assuming the terms were right) because the site was a near replica of the MCA property in Los Angeles. It was approximately the same size (300+ acres), bounded by Kirkman Road and I-4 versus Lankershim and Freeway 101 in Los Angeles, in the midst of a business district. Most importantly, International Drive was right across I-4 from the Major property.

Before one site visit, Keen's wife, Linda, told the crew from California that the palmetto-scrub terrain prevalent throughout the site contained many rattlesnakes. She suggested they put "flea collars" around their ankles to ward off the snakes. Everybody in the group believed her. Thank goodness there were no snakes around, for they were not protected. Keen and Linda sure got a good laugh.

Getting the contracts for all three sites simultaneously was not working out as planned, so the focus turned to the Major Realty site. The property was within the city of Orlando, a friendly jurisdiction, and owned by a motivated local real-estate company. Major held 323 acres of the original 423-acre track initially purchased by MCA. The Gulf Oil Real Estate Company (GORICO), a subsidiary of Gulf Oil, owned the other 100 acres. Keen tried to get MCA to purchase another property across the street that contained some bankrupt hotels, but nothing came of that.

Richard Swann listed himself as the buyer to keep MCA's identity secret. A price agreement was reached, first with GORIECO for their 100 acres at $75,000 per acre, and subsequently a verbal agreement with Major for their 323-acres at $15,000 per acre, for a total purchase price of approximately $12,500,000.

When the contract was in the final stages of acceptance, Jay asked Swann to come up with an announcement plan. Swann suggested following the Disney road map for the announcement of the contract. He suggested that Governor Bob Graham make the announcement as Governor Burns had done for Disney.

With the permission of Wasserman, Sheinberg, Dorskind, and Jay, Keen was given the authorization to track down Graham, disclose to him that MCA/Universal wanted to locate in Orlando, and that he had to call MCA Chairman Lew Wasserman for the "official" disclosure to be made. Keen relayed that it was Wasserman's request that Governor Graham make the announcement as the governor had been actively promoting motion-picture development in Florida during his term. MCA gave the governor full credit for his long-time efforts to get movie production in Florida, thus giving him ownership of the project.

Jay had drafted the original statement for the governor's use. The night before the announcement, after Swann's son-in-law, Terry McAuliffe, saw the remarks, he tore them up and said he would write something much better the following morning. He did, and Jay was delighted with the results.

An unexpected by-product of having the governor make the announcement was that he was helpful to MCA in moving the project through the development process. The governor was excited about the project and for being asked to make the announcement.

However, before the announcement could be made, Major demanded to know who was purchasing its land. Keen and Swann told them that they could not reveal the purchaser. The executives from Major refused to enter into a binding contract to sell the property, even though there was an agreement on the price, terms, and land area, unless and until the buyer was disclosed. Everybody was at a standstill.

Keen worked out a purchase-and-sale agreement for the sale of the property, and placed the fully executed contract into escrow, with the only condition for its release the third-party disclosure. That third party was Governor Bob Graham, who Keen knew from the last gubernatorial campaign.

Keen encouraged the governor contact Major and, without revealing the company's name, tell them that the buyer was a Fortune 500 company, a financial powerhouse highly respected in their field. The purchase and development of the Major Realty land would not only be significant for their company, but equally important to the Orlando area, as well as the entire state of Florida. Graham duly called Major, at which time the contract was released from escrow.

Shortly after the public announcement of the USF contract, Swann was asked to put together a group of area leaders for an introduction to the project. Some 150–200 attended the packed house presentation at the Robert Meyer Hotel in downtown Orlando. Swann was asked to be the M.C., and he made all of the preliminary remarks and introductions. All was smooth until it came to the main speaker, Sid Sheinberg. Swann did an excellent job describing Sheinberg's background and role, but as he wrapped up, he said, "So let me introduce you to Sid 'Steinberg.'". Swann was mortified, though he quickly corrected the error. Then, as an aside, he said remorsefully, "I'll be gone tomorrow." The audience chuckled, and Swann could imagine the other lawyers in the crowd licking their chops that a great client like MCA might be available soon. Sheinberg came to the podium giving Swann a wry smile. When he got to the podium, he said he wanted to thank "Billy Bob" Swann for that fine introduction, bringing a loud burst of laughter from the audience.

## Details, Details

There were other issues before the deal could be finalized. Swann negotiated the deal with one of the Major attorneys, a member of one of the most prestigious Orlando law firms at the time. The attorney assigned to the matter by Major thought Swann was negotiating too hard and called somebody at MCA to complain and asked to be allowed to negotiate directly with the person inside MCA overseeing the deal. Subsequently, Major's attorney asked MCA to remove Swann from the negotiations. Major's attorney was told that he was negotiating with the right person, and he must deal directly with Swann as if he was the equivalent of an MCA vice president.

The issues included a request to see the drainage plan. During the negotiations, Major had represented that the drainage plan for the property had been approved, and the easements to the outfall (Shingle Creek) were in place. Keen and Swann attempted to have them produce copies of the easements to attach to the contract. For whatever reason, they would not agree to furnish them until the due diligence period expired and USF's deposit was at risk.

When time was running out on USF's timeline, Jay authorized his Florida team to attempt to obtain the easements on Major's behalf. As it turned out, Major did not have the necessary documents. Swann extended the contract three or more times to give Major time to produce the easements. In the process, they determined that Major's drainage plan itself was outdated. Rules had changed and now required one inch of water retention onsite. Swann discovered that on government I-4 right-of-way plans a drainage pipe under the highway that was sized adequately to hold the flow of the water from the site even in its fully developed stage. Swann's personal real estate development experience and working relationship with a senior lawyer for the Florida Department of Transportation enabled him to not only identify the problem but also to find the solution. The easements became moot. A new engineer verified Swann's findings and was authorized to design a new plan in compliance with the new rules and process approval of the revised plan.

Then came the issue of land use entitlements. Major had represented that the property had vested development rights so that a development of regional impact (DRI) study would not be required. The development would not be subject to any of the requirements of the relatively new DRI regulations. In Swann's review of the statute, Major would be right so long as any change in the development plans would not be a substantial modification. The statute listed criteria setting mandatory metrics of several development issues such as transportation, sewer capacity, and other impacts, any of which if exceeded would trigger a DRI, and vested rights would be eliminated.

Working with Barry Upson, Swann prepared an application to the state to confirm that the property was deemed a non-substantial change. Upson calculated all of the impacts of the required metrics and determined all of them to be under the maximum allowed before the DRI requirement would be triggered, yet the application was denied because the *anticipated use* had been changed.

Upson and Swann went to the state capital in Tallahassee to meet with representatives from the Department of Community Affairs and argued that the change in use was a zoning matter and not listed as criteria in the statute. The staff told them that change in usage alone constituted a substantial change. They declared it was a matter of policy which could not be waived.

Swann had learned that Graham, as a senator in the Florida Senate before becoming governor, had been the sponsor of the DRI legislation. Swann found a pay phone in the Capitol (long before cell phones), called the governor, and explained the issue. The governor agreed with Swann's position and said it was never the intent of the legislation to have a change in use be a factor. He said he would discuss the policy with the governing agency. Not long after, USF got a determination that its plan was a non-substantial change. Swann was told by MCA that, if they had to be subject to a DRI, the time and expense of the DRI would kill the project. Victory.

Over the next twenty years, the Keewin Real Property Company and Swann & Haddock represented Universal as they purchased an additional 1,000 acres of adjacent contiguous land to the south, all the way from Kirkman Road to Sand Lake Road. This assemblage consisted of some 30 separate parcels.

Keen and Swann were responsible for making these deals and sometimes had to go to extraordinary lengths to secure an agreement. For example, Universal had to buy an old, wooden African-American church and some parcels of low-income homes on Wallace Road. Swann developed the strategy, Keen did the negotiations, and Swann handled the transactions. To get the church property, Keen brought Swann into the negotiations, as the church had obvious reluctance. USF agreed to swap some excess property and build the congregation a *new* church. Swann was impressed with MCA's generosity, as it funded the construction of a larger, modern, handsome church facility, accumulating goodwill with the displaced homeowners and surrounding neighbors.

Next was the purchased of a "choke-point" 1.5-acre parcel from the owners of Edwin Watts Golf Shop. On the property was a highly successful golf retail store that sat between two parcels owned by MCA. USF planners wanted to unify the separated parcels. Swann negotiated with Watts' owners to swap their property with the USF property separated from the rest of the super block. USF also agreed to replace the Watts building with a new facility on the swapped property. Everyone was a winner.

A cash-rich, powerful Osceola County family owned the largest amount of undeveloped property around USF outside of the Major Realty holdings. The family was not motivated to sell. They had plenty of money, and did not need more. Keen went to their "hunt-camp," deep in Osceola County, on several occasions; he sat by the campfire, sipped a little whiskey, smoked a cigar or two, and ultimately developed a personal relationship with the manager of the family's holdings. That led to an almost $10,000,000 contract for the land. Things were moving along well.

The Smith Sisters' property was the remnant of a family ranch dating back two or three generations. Keen brought them to the table with the outline of a deal. Keen and Swann met with the sisters and their lawyer to negotiate the contract. Swann had submitted a proposed contract as a first draft to work from. The negotiations began around midday and continued through the late night until the parties signed a contract. When the process was finally concluded, around 5:30 a.m., Keen and Swann went for breakfast at a nearby Waffle House in which Keen had an ownership interest. Swann paid. When the USF office opened, they called to let Jay know the contract had been obtained. They were congratulated, as it was the last tract the development plan required. When the staff was told that they stayed with it until signed, not leaving until 5:30 a.m., they were acknowledged by some as heroes and others as insane.

The experience left Keen with some takeaways. First, money could not motivate someone who had none if they did not know or care what it could do to their lives. Second, money does not always motivate those who had loads of money. For both type of sellers, it took a *personal* relationship before a transaction to occur. The lesson being, it is only those of us who have had a *little bit* of money who are motivated by it, not those who have been "without" or those "with."

On behalf of USF, Swann applied for an incentive grant to rebuild Turkey Lake Road, which at the time was a narrow two-lane country road in need of repair, to four lanes. The grant was awarded, but it would not be funded until USF began construction of its project. The award contained an expiration date for construction to begin. Time was ticking but MCA was not ready to move forward, due to lack of a partner. Swann worried that the grant would be lost. Even if an extension were given, USF was afraid that inflation would render the grant insufficient. The loss of the grant would have been a huge morale blow to MCA, and Jay was worried that Wasserman would kill the project. He was not going to let that happen.

Again, Swann called the governor and discussed the issue. He agreed to send the grant money to the city to hold in escrow until the construction of the project commenced. The escrow money was put into an interest-bearing account when rates were exploding (T-Bills at a rate of 18%). It turned out to be a bonanza for the project as early 1980s recession kept material costs relatively low, and the interest increased the pot. Not only was the cost of the Turkey Lake rebuild met, but there were also sufficient excess earnings to complete additional projects. Swann was told the arrangement of putting the money in escrow before beginning construction was a first.

The USF planners were worried that noise from fireworks would create issues with neighbors. Swann got a call from Tony Sauber, who had been in the class behind Swann at Duke Law School. Swann considered him a very smart guy, and they worked together in revising the city's noise ordinance. While most of the ordinance provisions were relatively standard, they accomplished having the noise level measured at the point of receipt, not emanation (which had been the customary standard). USF planners were triumphant with the new ordinance. It was especially useful when Islands of Adventure opened because, unlike USF, it had big, noise-making rides close to a school.

To have adequate access to the park, USF had to provide better access to I-4. While a plan for a new interchange had been approved years earlier, it had expired. Some said the plan would be difficult to reinstate since traffic conditions on I-4 had significantly increased. Swann worked with the US Department of Transportation, the Florida Department of Transportation, and city and local governments to get the plan reinstated.

Building the interchange was estimated to cost approximately $50,000,000, a major stumbling point with the budget. Swann told Jay that he thought he could get Trustees of the Internal Improvement Fund (TIIF) financing to build the interchange. No one believed Swann until he told them of his involvement with TIIF funding a similar purpose in Seminole County. With that, he was authorized to pursue the possibility of TIIF financing. He worked with USF's CFO and MCA's accounting department to prepare preliminary estimated numbers for the costs of construction versus the anticipated increase in property tax revenues to pay the bonds. Then, working with city and county officials, Swann obtained the local government's support.

A team was assembled to develop financial models, including the city's finance director, a county representative, and the city's bond counsel. One requirement was to qualify the bonds as municipal bonds. The taxing district had to contain at least five properties independent of USF, which was done. While it was a complicated transaction, it was successful. It could not have been done without the cooperation of the leaders and staff of the city (mayor), county (chairman), and finance teams of USF and MCA. While it was a rigorous task, it was win-win for city, county, USF, and the other property owners who joined in the taxing district. Though the project was estimated at $50,000,000 (representing about a third of new tax revenues to the city and the county), with USF's construction managers overseeing the outside contractor, the cost came in around $38,000,000. The interchange work went well, and the district became financially sound.

Early on, Swann had suggested they try to rename Orlando Vineland Road to Universal Blvd. The road was, at the time, the main road from downtown Orlando, if one wanted to avoid I-4. USF rightly thought a road to and from the tourist area would be more appropriate. The only problem was there was not such a main road with direct access to USF. However, when the I-4 interchange was built, it contained a flyover connecting Universal's main road to Republic Drive. With local government support, Swann orchestrated the name change from Republic Drive to Universal Blvd. It was a perfect moniker as it ran from Universal directly to the heart of the tourist district and all the way to the Orange County Convention Center, one of the largest in the country.

Years later, when Jay decided to explore the second park, Swann was asked to investigate the purchase of the remainder of Major's portion of the super block. Major said it was not interested in a sale, but suggested a partnership in which Major would contribute its remaining interest in the super block together with the rest of their properties in the immediate vicinity. It was an intriguing idea.

Swann prepared an outline presenting the idea to USF and MCA. He was given the authority to explore such an arrangement and, subsequently, to negotiate a deal. Major's corporate office was near Birmingham, Michigan, just outside of Detroit. Swann made two or three trips to Michigan to discuss the terms of such a partnership. When the discussion became serious, James M. Adams III, Major's CEO, turned Swann over to his outside corporate attorney who was with a prominent Detroit law firm. They would send drafts back and forth (by fax in those days) and, finally, had a deal acceptable to both parties. Because of the impact to Major's financials, Major was required to obtain its board approval.

Swann had a call from Major's corporate lawyer in Detroit who said that the board liked the contract, but before approving it, they wanted to see the plans for the super block development, including all of its elements. Swann arranged a meeting at MCA's corporate headquarters in Los Angeles for the Major board to meet Lew Wasserman and Sid Sheinberg and to review the plans. Jay and Swann were in the meeting with some MCA staffers. Major's attorney did not attend even though all of their conversations led them to believe he would be there. Swann believes he intended to be there. Adams spoke for Major and highly praised the project, the design, and expressed confidence that it would be a great success. Then the shocker—he asked, "How much are you going to pay us for our land?" Swann was shocked and embarrassed.

Sheinberg said he thought they were there to discuss a proposed partnership. Adams asked, "What partnership?" Swann butted in and said the partnership that they had been negotiating for the last several weeks with his outside attorney. The two lawyers worked together to set up the meeting. Adams responded, "What attorney?" Swann gave the name of the attorney and Adams denied knowing him.

At this point, the meeting was adjourned after a few pleasantries. Swann was humiliated and worried about Sheinberg, Wasserman, and Jay's reaction, thinking that he had misled them. Shortly after the meeting, Swann ran into Sheinberg and Wasserman in the commissary. He tried to apologize for the failure of the meeting, but Sheinberg said not to worry, it clearly was not his fault. Sheinberg said he knew that Adams was lying as soon as he denied knowing the lawyer. The stranger part was that the Major board of directors, consisting of five prominent, wealthy businesspeople, some nationally recognizable, would engage in such a charade. After a cooling-off period, Al Lawing, Major's head in Orlando, called to restart negotiations. Major needed a deal. MCA made one, buying the land for a much more attractive cost than the proposed partnership would have provided.

Now that the real estate deals were done, Barry Upson was sent to Florida to begin the planning process. He worked closely with Swann on development approval issues. He also needed a designer lead. Enter Bob Ward.

Ward was a former Imagineer and a talented designer who had been a part of the Disney design team in the creation of the Magic Kingdom. Swann assisted Ward in setting up his own design company in the early 1970s. After six up-and-down years on his own, Ward had traveled back to Los Angeles to explore themed entertainment work opportunities. He visited Imagineering and Warner Bros., who operated the Atari and Malibu Grand Prix destinations. He also met MCA's Herb Steinberg. Steinberg set up a meeting with Ward and Upson. Upson was impressed with Ward's portfolio and ideas, however, Upson pointed out that Universal was just a studio tour and they were *not* in the theme park business. It was a nice introduction, but that was it.

Not long afterward, when Upson got to the point of laying out the new park, he asked if Swann knew a good designer. Swann recommended Ward. Ward was hired immediately, and as part of the team, he played a significant role. Not only was he a great designer, but he was also an enthusiastic promoter of USF to prospective sponsors. Ward became such a star that Swann considered his reintroduction of Ward to Upson as one of his most significant contributions to USF.

## You Have to Find a Partner

Wasserman was interested in a Florida park. Nevertheless, his increasingly cautious approach toward business forced him to come up with one non-negotiable deal point. If Jay wanted to build in Florida, he had to find a partner. Wasserman made it clear that if expansion was such a good idea, then it would be no problem to find a partner to spread the risk. No partner, no park. Jay heard the ground rules loud and clear. Finding a partner was mandatory.

It made sense in Wasserman's mind. MCA and the partner would each put in equal capital and share the profits equally. However, in addition to MCA's share of the profits, they would also be entitled to a 5% royalty off the top to reflect the value of Universal's intellectual properties and their creative abilities. Also, the joint venture would pay for all of the MCA staff's development work and a portion of their executives' time. In other words, MCA's percentage return was higher for their 50% investment than it would have been—as a percentage, not in total dollars—from owning the whole business. Brilliant. The search was on.

From Jay's perspective, there was only one problem. Many of the partners that MCA would be approaching might have different agendas and financial requirements, and did not have the incentive to make the park great; rather, they wanted a sound investment and to get their money back as soon as possible. They may not be driven by MCA's desire to "out Disney, Disney."

Also, as the old saying goes, "You make someone a partner (or a producer) and then the next thing you know, they think they are a partner (or a producer)!" Jay knew this meant that any potential partner would want to put their two cents in and criticize his ideas, whether *they* brought any of their own skills to the table or not. It was a concept Jay's team knew was doomed to failure, yet Wasserman and Sheinberg were insistent that Jay find a partner, presumably because they did not have sufficient faith in the concept of the Florida park, and wanted the "vote of confidence" of someone else putting up half the money.

Sheinberg suggested they start with Paramount Pictures. He had claimed that Michael Eisner and Barry Diller, the men who ran Paramount, were his "two best, most trusted friends." Because of this personal relationship, he said, "It would have been unthinkable that we would have discussed this first with any company other than Paramount." The two studios had most recently done business when they formed the USA Network in 1980.

The meeting was set up for July 29, 1981, with representatives from both studios inside the "presentation room" bungalow on the Universal lot. From MCA were Wasserman, Sheinberg, Hal Haas, George Smith, and Jay. There were also a couple of creative people from P&D. Representing Paramount was chairman Barry Diller, Michael Eisner, and executive vice president Arthur Barron.

It was a happy place. Everybody was relaxed as they were amongst friends. In fact, Sheinberg was confident his "friends" would be a perfect fit, and they would jump at the chance to be MCA's partner. Jay knew Diller and Eisner casually, and Sheinberg and Wasserman were extremely close with both of them. Diller was a good friend of Wasserman's daughter and in his younger days spent a lot of time in their home observing and admiring Wasserman when he was on the phone. Diller spoke about this while delivering a eulogy at Wasserman's memorial service years later in the Universal Amphitheatre.

The presentation room, also known as the Dog and Pony Show, was full of color renderings of all of the proposed attractions, detailed models, a diorama of the site, and an audio-visual system with multiple slide projectors that showed confidential profit and attendance projections. It was a remarkable display and begged the question, "What do you need me for?" Over the next two-hours, MCA representatives took the Paramount executives on a street-by-street tour of the proposed park to answer that question.

Everything was going smoothly. Jay read Diller and Eisner as being pleased that all of their questions were satisfactorily answered. Everybody on the MCA side felt the meeting went well and that they had a real shot with Paramount. In the end, MCA and Paramount were not able to come to an agreement. *The Los Angeles Times* speculated that Charles Bluhdorn, chairman of Gulf & Western, Paramount's parent corporation, killed the deal. The leadership at MCA had no inkling what would take place a few years later.

Over the next few years, they approached RCA, Taft Broadcasting Co., Lorimar, and the Bass Brothers of Fort Worth, Texas, among others. Ironically, after the Bass Brothers learned of the opportunities in Florida, they became owners of 25% of Disney stock and helped to force future

Disney CEO Michael Eisner to increase investment in the Walt Disney World property, thereby setting up the battles to come.

Jay was still searching for a partner in 1984 when he made a presentation to Michael Milken, the junk bond king. Instead of investing in the park, Milken used the confidential information to convince casino owner Steve Wynn to buy just fewer than 5% of MCA's stock. Wasserman was furious.

After knocking on so many doors, a discouraged Sheinberg reflected, "I think there was a kind of feeling 'why is MCA looking for a partner if this is so good? Why don't they do it themselves?' We had simply decided that we did not want to expand into Florida all on our own credit." Jay would have to continue looking for that all-elusive partner.

Of all the potential partners, Taft Broadcasting came closest. Taft was already operating six theme parks including Canada's Wonderland and Great America in Santa Clara, California. They owned Hanna-Barbera Productions and many radio and television stations. Furthermore, they were there in the very beginning as MCA's partner in the Florida real estate transaction.

Jay went to Cincinnati to meet with Taft's chairman, Charles S. Mechem Jr. Jay stayed at Mechem's house and showed him the plans. He loved them. Mechem immediately contacted his executive vice president, Nelson Schwab. Schwab had helped Jay with the Florida land purchase many years before. For Jay, Taft was a partner made in heaven. They understood what Jay was trying to do and how they would fit into the project. They got to the point where they were drafting deal memos. Things were looking up.

Then came the announcement from Walt Disney Productions. On September 23, 1984, after a very public management coup, Michael Eisner became chairman CEO, and Frank Wells became president of Walt Disney Productions. It was not long before Eisner would start to test his old friends at MCA. It began with a conference call shortly after he took over at Disney.

During the call, a confident Sheinberg suggested to Eisner, "Let's get together on a studio tour in Orlando. We tried with your predecessors, but they were unresponsive. We think we can help you." Much to the surprise of the MCA executives, Eisner told his old friend, "We're already working on something of our own."

That was not the reaction Sheinberg, Wasserman, or Jay were expecting. "Ultimately, we were informed that they might want to do one of these tours themselves, and they did not want to be accused of somehow, whatever the word was, stealing or acting improperly if we had a meeting and they later decided to go on their own," Sheinberg then explained. "That signal really surprised us, to put it mildly. It was our first indication that they were off on a plan to do this."

The Taft executives took stock and realized that a partnership with Universal made sense at the original scope of the project, but with Disney's announcement, everybody knew that the game was moving to a higher level, and Taft backed out.

In October 1984, Lew Wasserman met with Florida Governor Bob Graham while they were both in Los Angeles. As an economic development initiative, Graham was trying to make Florida the Hollywood of the East. He said, "Florida has a special interest in the motion picture and television industry", and the project was "an important signal to the movie industry and the rest of the country and the country's business community."

Graham was not interested in another theme park. He felt that Disney was enough. What he wanted from Universal was a real working production studio. Using this desire to his advantage, Wasserman suggested that Florida loan MCA $150 million from the state's $8 billion pension fund to build the studio and tour. In exchange, MCA would build a bigger studio and park than they initially announced. The pension fund would hold the first mortgage on Universal's 423-acre property as security. Wasserman also suggested that the state invest $35 million per year for five years to produce films in Florida in exchange for a cut of the box office profits. Wasserman reminded the governor that Universal had already invested $40 million in developing its Florida property. He went one step further and had every executive in the Recreation Division donate to Graham's reelection effort.

Then came the announcement from Walt Disney Productions to their shareholders on February 7, 1985, about a studio and tour at Walt Disney World. To reassure stockholders, Eisner told the gathering that the studio theme park would be very different from any other Disney park. "Sensitive to the cost overruns at Epcot, we decided to build Disney-MGM Studios with a much smaller capacity, while leaving room to expand in the face of demand." Furthermore, Eisner said, it "meant that it could be less-finished in its look than our other two parks." Eisner also suggested that the price of admission might be less than the Magic Kingdom and Epcot Center. Disney's park would be half the size of the one envisioned by Universal. Eisner figured it would take Universal at least four or five years to build their park, even if they found their partner right away. Eisner wanted his park completed in *three*.

The partnership between Disney and MGM was a forced marriage. The Disney Imagineers recognized that their studio had a limited catalog of films that would interest adults. They needed recognizable intellectual properties fast and cheap. Ron Grover, in the 1991 book *The Disney Touch*, said, "The negotiations took about a month. In the end, Disney all but walked away with Leo the Lion's mane. Disney received almost free rein in use of the famous roaring lion and the treasure trove of old MGM movies. Most important, it got those rights for virtually nothing. Under the 20-year agreement, Disney was to pay only $100,000 a year for the first three years and $250,000 for the fourth year. The annual fee would increase by $50,000 in every year thereafter, with an eventual cap of $1 million for the yearly fee. Disney also got nearly unfettered ability to build other studio tours, for each of which it would pay half the fee agreed upon for the Orlando park."

Eisner also implemented a new strategy in his competition with MCA. He would try to be nice. On May 24, 1985, Eisner wrote Sheinberg and Wasserman denying any involvement in trying to prevent MCA from recruiting a partner. He was offering a truce. Eisner wrote, "We do not want to hurt you. If differences remain, let us keep them private as befits our companies as members of the same industry."

Along with the sweet came the bitter. Eisner warned his competitors that Disney's advantages in Florida ("our land, existing infrastructure, marketing commitment, hotels, monorail, research, and development organizations...and sources of financing") were insurmountable and that it would be unwise to proceed with their development plans.

## The Battle of the Burbank Backlot

The battles between Universal and Disney would not be limited to Florida or the parks in southern California. In 1987, Michael Eisner decided to bring the fight right to Universal's front door.

In the fall of 1985, Disney formed a partnership with James W. Rouse's acclaimed Enterprise Development Company. Rouse was a successful, well-respected, and socially conscious developer. Some of his best-known projects include the planned community of Columbia, Maryland, and festival marketplaces such as Faneuil Hall in Boston, South Street Seaport in New York, and Baltimore's Harbor Place.

The two companies began to look for opportunities to build family entertainment centers at key urban locations. The projects would have something for everyone by combining a festival marketplace, a Disney entertainment complex, and a regional shopping center. During the day, the festival market would attract both locals and visitors and become the regional shopping and dining destination of choice. Disney officials were quick to point out, though, that the compound was not a mini-theme park, and there would be a wide variety of entertainment, rides, shopping, and dining options to attract visitors. At night, the atmosphere would change to satisfy the adult seeking fine dining, "yupscale" entertainment, unique lounges, and venues such as the Adventurer's Club.

For 12 years, Burbank had been looking for someone to build a regional shopping center on a significant piece of vacant property on Third and

Magnolia. At one point, Ernest W. Hahn Inc. had an agreement with the city to build a conventional $158 million mall, but the deal fell through. When Robert R. Bowne, a Burbank councilman, heard the news, he suggested, "Why don't we let Disney dream a dream for Burbank?"

Without telling other members of the city council, councilwoman and former mayor Mary Lou Howard contacted Michael Eisner and invited him to have lunch with her and Burbank city manager Bud Ovrom. During the 2-hour lunch, Eisner sketched out on napkins and tablecloths some of his ideas for what to do with the property.

Disney proposed to build the Disney-MGM Studio Backlot at an estimated $150–$300 million. The 40-acre project would have featured a man-made lake, a fantasy hotel, and restaurants that change décor with the season. Other features included an animation production studio and radio and television media center.

City officials negotiated a property agreement with Disney at the bargain price of $1 million on May 5, 1987, to expedite the project. City Hall watchdogs claimed that the offer was too low and suggested the property was worth closer to $50 million. MCA officials were also troubled by the deal. They argued that they were denied the chance to bid on the property.

Even more sinister, after the deal was announced Disney executive Jeffrey Katzenberg called Cineplex Odeon CEO Garth Drabinsky (MCA's partner at the time in the Florida project) offering to drop plans to build in Burbank if MCA would abandon Florida. Stein described the communications as "blackmail tactics." MCA knew that the Burbank Back Lot development was a red herring. In June 1987, MCA filed suit to overturn the Burbank deal.

By October 1987, Disney was claiming that it had problems attracting a major retailer and that they were scaling back their plans. Internally, writer Michael McCall said they "overshot the target by misunderstanding the dynamics of translating down theme park attractions to the commercial environment dominated by malls, and transforming developer-driven retail merchandising up to the level of attractions." When Michael Eisner learned in February 1988 that the cost of the Disney project had skyrocketed to more than $618 million, he admitted, "I would say it's some time off before we break ground, a couple of years maybe." On April 8, 1988, Disney sent a letter to Burbank officials withdrawing from the agreement. When asked for his assessment, Sidney Sheinberg said, "I don't want to talk any more about anything that we feel toward Disney. We love everybody. Peace, love, and friendship."

Because of Disney's announcement, the leadership at Taft decided that their potential partnership with MCA would be too expensive. In the end, it was the rising interests rates and the cost of the project that scared them away. Although the entertainment industry was a cutthroat business, Sheinberg felt Eisner's actions crossed the line. His reaction was succinct. "The Mouse has become a ravenous rat."

## Frank Wells

Jerry Weintraub had managed artists including Frank Sinatra, Neil Diamond, and John Denver. The Universal Amphitheatre was frequently the venue for his clients. Later, he organized and managed large arena concerts. He then became a successful television and movie producer.

When Weintraub called Jay in July 1985, nothing seemed out of the ordinary. Jay had known the producer for many years. The two played tennis weekly, and Jay considered Weintraub a good friend. Also, Jay was always on the hunt for new ideas and new properties to exploit, and he relied on his relationships with producers to give him an edge. Weintraub told Jay that he wanted to meet privately as he had something crucial he wanted to share with him.

Jay prodded for more information, but Weintraub said that he could not discuss it on the phone. Jay told him that he was busy with the pre-production for Florida and could not afford the time to drive all the way out to Weintraub's house in Malibu. Weintraub then reluctantly divulged that *somebody* wanted to meet him. Jay agreed, and they set a date to meet.

When Jay arrived at Weintraub's house on the Pacific coast's Paradise Cove, he was met by Weintraub's wife, singer Jane Morgan, and she led him to Weintraub who was sitting outside alone, overlooking the ocean on that beautiful warm day. Morgan offered Jay a drink, and he ordered one of whatever Weintraub was drinking. Jane poured some lemonade and then left.

"Why all the mystery," Jay asked. Weintraub just smiled and said, "He just called, and he's running a little late; he will be here shortly." Ten minutes later, in walks a very tall, thin, patrician-looking man wearing glasses. It was Frank Wells, president of the Walt Disney Company. Jay recognized him immediately. Weintraub made the introductions, and they began about thirty minutes of talking about Wells' failed attempt to scale Mount Everest in 1983.

Jay was clueless as to why this meeting was taking place. Finally, Wells started talking about Disney and how their Florida parks were performing. He asked Jay numerous questions about how they do things and was effusively complimentary. Then Wells smoothly switched gears and said they were having some "leadership" issues. He told Jay that the man they had running their parks was a long-time loyal employee who was a good soldier, but he lacked imagination and creativity.

Wells was referring to Dick Nunis. Nunis had started at Disneyland just before the opening as one of the trainers and rose to the position of chairman of Walt Disney Attractions. Wells began to trash Nunis, saying that Nunis only knew how to do things one way, and was hesitant to introduce anything new. They were looking to make a change. Wells asked Jay, "How would you like to come work for the Walt Disney Company? You can build the park you want. What would you do differently in our parks?"

During the conversation, a helicopter was circling over Weintraub's house. Jay noticed Wells beginning to show signs of sweat under his shirt. He was growing very uncomfortable. He finally asked Jerry, "What the hell is going on with that helicopter? Why is it circling your house?" Weintraub began to laugh, "It's nothing Frank. It's Bruce Jenner. He does this all the time."

Now the helicopter was hovering with its pilot looking in their direction. At this point, Wells stood up and said, "I don't want to continue our discussion at this time. That helicopter is bothering me! I just don't like it." Weintraub again tried to convince Wells it was only Jenner "doing his thing." Wells was not persuaded. The meeting lasted only a couple of minutes longer before the nerve-racked Wells felt like he was being set up. They all quickly shook hands, and he left abruptly.

Once Wells had left, Jay asked Weintraub what the purpose of the meeting was. Weintraub replied, "They were trying to steal you away." Jay was not so sure about the offer. He never heard from Wells or Disney again. Jay has kept this meeting a secret until now, for this book. Only Tony Sauber and Bob Finkelstein knew of the offer.

There were several occasions over the following years when Jay was publically criticizing Disney and Michael Eisner often responded, "Stein is only mad, angry because we did not hire him." Every time these remarks came up in print, Jay expected a call from Sheinberg or Wasserman demanding an explanation. They never called, nor did any of Jay's employees ever question if this were true. Eisner's credibility within the ranks of MCA was so small and insignificant that everybody just ignored his remarks.

On July 6, 2015, Jerry Weintraub passed away. The day before, he and Jay had breakfast, and they reminisced about the meeting with Wells. Jay speculated on what would have happened if Wells had not been interrupted and had put a firm offer on the table. Jay's first action would have been to go to Sheinberg and tell him about the offer. He felt that would be the honorable thing to do. If asked to stay, Jay would only ask for two conditions. First, MCA would have to match the Disney offer. More importantly, Sheinberg would have to give Jay an iron-clad commitment that they would build the Florida park with or without a partner. Unfortunately, for Jay, the search for that elusive partner would have to continue.

## On Hold

The difficulty in finding a partner combined with the aggressive Disney tactics were challenges that seemed insurmountable. However, it was the world economy that finally put the Florida project on the shelf temporarily. By 1984, prime interest rates were skyrocketing to close to 18%. Jay was concerned and had Peter Kingston rerun the calculations. What he found was very disappointing. If the economy kept on its current track, the park would be financially unappealing as an investment. The internal rate of return would not satisfy *any* potential partner.

There were other factors. Gasoline prices were historically high, and the 1984 Los Angeles Olympic Games hurt attendance at every southern California theme park. Locals left town, and visitors only went to the games.

In early 1985, in a pivotal meeting called by Wasserman and supported by Sheinberg, the men explored their options. They could cancel the project and sell the land. They could rush ahead without a partner and build their park before Disney by cutting corners, or they could go back to the drawing board and design a bigger and better park with the determination to win.

The decision was to put the project on hold. Shortly after the meeting with his bosses, Jay gathered his troops. He told them that although he was discouraged, he thought that the economy would eventually rebound and, if they kept their powder dry, they would live to fight another day. He said, "You can leave if you want to, and I won't hold it against you." Nobody left the room or the company.

Upon reflection, Jay believed that the dire economic situation of the mid-1980s contributed to Wasserman's belief that MCA needed deeper pockets to compete against Disney. Wasserman calculated that if he could not find partners for his various initiatives, then MCA being acquired would eliminate much of the risk and protect his net worth. This plan would make sense if Sheinberg could continue to operate the company with little interference from the new parent.

## Everything Would Have Been Different

In the early 1980s, things were not going smoothly at Walt Disney Productions. At the time, Disney was best known for its theme parks, bad live-action films, and re-releases of old animated classics. Disney's new president, Ron Miller, was trying to move the stagnant studio forward, but the conservative chairman, Card Walker, hampered his attempts. Miller was responsible for Disney's entry into the home video market, Tokyo Disneyland, Touchtone Films, the Disney Channel, and many other innovations. However, a behind-the-scenes power play by Roy E. Disney, son of the company's co-founder, Roy O. Disney, was brewing.

In 1984, Walt Disney Productions became the target of numerous takeover attempts. One person taking a serious look was Lew Wasserman. Miller and Wasserman were old friends. A meeting was set up between Miller, Wasserman, and Disney's new chairman, Ray Watson. It seemed like a deal was possible. The only thing left was deciding who would be president of the new company.

Watson wanted Ron Miller to get the job. Wasserman preferred his right-hand man, Sidney Sheinberg. When Sheinberg recognized that he could be the deal breaker, he declined the position for Miller. However, Wasserman would not be deterred. He continued to insist that Sheinberg should get the job.

Felix Rohatyn, the investment banker advising MCA, told Wasserman, "Do it. A year from now you'll get rid of Miller and make Sid president." Wasserman did not take his advice. MCA could have likely purchased all of Disney for $1.5 billion at the time, but Wasserman opted not to. Barry Diller said of his friend, "It was Lew's inflexibility that caused him to blow deals he should not have blown. He and Jules [Stein] had built the best company. They should have owned the world. And had they made this deal with Disney, everything would have been different."

Years later, Jay speculated if the merger would have taken place, Disney California Adventure, Disney's Hollywood Studios, and Disney's Animal Kingdom would not have been built. Disney wasted a lot of money on inferior themes. ESPN Wide World of Sports would have been dramatically more imaginative and cutting edge.

*Chapter 6*
# Universal Studios Florida: Take Two

## Steven Spielberg

On July 9, 1985, Michael Eisner made good on his pledge and Walt Disney Productions began development of a new $300 million theme park in Orlando based on how movies were made. The park would have capacity for 25,000 guests.

Jeffery Katzenberg, Disney's head of production, suggested that Disney would ramp up annual production to 15 or more live-action films, 15 or more television movies, and 6 cable films, and that he could use the additional studio space. He also quietly mentioned that MGM was not planning to use the facility for productions of its own.

MCA cried foul. The plans Disney announced sure looked *a lot* like the plans MCA presented to Michael Eisner when he was at Paramount. Erwin D. Okun, senior vice president of Corporate Communications at Disney, said, "It is a totally fabricated fantasy. Who needs a plan when you can buy a ticket for $15 and go on a tour? Disney does not intend to be drawn into a manufactured controversy. We will not lend the series of unattributed and/or personal assertions dignity by responding to them individually, but we do deny categorically: (a) that Disney ever stole, borrowed, or misappropriated anyone else's ideas for the Disney-MGM Studios—or that Disney will ever do so, or would have to do so; and (b) that Michael Eisner saw or discussed any plans or drawings of anyone else's studio tour proposals before or after he came to Disney."

An unintended consequence of the war with Disney was the need to start paying other studios for the theme park rights for intellectual properties. Disney, due to its rather limited catalog of titles that would appeal to adults, had to open its wallet to other studios, and that bid up prices. Universal was used to getting the rights free. Jay and Tony Sauber spent a lot of time reassuring producers that the exposure outweighed any need for financial compensation. With that said, they did pay key actors and creative personnel for their cooperation and consents. Disney ruined that. Making matters worse, Universal could not start paying for new properties without reopening the agreements with those producers already on board. Sauber wrote Jay, "If we pay other studios for rights, we are opening a 'can of worms,' with wide-ranging ramifications, but that may be the only way we can get other studios to cooperate, given the changed marketplace that Disney has caused."

In the past, Jay had access to productions well in advance of their completion. More recently, his division had been kept in the dark on some story elements that could be highly relevant in designing an attraction. For the first time, they were being treated as outsiders by filmmakers. This happened with the team producing *Back to the Future II*.

With dollar signs dangling in front of producers for the first time, the market began to dry up and what few properties were out there became very expensive. For example, Disney paid Paramount Studios $400,000 to use film clips at Disney-MGM. Jay suggested that the parks should get involved in the earliest planning stages of their big-budget films that have the potential for exploitation in various formats. He used Disney and *Dick Tracy* as the example of doing it right. They were planning stuff while the film was still on the drawing board. Unfortunately, for that potential franchise, the film turned out to be a flop.

There was one rights agreement that became central to the success of the Universal theme parks. Jay wanted to work in close collaboration with Steven Spielberg to maximize the potential of his projects. Jay needed Spielberg. He needed him for his properties, his stature, his creativity, and all the entertainment credibility he brought to the parks. Without Spielberg's support, USF would not have been possible.

The rule was clear. MCA executives remained in the background. The star was the star. MCA was not a "me-me thing" but a team effort run by Lew Wasserman for the benefit of their clients. That is why the MCA executive wore a black suit and stood in the background.

Talks began in 1986, soon after Spielberg had been exposed to the King Kong audio-animatronics figure. Sheinberg took the lead in setting out the Spielberg deal. Spielberg would let his name be used in marketing (subject to his approval) and would perform as a "creative consultant." In exchange, Spielberg would get a percentage of the absolute gross for all revenues of that park, and the deal would apply to all future Universal movie theme parks (other than the pre-existing park in Los Angeles). The exact percentage was specified as confidential, but it has resulted in extraordinary payments to Spielberg. This deal was part of a larger deal that was more important to Sheinberg—that Spielberg would make his production home at Universal. Spielberg was family. Sheinberg was his dad and Wasserman was his uncle. They were very close. For the theme parks, Steven Spielberg would get the creative credits.

Jay recognized early on that if the public wanted to believe that Spielberg was the creative master behind the attractions at Universal, then they should ride that horse. That is why he never flinched at his management fee. His name, his films, and many of his suggestions gave Jay's team credibility that surpassed anything they could do on their own. Spielberg's validation of what the Recreation Division was trying to do provided an invaluable level of comfort to Wasserman and Sheinberg.

On the one hand, Jay was happy to have Spielberg's creative help and his self-interested support for the park, and to be able to use his name in marketing, and was especially glad that this phenomenal payday for Spielberg would make it much more likely that they would get USF built. Also, it made it much more likely that Spielberg would allow Jay to use his films as attractions as well as those he did at other studios.

Jay warned Sheinberg, "While Disney won't catch up with us with attractions based on *Honey I Shrunk the Kids*, if we let Steven take his big, attraction-oriented projects there, and if they develop rides around some of Steven's mega-projects then we will have a problem." This was no idle threat. Jay had heard rumors about Amblin's spider-themed project *Arachnophobia*, although he felt such an arrangement was prohibited by their agreement.

On the other hand, Spielberg's creative input, in reality, was not as important to Jay's team from a strictly artistic point of view. When the team conducted presentations, Spielberg would just about always approve enthusiastically and perhaps offer some minor "tweaks." He was a great audience. Jay said that Spielberg had an exceptional ability to think three-dimensionally. The Universal team would come up with ideas and bounce them off Spielberg. He asked penetrating questions and suggested changes, especially when it came to his movies. He would step in quickly to pick up the weakness of any concept. He was generous with his praise.

Spielberg would help sell the ideas to Sheinberg by showing his enthusiasm. When he endorsed a ride or show, it *meant* something. Even when Speilberg only tweaked or approved a project, Jay wanted him to take as much creative credit as Speilberg was willing to accept. To be fair, he always underplayed his role, reluctantly taking partial credit. Jay felt that his imprimatur was of much more value than something generated by "Jay Stein and Planning and Development." However, Spielberg's creative proposals were relatively minor and frequently would be too theatrical to be practical, such as things that could not be done repeatedly every few minutes.

The only drawback to the deal was economics—Spielberg's percentage of every penny that came into MCA coffers took away a big part of their profits.

Jay's relationship with Spielberg was respectful but not warm and personal as was his relationship with Sheinberg and Wasserman. Spielberg's loyalty was unwavering toward Sheinberg and Wasserman. The several times Jay wrote to him confidentially to gain his support on projects (rides, shows, budgets, etc.) where either Sheinberg, Wasserman, or a partner were uncommitted, Jay always got something approved. He would not get a reply from Speilberg and the director never betrayed Jay's confidentiality request. To this day, Jay is unclear about what role, if any, the director played in getting approvals, but he believed he was batting very close to 1000 after requesting his help.

One other factor influenced Jay's relationship with Spielberg. Jay was at war with Disney in the press, claiming that Disney had stolen Universal's plans. Michael Eisner and Jeffery Katzenberg were busy denying the charges. Jay wanted to sue Disney for stealing the plans. He had Terry Winnick put together the entire case, and they were about to file for an injunction.

Then Jay received a strongly worded letter from Spielberg telling him to "stand down." This was followed by a confirmation phone call from Sheinberg. Jay later learned that Katzenberg was one of Spielberg's closest friends. Jay believes Katzenberg asked Spielberg to intercede to stop his aggressive charges.

After this encounter, Jay became obsessed with outdoing everything that was going into the Disney-MGM Studios by building his own studio with superior production facilities, set streets, rides, shows, theming, and overall ambiance. After all, Disney's plans were public, and Jay estimated that 70% were taken from Universal. Ironically, Katzenberg and Eisner had a major and very public falling out when Katzenberg left Disney to form a partnership with Spielberg and David Geffen called SKG.

If he could brainstorm with Spielberg and other producers to learn what was in the pipeline, Jay promised that the parks would commit to a mini-attraction to open simultaneously with the major feature. Planning for a mega attraction would begin immediately and be ready if the film was a hit. Jay was diplomatically planning for growth and a headstart toward other projects.

## Home Run!

It had been more than five years since Jay had gotten the green light contingent upon finding a partner. Five long years and nothing to show for it. In September 1986, everything changed.

Sid Sheinberg and Garth Drabinsky were having lunch in the MCA commissary. Drabinsky was the head of the Canadian Cineplex Odeon movie chain. With the help of Seagrams, another Canadian company best known as the largest distiller of alcoholic beverages in the world, Drabinsky created the second biggest chain of theaters in North America and the United Kingdom with 1,818 screens. Along with Myron Gottlieb, Drabinsky's partner, he also dabbled in movie and Broadway stage production and they became high rollers in the world of finance.

After the Cineplex Odeon complex in the Beverly Center had become the biggest grossing theater in Los Angeles, Hollywood insiders took notice. Drabinsky worked out a deal with MCA to build the world's largest multiplex adjacent to the Studio Tour in Hollywood. After they had made the deal, Sheinberg had no doubt that Drabinsky's ambitions were to take over his job. Drabinsky's provocative and ruthless personality earned him the nickname "Garth Vader." Nevertheless, Sheinberg was impressed enough that MCA took a 49.7 percent interest in Cineplex Odeon for $150 million.

Jay and others at MCA described Drabinsky as another "genius of the month." Frequently, Sheinberg would "discover" someone outside the company and put him in charge of some area with jurisdiction over long-standing executives or place him in a high corporate position with the power to comment on what the divisions are doing. For many of these *genius de mois*" it would not be long before Sheinberg would realize they were not as talented as he first believed and they would be gone.

After lunch, Sheinberg and Drabinsky wandered down to the P&D office to see the projects underway for the Studio Tour in Hollywood and Universal City Florida. As the men entered the room, they saw Bob Ward working on the Earthquake attraction. Ward was an enthusiastic, loyal team player. Jay spent many hours working alone in his home with Ward because the latter was able to grasp his boss's ideas and almost immediately sketch his thoughts on paper. Ward *got it* and was an indispensable player who deserves much credit for his immense creative and practical contributions to the Universal parks. Emotionally, he was the heart and soul of Planning and Development.

"We were at the drawing stage," Ward said. "We had storyboards and were starting to build a hydro model. The concept had telephone poles moving. Power lines sparking. Transformers blowing up. A couple of houses collapsing. There was a pause so that this would be perceived as the show. Then the second whammy. The road erupted, a gas line broke. Huge flames. A crack in the dam. Vehicles overturned. Then a wave of water—100 to 150 thousand gallons—came directly at the tram, went over the top of the tram." The plan was to duplicate the attraction for both Los Angeles and Florida. Drabinsky wanted to learn more.

Jay invited him to see the highly polished partner presentation. Jay started with some background and introduced Peter Alexander, who went through their usual briefing. Drabinsky loved it. He seemed impressed with every component. "He [Drabinsky] was jumping out of his chair," Bob Ward recalled. "He said this is the greatest thing going. He was actually jumping around." He kept yelling "home run" and turned to Sheinberg and said, "Sid, if you don't do this you're an idiot. What are you waiting for?" He could not have been more complimentary. Jay thought to himself, "Where did this guy come from?"

Not long afterward, Sheinberg arranged a meeting with Drabinsky, Spielberg, Wasserman, and Jay. Drabinsky waxed eloquently about how impressed he was, and that he would love to be a partner. He told Spielberg that he was confident that they had a winner. Once again, he called the Florida project a "home run." His enthusiasm boosted confidence at the top. Spielberg was excited. Even Wasserman chimed in with a compliment or two.

Jay remembered Spielberg looking at Drabinsky trying to assess if this guy was for real. Spielberg turned to Jay with a quizzical look on his face. Jay just kept quiet, faintly smiling like a Cheshire cat, enjoying his happiness after so many years of effort and disappointment. It was a love fest. USF was now going to be a reality.

In December 1986, a handshake deal between MCA and Cineplex Odeon was announced at a MCA management meeting in Newport Beach. Jay's dream took a major step forward. Jay had been fighting with Wasserman and Sheinberg for years, and he never gave up. Drabinsky gave Sheinberg and Wasserman the validation they needed to build USF. Over several days in Toronto, Tony Sauber worked with Cineplex Odeon lawyer Murray Pearlman (Murray the Pearl) drafting an agreement.

However, it would not take long before Jay would learn that what first turned out to be a blessing would soon become a curse. A week later Drabinsky asked to change some of the terms of the deal. He wanted to have 50% of the management fee since he was a 50/50 partner. Also, he told Jay he wanted the woman he was traveling with to be part of the team. Jay said no. Wasserman and Sheinberg were taken in by a guy with very little capital investment capability, with the goal of taking as much money out of the project, while Jay wanted to reinvest and build the project to its full potential. It did not take long before Jay realized that Drabinsky was an egomaniacal, dishonest person who had little knowledge of the businesses in which he was now a partner. Sheinberg's said, "Lew and I woke up to realize we were in bed with a madman."

Drabinsky hired Jeff McNair to represent the Cineplex interests in Orlando. McNair had a marketing background and Drabinsky's trust. He was given access to all of the day-to-day joint venture information and was invited to all project, financial, budget, and marketing meetings. What the MCA team soon learned was that he was sending misinformation or misinterpreted information back to Drabinsky. Drabinsky would then call Wasserman or Sheinberg and tell them what he was told and often with his own spin and most often without verification from Jay, who would then receive a call and a witch hunt would begin. As a result, the MCA team became very cautious around McNair, who always had a grin and seemed to enjoy watching people scramble.

## The Joint Venture

It was up to Tony Sauber to get the deal with Cineplex Odeon locked up. He was the only lawyer for the entire Recreation Division, which was already ramping up with land development and construction contracts. He was also drafting the complicated deal with Steven Spielberg to become the creative consultant. Assisting him with the heavy work on the two contracts was Jerry Nagin, a competent, detail-oriented lawyer from Rosenfeld, Meyer, and Susman. The firm had historical ties to Universal.

Sheinberg made the basic outline for the deals in just a sentence or two. Because it was difficult to cover all contingencies, both agreements took a long time to draft and were incredibly complex. The formal agreements became huge, and it seemed only Nagin understood everything. Sauber tried to simplify the contract language and summarize the issues in ordinary English for Jay and to work to strengthen MCA's position on the issues.

Sheinberg told Sauber and Nagin to consult with Charles "Skip" Paul on any issues that were not going well. Like Drabinsky, Paul was considered by many to be another one of Sheinberg's "genius of the month" club members. Paul was well educated, earning his law degree from the University of Santa Clara and serving as a law clerk for U.S. Supreme Court Justice John Paul Stevens. Paul was bright, congenial, acted interested in other people, and was always very well dressed—in a country-club manner. He enjoyed discussing strategy and was accomplished in thinking several moves ahead. Years later, Paul would join the MCA board of directors.

Paul was responsible to Sid Sheinberg and the corporation and not to any one division. He was an early advocate of Garth Drabinsky and the MCA person overseeing the investment in Cineplex Odeon, which Paul was confident would be a goldmine.

Paul was also put in charge of international development. Under his leadership, MCA looked at building a park just east of London. Paul introduced Lew Wasserman to Margaret Thatcher, but the project did not progress much further. Paul talked with officials in Spain after they were left at the altar by Disney. Spain was more than happy to make a deal. Paul and

Frank Stanek also found a location south of Paris that was superior to the Disney site. When they met with officials, Disney executives went ballistic.

Those in the Recreation Division thought Paul was not a team player. His peers described him as smart but rather devious. He used to tell everyone in the Recreation Division that he thought *they* were the sharpest and most fun to be with of all the MCA divisions. They did not believe him.

Although Paul was a supporter of the division and wanted to see the Florida park built, he would turn around and occasionally toss a colleague under the bus. Tony Sauber recalled such an encounter while seeking the rights to use *Star Trek* as the featured intellectual property for the Screen Test Theatre in the Los Angeles park. The premise for the show was that audience volunteers would appear to be acting in a *Star Trek* episode, in costumes and on the bridge of the *Enterprise*, and ultimately their performances would be played back, so it would seem that they were interacting with the actual *Star Trek* cast (using pre-existing footage). Sheinberg approached someone high up in Paramount and got approval in concept, and left it to Sauber to negotiate the deal points and finalize a contract. Sauber also had to get permission from Gene Roddenberry and all the performers. That was no easy task.

Sheinberg told Sauber to report to Paul once everything was resolved. There was a trivial "give" that Sauber had to allow Paramount, which he knew would not matter in reality. Paul approved the deal, and Sauber forwarded it to Sheinberg. Not long afterward, Sauber got a call and was told to come up to Wasserman's office right away. For some reason, Wasserman and Sheinberg were clearly upset about the "give", at which time Paul said, "Yes, Tony, why did you do that?" (the implication being he knew nothing about it). Paul would also make disparaging remarks about Jay with the implication that he would do a better job running the division. For those loyal to Jay, this was troubling.

Moreover, many in the division believed that Paul sided with the other party in the Cineplex and Spielberg negotiations. The result was that the Cineplex Odeon and Spielberg agreements were unfavorable to MCA Recreation, considering what they were bringing to the table. Paul felt the Spielberg deal was important for reasons unrelated to the theme parks. As part of the deal, a bungalow complex on the lower lot was developed at great expense for Amblin, Spielberg's production company. The complex replaced the tour staff offices. The staff was moved into a "Butler-type" metal warehouse building. A few years later, the structure on the lower lot was recycled into tour offices at the top of the hill.

Under Sheinberg and Wasserman, there was no interest in providing the Recreation Division with decent offices. For many years they were in trailers and had to walk outside to go to the centralized bathroom trailer.

If the expenditure could not be seen by the ticket-buying public, they were not interested in making it, even if it might increase efficiencies or encourage recruitment of talent.

Paul was looking at the bigger corporate picture and Spielberg was essential to financial health at MCA. He has also boasted that Drabinsky was "a pearl without price" and he had MCA give in on most issues. Both contracts were finalized and awaiting signatures. Spielberg signed his right away, but Sauber waited for the Cineplex Odeon team to return theirs.

A critical milestone in the creation of Universal Studios Florida was achieved on December 15, 1986. Over the course of two days, the Joint Venture management team met for the first time. On one side of the table sat Jay and the P&D group from MCA. On the other side sat Garth Drabinsky and his crew from Cineplex Odeon. The tension was palpable from the start.

Jay's team went first. The discussion began with a review of MCA's 1982 plans. Those plans revealed a park capable of satisfying 3.5 million guests a year at an estimated cost of $219 million. The park would be similar to the Los Angeles Studio Tour but without the tram. The Florida site was flat; there was no need for an expensive tram system.

The MCA plan had the stunt and animal show staged in open-air arenas with the roofs over the seating and performance areas. The set streets behind the core "front lot" were much smaller in scope, with the surrounding "back lot" consisting of low-cost elements such as wilderness, desert, jungle, Red Sea, and Amity sets. The special effects were demonstrations, not shows or rides. The studio section was purely functional with bare stages for four-wall rentals. Barry Upson thought they could build that project no later than December 1989.

Drabinsky was not impressed. He considered cloning the Los Angeles Tour as "obsolete and ancient history." He rejected the stunt "fort" and said that Westerns were dead. He wanted a tall structure visible from exterior roads to signify where the park was located. His other demands included the purchase of an additional 30 acres and a special facility for cultural events hidden behind classic movie theater facades. Drabinsky also wanted fine dining added to the mix. Finally, he insisted that Lynda Friendly, his girlfriend at the time, review the merchandise program. There was no way that Jay could build a park with those changes for the money he had available, nor were his ideas merit worthy.

The heated discussion continued. Each side stood proudly by what they had done but now was the time for collaboration and compromises. That's how Jay worked. As a result, the overall concept of the park changed from a "two-ride park" with one land-based system and water-based system to a "show/ride" park featuring familiar characters from such films as *King*

*Kong* and *Ghostbusters*, a water mini-tour based on *Jaws*, the ice tunnel, and the Hollywood Hills earthquake. Added to the roster were a motion picture museum, the Cinemafantastic show, and expanding the streets from tram-tour size to walking-tour size.

After the meeting, everybody went back to their corners with the hope that the next gathering in January 1987 would be more productive and collaborative. In reality, this was the peak of cooperation and the beginning of a downward spiral.

## Bummy and Newberry

In January 1987, Jay felt confident enough about the progress to arrange a meeting with Wasserman, Sheinberg, and Spielberg. Spielberg liked what he saw and was so pleased that he recommended that it was time to add more "mega" rides to the offerings. He recommended the addition of a James Bond-themed live-action show, an indoor stunt show (bar brawl), an IMAX presentation, and food (Hard Rock Café). Other ideas that gained traction were a much larger, three-scene King Kong ride, and expanding Jaws into an animated boat ride. The leadership's growing enthusiasm for the park took a significant step forward during this meeting. The budget increased to $288 million.

Jay should have been elated about the prospect of building a more sophisticated park, but instead he began to worry. Although the Joint Venture team had already started working together, there was still no formal agreement between MCA and Cineplex Odeon. Drabinsky was dragging his feet. Jay did not anticipate this. He thought, because of Drabinsky's verbal enthusiasm, that he would be able to check off that box quickly once the MCA attorneys submitted an agreement to Cineplex Odeon. It would not be long before this status would become a dark cloud hanging over the project.

Nevertheless, Jay had to press on. Time was an issue. Since the Joint Venture meeting, Jay had his design team draft five different site plans that responded to the discussions. In all cases, the footprint expanded by as much as 68% since the December meeting. The stunt show that Drabinsky dismissed but Spielberg requested was expanded into a 360-degree wrap-around set with up to 20 costumed guests included in the show. The visible "out of the park" icon would be the Hollywood sign perched on top of the show building that enclosed Earthquake.

One thing that became non-negotiable was Jay's insistence that a state-of-the-art, authentic, and functional back lot was critical to beating Disney. He carefully studied photographs of all the movie studios in Hollywood and tried to incorporate the most visually identifiable features from each of them to provide the look he was striving for. Bob Ward said, "We studied what would be the most utilized sets for production companies. We did set environments."

In fact, Universal Studios Florida's back lot would be better than Hollywood. Jay was elated when Lloyd Henry "Bummy" Bumstead and Norman Newberry joined the project. The two men were the best in the business when it came to the design and layout of set streets on a back lot. Jay met Bummy at a screening of *The Sting* at producer Jenning Lang's home in 1973. He was a two-time Academy Award-winning cinematic art director and production designer (*The Sting* and *To Kill a Mockingbird*). Bummy had once worked for Disney and Jay made a mental note (just in case) for his Florida park idea. He knew that Bummy would be the only man who could create the look and feel of what he was trying to achieve.

Norman Newberry was an art director and production designer for *Staying Alive*, *The Best Little Whorehouse in Texas*, *History of the World: Part I*, and many others. Jay found Newberry to be one of the most talented and cooperative people he ever worked with. Newberry was unflappable and always striving for perfection. He seemed to have a solution for everything.

Confident that they had found the perfect creative team for the street sets, the budget was substantially increased. Every inch of the property would be a collection of excellent locations and shooting streets, a truly authentic experience. Disney may offer a fantasy version of Hollywood, but Universal would give the public a real working studio back lot to experience with a level of detail that would *destroy* what Disney was planning. Bob Ward said, "With our layout, you can see environments from many points of view. It's like any studio in Hollywood. The Disney back lot isn't like that."

While the MCA team was responsible for the principle design and construction of the park, Cineplex Odeon pledged to use its experience building movie theaters to find up to $20 million in construction savings without affecting the show. While Jay was skeptical about this claim, he did not want to challenge Drabinsky and lose their momentum. Drabinsky also suggested his relationship with Columbia Pictures was so healthy that he could get the rights to the popular *Ghostbusters* franchise at no cost. The Western stunt show and the Conan show were dropped for an expansion to the make-up show and other enhancements to the primary rides. By March, Barry Upson was getting ready to lock down the full schematics within two-and-a-half months. All of the changes meant a new budget of $295.7 million versus the proposed $239.6 million at the time of the first Joint Venture meeting. Things were coming together, and the Joint Venture team was just about ready to go to the banks.

## You Can't Have It Both Ways

Then Drabinsky decided to throw a giant wrench into the works. He threatened to pull out of the project unless MCA dropped their management fee and renegotiated with Steven Spielberg. Drabinsky had still not signed the joint venture agreement, and he was about to fall behind $9 million in payments for the development costs. Even though Jay, Sheinberg, and Wasserman thought they had a deal, Drabinsky began trying to change many of the agreed-to items and thought he was in a good position to negotiate.

Jay found these changes to be outrageous and in violation of the letter as well as the spirit of the deal memo. Despite his start as the "savior" of the project, Drabinsky was turning into Jay's greatest foe. Jay wanted to build a theme park. Drabinsky wanted to play accounting games to benefit Cineplex Odeon.

Problems were continuing to mount. Not only was Jay fighting with his partner, but he was also having little luck securing contractors who could build the back-lot sets within the original budget. No one had ever made sets to last years in the Florida climate, and there was a large "fear factor." All of the bids were coming in well over the budgeted amount.

Despite these struggles, the project finally did make it to the banks. With their approval, Jay thought he could refocus on getting the park designed and built. He was still dueling with Drabinsky. After a drafting session in late May, Jay submitted a new agreement and reminded Drabinsky that it "contained substantial concessions from us."

As for the park, even with one production studio dropped from the plans to save money, the budget grew from $295.7 million to $318.8 million. With financing costs, that number would increase to $372 million.

By August 1987, things were deteriorating quickly. On August 24, Drabinsky called Sheinberg to complain about the cost overruns. Sheinberg immediately contacted Jay and asked him to explain. "Sir!" That is how Sheinberg addressed everybody. Jay reminded Sheinberg that he would never delay reporting bad news. That was the MCA way. The numbers that Drabinsky were complaining about were raw numbers and did not reflect changes Jay had made a couple of days earlier.

Jay was feeling a lack of support from Sheinberg. In the past, he could always count on Sheinberg to be on his side. Now, he was not so sure about his boss. "On at least four occasions I can name, you have given Garth [Drabinsky] an audience to present his side of a dispute with us and have sided with him to the detriment, in my opinion, of the project." In a candid moment Jay further wrote, "While I recognize that you might find my point of view wrong and overrule me, what bothers me is that you did not follow the procedure you always insist upon when there is a dispute between executives—calling the affected people together to hear both sides. Garth clearly feels he has your ear, and when he and I cannot reach an agreement, he has learned that he can get a favorable reaction from you outside of my presence."

Jay felt Drabinsky had been using his access to Sheinberg to berate the MCA team and their efforts. He knew that Drabinsky and McNair were trying to portray the project as a fiasco, and drastic measures had to be taken. Jay already had Barry Upson prepare a list of potential changes and the cuts necessary to bring the project back in line. Jay told Sheinberg that was going to be the topic at a Joint Venture meeting the next day. Drabinsky never accepted that he was the only one responsible for the increase in show costs. Not only were the costs going up, but the already tight project schedule was also beginning to slip. Drabinsky had jumped the gun.

"There is no question—Garth has helped the project enormously," Jay wrote to Sheinberg. "He has had the vision and enthusiasm to raise the project to a higher level of entertainment value (and cost) than originally contemplated. Universal Studios Florida is bigger and substantially better than we envisaged in 1986 and Garth has been a moving force in achieving this. Cineplex also got us the hotel deal and played a key role in obtaining the loan commitment."

However, the downsides were beginning to outweigh the advantages. Jay and his staff found working with Cineplex to be debilitating and counter-productive. Things had to change immediately, or he was gone. He told Sheinberg, "The events preceding and following [the meeting] have brought the project to a very critical point and also serve to highlight major problems inherent in our relationship with Cineplex Odeon."

Frustrated, Jay wrote Drabinsky a handwritten note. "You threatened not to sign, and we have no deal if we didn't change the deal. You were told if you want out okay but the deal remains as written and either sign or withdraw but stop trying to negotiate with threats. You want all the benefits but not all the risks. We have to make commitments, and there are risks, which need to be shared. You made it very clear that you wanted to be a full and active partner, not a second-class partner. That you would be an active contributor entitled to full benefits. You can't have it both ways."

## Happy to Step Aside

To build a case against Drabinsky, Jay outlined some grievances for Sheinberg's consideration. First was Drabinsky's lack of candor. He would frequently agree to something and then quickly disassociate himself from the joint efforts. Then he refused to discuss cuts and would go directly to

Sheinberg and misstate the facts. Jay refused to believe that Drabinsky was sincere. He believed that all of this new concern about budgets was a just a front and excuse to renegotiate the deal under stressful conditions. Instead of working as a real partner, Jay felt that Drabinsky was always negotiating. He was always trying to achieve some advantage.

In a calculated move, Drabinsky had not signed the loan agreement and by drawing out the process until Jay was "under the gun," he could extract terms that would never have been agreed upon under other circumstances. He was always making change orders, creating significant delays.

Unfortunately for Jay, the strategy seemed to be working. Drabinsky wanted a collection of fine dining establishments hidden behind the facades of famous movie theaters. He also wanted to build a Roman-style amphitheatre. He felt that advertising on television was unnecessary and that newspaper ads would be enough. Drabinsky also suggested placing billboards near the airports of the top twenty to thirty markets two years before the park opened. None of this was helping to get the park built. Jay thought these suggestions idiotic.

Then there was the lack of respect. Jay thought Drabinsky was rude, inconsiderate, boastful, insulting, and prone to gross exaggerations. He would frequently make statements with no backup. Most importantly, he had no respect for MCA people at any level and in every division and was indiscriminate with whom he shared his views. MCA was a tightly run ship, and Drabinsky's inappropriate behavior with regard to meetings was hurting the project. He would frequently show up late, talk on the phone during the meeting, take long lunches, and then leave well before the meeting was over to go somewhere else.

Jay confided to Sheinberg that they had a partner who believed that they were incompetent. Drabinsky had no confidence in MCA's ability to control costs, and he was hoping and predicting Jay would fail. Jay argued that Cineplex Odeon had contributed nothing constructive and sat on the sidelines with an unsigned contract waiting to see another card.

It was Jay's belief that a partnership is where both partners share risk. He reminded Sheinberg that Drabinsky was given a chance to withdraw in August. He chose to stay but had still not signed the joint venture agreement. Because of this, Jay just did not trust them.

He was also annoyed that Drabinsky had no desire to learn about the theme park business. He refused to visit other parks beyond Epcot Center and Sea World. "Garth is not used to having anyone tell him he is wrong; every time he makes a claim or suggestion, even if we know it is totally wrong, it becomes very time-consuming as we must make the effort to consider it and then prove it is not appropriate," Jay wrote to Sheinberg. "All of this is a diversion of our efforts."

Jay was also counting on Drabinsky to deliver on some of his earlier promises with no luck. Getting the rights to *Ghostbusters* was on the top of that list. Drabinsky said his team could find ways to shave costs during the construction process, but they failed. Cineplex Odeon promised to create and promote a new event, the Orlando Film Festival, but that effort did not see the light of day either.

"It's the biggest project in the history of MCA coupled with the simultaneous largest expansion in the tour's history; we must work in a very compressed time period; the relationship with Steven [Spielberg] requires great care; and we must meet the Disney challenge," Jay said. "Further, given the history of this project since the late 1970s, our people (both veterans and newly hired) are paranoid enough about how real our intentions are, without having a partner threaten to pull out. People who do not believe we are serious will not make the same effort as those who know we must meet our deadlines."

Finally, Jay placed an ultimatum on the table. "All my career I have met similar challenges and I have been preparing for Florida for over 20 years," Jay told his boss. "I am confident I possess the executive leadership and the creativity to make this project happen. But I need support from top management." He warned, "I do not feel it is feasible to continue the relationship as it presently exists." Jay suggested, "If you believe there is someone else who can handle these pressures better, I'd be happy to step aside, but I cannot continue to be effective under the existing conditions."

Sheinberg had no choice. He knew he had to back up his longtime colleague or see the visionary force for the entire project walk out the door. Also, Jay was one of them; a true product of the MCA ethos. Sheinberg smartly decided to put his money on Jay.

On September 1, 1987, at the Isleworth Country Club in Orlando, in a meeting with Lew Wasserman and Jay, Drabinsky proposed that MCA should eliminate their management fee in response to the project overruns. Wasserman looked Drabinsky in the eye and told him that he was free to drop out, but MCA would not renegotiate. Although Wasserman had called his bluff, Drabinsky would not give up. After the meeting, he asked if the deadline to sign the joint venture agreement could be moved from December 7 to mid to late January 1988. Jay told his bosses that Drabinsky was trying to postpone his "escape" date to get to see another card, and he would try to use the pressure of closing the loan deal to accomplish this.

Jay outlined four reasons why MCA should say no. First, all of these changes were not the way to deal with a partner. Second, Drabinsky knew that there would not be a full budget estimate by December when he had to make a final decision, creating yet another excuse for a delay. Things were not set in stone yet, and eliminating elements could make cost savings.

Finally, Jay knew that Drabinsky was going to do the same thing in January, so why wait? He felt that Drabinsky was a "dishonest pig who got in over his head" and "went from being our angel to being the devil."

## The "Barry Upson" Clone

Drabinsky's next tactic was suggesting Jay hire a "Barry Upson clone." Jeff McNair recommended Mike Bartlett as project manager, and Jay thought they had hired a problem solver. Bartlett was the vice president of construction for Taft's Canada's Wonderland, which opened in 1981. Jay felt his familiarity with major international ride manufacturers would be an asset. Bartlett also recruited some knowledgeable people such as Keith James.

Unfortunately, instead of advocating solutions, Bartlett let everyone know that the project was too ambitious and in no way could be built on time. On November 19, 1987, he delivered his assessment of what it would take to complete the project, and the news was not good. Bartlett told Jay and Barry Upson that it would cost at least another $40 million to get the job done. Although his analysis was "based more on informed judgment than hard fact," he said that "decisive action is required to establish a realistic budget and plan that will immeasurably improve our [my] chances of successfully managing the budget and delivering the project on schedule." Jay realized that the project was simply beyond Bartlett's comprehension and capabilities.

Bartlett then went on to lecture his bosses. "I can certainly understand your reluctance to retract your position, the repercussion of acknowledging significant problems early are never as difficult as later when corporate management has less opportunity to influence the future of its investment," Bartlett said. "The Joint Venture is spending cash and making commitments at an accelerated rate on a product the current budget can't afford." He added, "I've been in similar circumstances and know without the slightest doubt that the sooner you at least acknowledge the probability of a budget problem the better our chances are of developing workable alternatives." Bartlett outlined four options for Jay and Upson to consider.

The status quo would be a national attraction. The Joint Venture would have to continue as planned and just ask for the money when the time comes. They would need to prepare an aggressive marketing and sponsorship campaign and get ready for expansion within three years with San Francisco Earthquake, Live-Action Arena, Hanna Barbara, and the European street sets.

Another option was to downsize the park with a regional marketing focus. To do this, they had to stop the project and "give up all thoughts of being a national attraction and concentrate on producing a lower risk business plan that markets against the tourist visiting Central Florida." Jay immediately discounted this option.

A third option was an aggressive national attraction plan. Universal would build everything. "Establishing, without question, our national action credentials and leaving our competition in the dust." This option would be the best course of action if the ultimate goal were to expand into Japan and Europe. This was Jay's vision.

The final option was to phase in the national attraction. This meant not building the Live-Action Arena and Hanna-Barbera, and opening Back to the Future and Ghostbusters *after* the grand opening. Bartlett suggested that Back to the Future would open on May 1, 1990, just in time for the park's first summer season. He also recommended convincing Pepsi to sponsor the attraction and have Michael J. Fox as the spokesperson. He even suggested changing the ride's storyline to serve the sponsor's needs if necessary. Ghostbusters would open for the 1990 Christmas season. Then, in May 1991, the San Francisco Earthquake ride would open. He even suggested that the creative team should be open to the idea of adjusting the Earthquake storyline to meet the needs of AT&T, a potential sponsor. The changes would result in $25.5 million in savings.

"I hope you know my preference is Alternative 3, building the complete concept and assuming the risk that we may not raise all the funds from corporate participants," Bartlett wrote to Jay. "The Phased Alternative is also acceptable as long as there is an absolute commitment to add the three major attractions within eighteen months of opening, and accept the risk of not raising all the funds from corporate participants."

Jay found Bartlett's assessment to have missed the mark and not helpful. "The problem is severe, the entire project is in jeopardy, and by taking the position you have, you have failed to give USF the support you were hired to provide," Jay told Bartlett. "Advising me to act on speculative corporate sponsorship support or change the overall scope of this project is not giving me alternatives. You should be using your claimed expertise in this field to develop ways in which shows, sets, and rides can be built more economically, either by redesign or using more innovative manufacturing and construction techniques. In other words, you must get your hands dirty in the details." Jay suggested, "You should work with them [contractors Bartlett and Peter Alexander hired] toward that objective and stop looking for alternatives to build or market a different attraction."

It seemed the battles with Drabinsky and McNair were endless. By December 1987, Cineplex had signed off on the Jaws and E.T. rides, the Creep Thrills show, and the street sets. Originally, the How We Shoot Movies demonstration was outdoors and based on a *Miami Vice* theme similar to a very popular and innovative show at Universal City. McNair never saw the show in California and insisted on moving the show indoors and using Alfred Hitchcock as the theme. As an alternative, he offered the Hanna-Barbera characters instead of the esteemed director.

With budgets already tight, Jay agreed to the changes but reminded McNair that it was going to cost another $40,000 for show design and research. "Remember, exciting creative concepts do not magically materialize free of cost," he wrote to his adversary.

Another frustration was McNair's demand that Jay's team fully design attractions before the rights had been secured. This meant more money spent with nothing to show for it. Jay wrote McNair, "The way to maintain this budget and achieve our mutual objectives is not by advocating unrealistic and, quite frankly, unprofessional demands which show no understanding nor appreciation for the creative design and budgeting process."

As an example of Cineplex's lack of vision, they did not want to invest in an innovative dual water pipe system. Dual water systems feature two separate distribution systems that supply potable water through one distribution network and non-potable water through another. The two systems work independently of one another. It was an opportunity to save money. Such a system can substantially reduce the fire insurance premiums, it has a rapid payback, and it was the right thing to do environmentally.

Arguments over budgets were constant. Drabinsky claimed that Jay constantly wanted to reduce the quality. Jay was having none of it. He just knew how to get the biggest bang for the buck, like any Hollywood producer. For example, his team revised Jaws to include an interior boathouse scene that greatly magnified the thrill factor of this ride. Although the boathouse replaced a more costly collapsing dock and a helicopter fire/explosion sequence, the less expensive alternative improved the overall quality of the experience.

In a meeting in early December 1987, the pins were pulled from the hand grenades and explosions could be heard everywhere. Jay and Drabinsky were locked in a battle over compromise. Drabinsky said he did not want to compromise. Jay said, "Neither do I. Compromise, however, is very much a reality in our complicated endeavor. Although painful, let me remind you that you have personally experienced the sting of compromise during our venture. The rights for *Ghostbusters*, despite your strong relationship with Columbia and Coca-Cola, did not come free of cost; and our hotel deal was not limited to the ten to 12 acres of land usage you had claimed it would require."

Jay pointed to another example. Spielberg was making changes to E.T.'s home planet section of the ride. The attraction was based, in part, on the book *The Green Planet* by William Kotzwinkle. Peter Alexander said,

"[Spielberg] insisted on a happy alien planet for E.T. Most of the time alien planets are gloomy." Terry Winnick recalled, "Steven came over at lunch, looked at a sculpture of the young E.T. in clay, and said it must be done differently. He showed us how."

The additional changes added another $5 million. Jay asked his partner, "Should we compromise and increase the budget, eliminate other elements, or simply ignore his suggestions? It is obvious that we cannot ignore his suggestions. We must continue to design, storyboard, and budget each of his ideas. If the decision is made to *compromise* because his creative approach will not permit us to stay within budget, it will not be a decision that I will make. It will be a decision that *we* will make."

Jay reminded Drabinsky that the real enemy was Disney. "What neither of us know are what actions this fierce competitor might take when it discovers more details of our project. Just as I pointed out in the illustration regarding our creative consultant, the decision to compromise our original plans, if necessary, to meet an increased competitive challenge would be one that we will make *jointly*." The two men were attached at the hip and would either prosper or perish together.

Jay's vision was clear. USF would be a real working studio. Authenticity was everything. For twenty-five years, "going behind the scenes" topped the exit surveys in Los Angeles. One of Disney's weaknesses was that their Florida studio was not a credible "working" studio. Jay always reminded his team that it was essential that the public feels it is learning something about movie making; otherwise, they will view USF as just another amusement park.

To accomplish this, he proposed a $19 million package that included the Special Effects Stage, the Post Production Theater, and a nighttime live action stunt spectacular. He felt it imperative these become opening day attractions.

The Special Effects Stage would be an updated version of the show in Hollywood. For the Post Production show, Jay had convinced award-winning actress Angela Lansbury to host as her character on *Murder, She Wrote*. Jay said the latter deal "filled the 'TV' niche, the 'behind-the-scenes' niche, and the 'star' niche."

Jay also wanted to add an $8 million nighttime live-action stunt spectacular as a counter to Disney's Indiana Jones-based show. Jay felt Universal owned the stunt show segment. He suggested a show based on the popular television series *Miami Vice*. "There is no stronger 'Florida' product in the entire history of the cinema." The action theme would attract teenagers and young adults. Also, Jay would be able to avoid the noise problems he had to deal with regularly in Los Angeles. He suggested that by making noise *today*, it would prevent future residents moving into the area from having the right to complain.

He suggested the new demonstrations would add to the "critical mass" necessary to make USF a two-day attraction with all the important "themes" covered (thrill, animation, behind the scenes, sets, production, comedic stunts, TV, special effects, etc.).

"As pretentious as it sounds, every major component of filmmaking will be presented in our major stages, shows, rides, sets, or demonstrations," Jay told his team. "No matter how much Disney spends, they will not be able to offer an element that we have not already provided in a highly interesting, entertaining, or exciting way; and most importantly, all our elements will be associated with outstanding hit properties." He added, "If we win overwhelming in Orlando, our path for expansion worldwide is assured."

Another opportunity where Cineplex dropped the ball was securing the rights to *Ghostbusters* and the iconic theme song by Ray Parker. Drabinsky claimed that he had strong relationships with Coca-Cola because Cineplex Odeon sold their products. Coca-Cola owned Columbia Studios. Drabinsky said he could obtain the rights at no cost. This would be a huge addition to the roster of attractions for the Universal parks.

By March 1988, it was obvious that he had overpromised. Drabinsky told Tony Sauber to give a call to his contact at Columbia to finalize the deal. Sauber had thought that the deal was a *fait accompli*; to his surprise, it was anything but. Sauber was told that in no way was it a "done deal" and it took much salesmanship to strike a compromise. Sauber argued that the attraction would be good exposure for the property; the park would carry merchandise and even Columbia VHS product.

Instead of a straightforward licensing agreement, Drabinsky agreed to a deal contingent upon getting the consent of the director and the three primary stars: Bill Murray, Dan Aykroyd, and Harold Ramis. The process took more than a year, and after considerable negotiations and at significant cost ($250,000 per year per location plus a share of merchandising revenue) these consents were obtained without any right to use their names or likenesses. Then, at the last moment, Ray Parker's agent put on new demands. Worse still, the deal was only for Florida. Despite Jay telling Drabinsky a year earlier to secure the rights for *both* coasts, Drabinsky claimed he had no choice and threw MCA under the bus.

Jay was furious. Without Columbia and Coca-Cola already committed with a Ghostbusters attraction, it would limit MCA's ability to negotiate a sponsorship deal with Pepsi at either park if they chose to do so. He fired off a memo to Drabinsky and said, "I am truly offended by the way the *Ghostbusters* negotiations have been conducted. It is inexcusable for Cineplex to exclude us from the process as decisions are being made which adversely affect us in particular and the project in general."

## Production Begins

The production facilities would be the first thing to open. In October 1988, the *New Leave it to Beaver* series began production on one of the soundstages with original stars Jerry Mathers and Barbara Billingsley.

More importantly was Ron Howard's feature film *Parenthood*. Jay put pressure on Wasserman and Sheinberg to find a production in the pipeline that could cast legitimacy on the facility. Due to a lack of experienced technicians in Florida, Universal was forced to fly out the cast and crew and house them, negating any cost savings. However, the marketing team was able to use the movie in advertisements.

Universal boasted in a press release that its new facility was "the largest motion picture and television production studio outside of Hollywood." Within the first year, 13 feature films and 500 television episodes would go before the cameras at Universal Studios. The credit goes to Dan Slusser, who started in Yosemite and became a well-respected member of the Recreation Division team and, at this time, was the manager of the studio in Los Angeles.

Rewind the tape to early 1980. Slusser got a call from Lew Wasserman asking, "What are you doing for breakfast in the morning?" Being a fast thinker, Slusser said, "Whatever you want me to do." The next day, they met at the counter in the commissary at 8:00 a.m. After a little bit of small talk, Wasserman said, "You know Joe Hiatt is very sick." Hiatt was in charge of the studio operations and struggling with a losing battle against cancer. Wasserman continued, "The office next to him on the 14$^{Th}$ floor is empty, and I want you to move in there and work with Joe. I'm very worried about his health, but I am also worried about the studio. There is too much going on there for it to be managed on a part-time basis."

Stunned, Slusser asked, "What do you want me to tell Jay?" Wasserman replied, "I'll talk to Jay." The next question from Slusser was, "When do you want this to happen?" Wasserman said, "Today."

Slusser moved to his new offices that day, and it felt awful because he had no chance to talk with Jay. When he did talk with Jay the next day, he was not happy. In fact, Slusser was not happy for a while. A few days later, Bernie Fisher paid Slusser a visit and said he had spoken to Jay. It seems that Jay was happy that Slusser got the promotion now that he realized that he was in a position to be helpful in getting Jay's Florida project built.

Jay was a big fan of Slusser and hated to lose him when he was put in charge of running the studio at Universal City. Slusser was street smart, honest, fearless, diplomatic, and a tenacious negotiator. Under Slusser's leadership, the California studio turned a profit for the first time. He was renting space to every studio in Hollywood. At one point, the Disney film group became his number-one customer.

Slusser also had an eye for talent and hired both Glen Gumpel and Jack McDaniel. McDaniel, a competent lawyer, would become an executive vice president overseeing special projects for the Recreation Division.

Glenn Gumpel was a lawyer who worked at the Director's Guild before joining MCA. Jay thought so highly of Gumpel he wanted to put him into a high position in Florida. However, Sheinberg objected. He felt Gumpel lacked experience. Jay and Sheinberg had at least two heated arguments over the matter, but Sheinberg stood firm. In his entire career, no one had ever interfered with Jay's autonomy in making personnel changes. Jay was angry and dumbfounded. What Jay did not know was that Garth Drabinsky and Jeff McNair were behind the decision. They both objected to Gumpel's promotion. Sheinberg wanted to placate Drabinsky. Gumpel, disappointed by the decision, left MCA and returned to the Director's Guild in 1987 as executive director. He saw no future at MCA.

Gumpel was rehired by Ron Bension to be his number-two person once Jay retired. His role was to be sort of a hatchet-man for Bension regarding disputes with other divisions within MCA. He would later go on to run the Universal theme park in Japan.

On a somewhat reoccurring basis, Wasserman would bring up the subject of Florida during other conversations with Slusser. When they were having coffee in the morning in his office, which they often did, Wasserman would stop in the middle of a conversation and ask, "This Florida project is moving along. Do you think it makes sense?" Slusser's response was always the same. "The theme park business continues to grow, and it makes logical sense to look at expansion." Slusser always believed that the Recreation Division was a real asset to MCA. That is where he started. It was a stable business. The Motion Picture and Television divisions were a high-risk, high-reward business. As time moved on, the questions from Wasserman were becoming more frequent. In one early morning conversation, Wasserman said, "Are you aware that Jay has this vision of building a functioning studio?" Slusser told his boss that he was aware of what Jay was trying to do and agreed it had to be a real studio. You cannot fake production.

Slusser started to realize that Wasserman was using him as a sounding board. At the same time, Slusser began to get calls from labor leaders from all over the country pleading with him to meet with them to talk about a deal in Florida. Slusser repeatedly told them that it was not in the cards.

Then one day Slusser got a call from Herm "Blackie" Leavitt, an old friend. Leavitt was the head of the Hotel & Restaurant Employees International Union. He asked Slusser to have lunch with him, Bill Robertson, and some other labor guys. Slusser and Robertson had been friends for years. He was also close to Wasserman and Mayor Tom Bradley of Los Angeles.

At the time, Slusser was the chairman of Mayor Bradley's Los Angeles City Film Development Committee. They agreed to meet at Jimmy's in Century City. When Slusser arrived, there must have been eight or ten International Union presidents at the table. He believed every union that had a contract with Disney was at the table. Slusser addressed the group, "Gentlemen, am I the lunch speaker or am I the lunch?"

It was an enjoyable meal, but he kept repeating to himself, "There is no deal here after we are open, and you can get a showing of interest from the employees, and if you prevail in an election, then we'll see you at the table." He reminded the group that MCA was still looking for a partner. Then Leavitt said, "If we can find you a partner, would that be helpful?" Slusser asked for clarification. "I'll call you," Leavitt said.

A couple of days later he did call. Leavitt asked, "Do you know Bobby Georgine?" Slusser replied, "The Chicago construction union leader?" Leavitt said, "Yes, but he is now CEO of the Union Labor Life Insurance Company (ULLIC), and they are looking for investments." Intrigued, Slusser said he would ask around and see what kind of response he got.

He immediately briefed Jay. They talked about the pros and cons. They decided they should talk with Wasserman and Sheinberg together. After much discussion, Slusser got the go-ahead to see if there was any real interest on their part.

After consulting with Leavitt and Georgine, it was decided the best course of action would be to make a presentation to the ULLIC board at their headquarters in Washington, D.C. Representing MCA was Wasserman, Sheinberg, Jay, Barry Upson, Bob Ward, Skip Paul, and Dan Slusser. After the presentation, the MCA team and members of the ULLIC board went to Florida to see the land they had purchased. They ate a lot and talked a lot. Then the ULLIC folks said they would get back to them. When Georgine called to say they were going to pass, he was very complimentary about the project. He said, "They had some other opportunities that were a better fit for their fund."

Therefore, Slusser focused on the original mission of building the Florida production facilities. Disney had started construction on their complex and Jay was concerned that MCA would not be able to compete with them. Slusser, Bill DeCinces, and Ray Brandt started contacting different individuals in the industry and piecing together some accurate information. They still had concerns, because some things they were being told did not make sense. Slusser reverted to his military training: if you are not sure about what you are being told, then look at it for yourself.

They went to Florida, rented a helicopter with a Vietnam veteran at the controls, and said to get as close as possible to the construction site so they could read the signs on the men's room door. He did what he was hired to do. DeCinces, a former art director and a licensed architect, took a ton of pictures, and they came back to the studio and built a model to show Jay. All of the rumors about what Disney was doing were cleared up, and they moved forward with the studio production facilities.

After reviewing the plans for the production complex with Jay and his team, Slusser was able to start getting bids and preparing a construction budget. The budget was approved, and construction commenced. They built four soundstages and an office complex. That was the same number of soundstages that Disney had in Burbank. Slusser gave Jay a real working studio—the heart and soul of the new venture.

Another benefit of getting the studio up and running was strategic. Steve Lew and Tom Williams focused on getting close to Orlando Mayor Bill Frederich and Florida Governor Lawton Chiles. Slusser started to conduct studio tours to keep them up to date on the construction progress. Governor Chiles has been particularly interested in bringing filming to Florida and appointed Slusser to the Florida Film Investment Board.

One of the more outrageous favors for a local politician came from a request by Mayor Frederich. He had just built a new city hall and could not find anyone to buy the old building. He said it was worth more as a vacant lot than with the building on it. That night Slusser called an old friend, producer Joel Silver, who was shooting *Lethal Weapon II*. He asked him if he wanted a building to blow up. Two days later he was in Florida. Slusser put him together with the mayor and it worked out. It made a great shot in the movie.

Assisting Lew and Williams was Denise Brock. Later, she would serve as Jay's secretary. As one can imagine, Jay was not the easiest person to work for. Brock was in a class by herself. She handled everything Jay needed or wanted and tried to anticipate (with unbelievable accuracy) his next request. She always stood up to Jay and told him the truth. If Jay was the commander during wartime, then Brock was his chief of staff.

Unlike his predecessor studio managers, Slusser liked the tour and tried to accommodate its growth. Parking for the tour in Hollywood was a problem on the weekends during the summer (a five-month period), and Wasserman asked Slusser if he could make room in the transportation lot. Slusser did. He also told his boss that the entire studio had a parking problem, and they should build a parking complex in the area next to Technicolor. Slusser promised he could have the project completed by the next summer season, and that it would solve everyone's problem. They built a parking structure, and it worked.

In Hollywood, Slusser had to find the right balance between production, Jay's Recreation Division, and Albert Dorskind's development group. A lot was going on, considering the expansion of the theme park at the time, and every time Jay's division made a presentation to Wasserman or Sheinberg, Slusser would get a call to join them. It was always the same.

"They want more of your land." Slusser usually told him he had seen the presentation and thought it was a "win-win" for both the studio and the theme park. Every time the theme park expanded, the studio was able to build new facilities such as a new prop house, a wardrobe facility, a new transportation department, a new construction mill, a new art department, a new office complex and much more.

One of Universal's weaknesses was the lack of children's stories to tell. Woody Woodpecker was not enough. That is why the announcement in March 1988 that Universal had acquired the theme park rights to the Hanna-Barbera stable of characters was such a breakthrough. The animation studio was famous for its family-friendly television productions like *The Flintstones, Yogi Bear, The Jetsons, Scooby-Doo, Jonny Quest, The Pink Panther,* and many others.

Around the same time, Dan Slusser was in discussions with Nickelodeon to do a one-time special at the Florida studio. Nickelodeon was a new, popular children's television channel owned by Viacom and MTV Networks. Slusser spoke at length with Geraldine Laybourne, executive vice president and general manager of Nickelodeon about the value of shooting at the studio. There was much interest. Slusser then began to press the idea that the Florida studio could become the new permanent home and worldwide headquarters for Nickelodeon. To facilitate the discussion, Slusser contacted McDaniel and asked him to see if there was interest on the theme park side. Jay's team became very excited about the idea.

In January 1989, McDaniel and Sauber went to New York for five days to meet with the Nickelodeon people with the goal of reaching a signed agreement before returning home. The deal would include Universal building two production stages and production offices for Nickelodeon at USF. Nickelodeon would do virtually all of their television production from soundstages located there, and theme park visitors would be able to be contestants and watch the taping of Nickelodeon's successful children's and young adult programming. USF would become "Home Base for Kids." Also, Nickelodeon offered family entertainment that, at that time, was less bland than Disney. Sauber and McDaniel felt the deal was a "win-win-win."

The time pressure was not just a negotiating tactic. Both sides had to reach an agreement as the facility had to be ready when the park opened. It took Nickelodeon's Laybourne to cut through the small stuff and keep the parties moving toward an agreement. That agreement lasted until 2005.

With the win, Jay told Sheinberg and Drabinsky, "This package, in one bold stroke, delivers a level of instant national market recognition, continuous production credibility, and the hard-to-attract kid/family franchise that Disney has dominated and exploited over the past several decades."

If visitors wanted to see an actual production and maybe even participate, they only had to visit the Nickelodeon Studios at USF. Because Nickelodeon produced so many game shows Jay knew, "We will have finally achieved the ultimate Screen Test Theatre guest experience that we have been seeking for Florida in that the guest will have a realistic chance of seeing, and even appearing in a real, live television program."

## Appropriately Timed Coverage

*Good tactics can save even the worst strategy.*
*Bad tactics will destroy even the best strategy.*
—General George S. Patton, Jr.

On May 13, 1988, Jay's carefully planned strategy to beat Disney was pushed aside by a significant tactical error by his partner, Garth Drabinsky. In a self-serving move, Drabinsky decided to leak the plans for USF to Cineplex Odeon shareholders without consulting Jay. With Cineplex's stock trading at its 52-week low and losing half of its value in the last 12 months due to perceived over-expansion, Drabinsky was happy to throw Jay's plans into the fire if it meant refueling his stock price.

Drabinsky told his investors that the plans have "been kept under tight wraps until now." For the first time publicly, the $450 million cost of the project had been disclosed. Drabinsky prematurely released photos of the project layout and key attractions. He also revealed specific design details such as the inclusion of the façade from New York's Plaza Hotel. Drabinsky quipped, "The hotel's inclusion appears ironic since it was recently acquired by New York real estate developer Donald Trump, who threatened in February to acquire nearly 25% of MCA." In fact, Trump had not granted the rights to use the façade.

When Jay learned of the betrayal, he was livid. In a memo, he told Drabinsky, "Most incredible is the publication of a slide depicting our detailed site plan. You might as well have given Disney the combination to our vault, knowing their propensity for stealing our concepts and architecture." Jay went on: "In short, I feel the disclosure of the unauthorized, sensitive, and confidential information in this manner takes a media event of international importance and reduced it to a second-rate business story, showing absolutely no understanding or appreciation for the meaning of a Joint Venture. I want to go on record as expressing my contempt and disgust for this unforgivable behavior."

He added, "Words cannot express how far apart I feel we are as to the damage you have done in releasing, unilaterally, photographs of our project layout and key attractions, a listing of the key attractions and set streets, a description of the E.T. attraction, and the overall disclosure. It assists Disney, and it damages our chance for appropriately timed coverage."

Jay was concerned that Disney would steal ideas or increase the scope of their project to meet the challenge, which they had previously done. The surprise was a key strategic element. Due to the announcement, for the first time readers would learn that E.T. would have aerial bicycles, something Disney had tried but abandoned as too complex. Moreover, the photo of the model would tell Disney how the facility fit into the larger picture. Jay was aware that Disney was doing frequent fly-overs. Another piece of information was the cost of the project. Jay wanted Disney to think they were spending $350 million. Drabinsky suggested it was closer to $450 million. Once again, Jay wanted Disney to underestimate him. The premature leak upset a carefully planned rollout of information.

Drabinsky's first instinct was to blame reporter Katie Harris for lying to Cineplex's public relations person. When this ridiculous argument fell apart, he then suggested to Jay that he was overreacting. "To claim the Harris article severely affects our competitive position with Disney is totally ridiculous and insulting," Drabinsky said. When that argument went nowhere, he then blamed Jay for not telling him about the expansion plans for Hollywood, which was untrue.

Finally, Drabinsky told Jay he had no choice. "We have been under attack for many months in relation to our investment in Universal Studios Florida," he said. "This investment represents almost 25% of our shareholders' equity and is the largest capital project of its kind for Cineplex Odeon Corporation; however, the analysts give us zero credit on our USF cash flow estimates. They see us spending significant sums to dethrone Disney, all the while refusing to give any details when Disney is so much bolder than the Joint Venture in providing product detail, and in fact, they seem better at making their dates." It was evident to Jay that Drabinsky made the announcement to cover his ass with his shareholders.

Drabinsky was as big a problem as Disney. "Assuming you disagree and continue to feel your release did no lasting damage to USF, competitively or media-wise, I hope you would at least agree that such disclosures of critical elements of USF, for the first time, should have been discussed between us in advance," Jay told Drabinsky. "I cannot believe you felt you have an absolute right to give out this information we have all treated as confidential, and for which our pre-opening marketing plan had included a careful, calculated release, just because you think it will help Cineplex with its shareholders, especially without consulting the largest shareholder." Unfortunately, the relationship between the two men continued to deteriorate.

Then there were Jeff McNair's continual attacks on Steve Lew. McNair had lost faith with Lew and wanted to promote Mike Bartlett. Jay did not want that to happen. He wanted to elevate Tom Williams to the status of executive vice president for USF. After seventeen years of experience in Yosemite, Williams possessed the managerial qualities to lead highly motivated professionals. McNair disagreed and said he was "only an operations guy who knows nothing about marketing." That battle would continue.

With all of the adversity, there was some good news. The *esprit de corps* of the management team was developing into nothing short of magnificent. The petty grievances that had compounded their efforts in the early months were rapidly being replaced by a single goal. *They all wanted to beat Disney*. The overriding sense was that they were doing something that had never been done before.

## Miami Vice vs G.I. Joe

If the Magic Kingdom and Epcot had nighttime spectaculars to keep people in the park until closing, then Universal Studios Florida would have the same, but bigger and better. At least that was the thinking. The fireworks show at both parks had become signature entertainment pieces and huge draws. Steven Spielberg liked the Disney fireworks shows.

Jay quickly learned that they were expensive. For Florida, the cost to produce and maintain the show was $15–$20 million—two to three times what MCA wanted to spend. His solution was to check two boxes from the Disney attraction inventory with one show. By 1988, Universal did not have a stunt show that would compete with Disney's Indiana Jones live-action show. By placing an action stunt show in the middle of the lagoon, Universal would be able to accommodate as many as 14,000 people. With a show of this size and scope, it would eclipse Disney at their own game.

Once again, the main objective was to find the perfect intellectual property to base the show on. Early concepts were based on *James Bond* and *Superman*. The rights to both franchises were not available. At one point Peter Alexander had suggested a show based on G.I. Joe, the toy and Saturday morning animated series. Jay thought it was a dumb idea. He felt it would be very hard to make a funny show with a military/war/battle theme. Moreover, army men made no sense as a show on a water stage.

Jay suggested *Miami Vice* as the theme. Obtaining rights would be a breeze; it was a Florida-based show, it had all of the proper elements, and guests enjoyed the show in Hollywood which used the same characters. "It really is a 'natural' for our Florida park," Jay said. However, Jay gave Alexander the benefit of the doubt and *Miami Vice* and G.I. Joe were tested in a poll. It found that G.I. Joe was significantly less popular than *Miami Vice*, which was then in its fifth season on television. Jay moved forward with *Miami Vice*. Jay earned yet another "I told you so."

Spielberg was concerned. He told Jay that the *Miami Vice* theme would leave "visitors with an excessively violent experience." Instead, Spielberg suggested a show that would combine different properties such *E.T., Back to the Future, Jaws*, and *Miami Vice*. Jay argued, "The re-use would somehow lessen the impact and show tremendous value of that attraction which are already fully developed for the park. A duplicate use could cheapen the value of our existing attractions and even confuse our guests." He knew that Universal did not do generic well. That was a Disney thing. Universal's greatest successes came from strong intellectual properties.

To sell Spielberg on the concept, Jay suggested that the show could be presented as an opportunity to peek backstage at the production process while also being a comedic thrill show. Peter Alexander revamped the show with more humorous elements, especially the finale. Despite the changes, Spielberg was still not sure and could not reach a decision. This was the summer of 1988, the clock was ticking, and opening day was only 17 months away. Jay was getting concerned. This pressure was starting to reflect on his relationship with his staff.

As a leader, Jay had a reputation that could be harsh and unforgiving when his employees did not perform to his expectations. A good example was captured on August 18, 1988, in a memo sent to David J. Sparks, part of the Florida marketing team. Jay recalled Sparks as a young, cocky, well dressed, tall and good-looking man with impeccable credentials working at a notable advertising firm in New York. He was also a McNair man.

Both McNair and Sparks had a background in retail marketing. For the two men, press relations was fluff, something they could ignore. They felt the real muscle was in television advertising. Therefore, they built a marketing budget loaded with expensive ad buys and little attention paid to free media, a staple of the movie business.

Jay was always emphatic and demanding about press coverage. It was Sparks' responsibility to respond to a series of Disney press releases. Jay was furious that he wanted to take credit by distorting the facts. "You failed miserably: *The New York Times* ignored our story, *The Los Angeles Times* buried it, and coverage in the target markets appears to be minuscule," Jay told his young staffer. "Someone reading your memo to me of August 17 would come to the conclusion that your handling of the production announcement was a resounding success. In fact, it was a dismal failure, not meeting even our minimum objectives, and no amount of self-aggrandizement on your part can change that fact." Jay recommended that Sparks rethink how he approached his work. For Sparks, it was a clear threat to his job.

It became apparent to Jay that those who used to work for McNair had no marketing background other than advertising and that background was in the service of established brands. They were in over their heads.

Frustrated, Jay stopped talking to Sparks and appointed Jack McDaniel as shuttle negotiator to force Sparks to change his excessive budget recommendation. McDaniel pressed Sparks with Jay's message that the mission was *content*, which, in turn, would become compelling news with vastly greater value than a mountain of 30-second spots. Sparks would not bend. At some point during the discussion, McDaniel realized that it was hopeless, and he fired Sparks.

When Jay first learned of the firing, he was concerned about Drabinsky and Sheinberg's reaction. When McDaniel told the two men, Sheinberg was perplexed, and Drabinsky said he "never liked that prick."

## We Are at War

Jay's most important ally was Sidney Sheinberg. Jay would always try to engage him in the creative process. When Sheinberg came up with an idea, whether it was good or bad, he would often say, "Now I know why they made me president." Jay quickly learned if you accepted one of Sheinberg's suggestions, which were often quite good, he became supportive.

Somewhat risk averse (probably because of pressure from Wasserman), Sheinberg never wanted to "go all in" alone. He was a lawyer by training, vehement yet tender, bellicose yet reserved. Sheinberg could be passionately angry one moment and coolly rational the next. Most found that Sheinberg could be brutally forthright. He would sometimes refer to business opponents as "idiots" and ideas with which he disagreed are "just stupid." He was a master negotiator, but often a poor judge of character. Nevertheless, he was always loyal and supportive to Jay and always had his back.

At first, it was tough on Sheinberg. People were used to going straight to Wasserman for approvals. People were told to go through Sheinberg instead of Wasserman. Nevertheless, they did not listen and continued to go directly to Wasserman. Every time Jay had a private meeting with Sheinberg, Wasserman would walk in. Wasserman was not sensitive to this and for the first two years, it was uncomfortable for everyone.

During the Hollywood expansion and the Florida project, both men were highly motivated by what they considered was a rejection and double cross by Michael Eisner. Sheinberg had his limits. He was operating within a self-imposed risk tolerance that required Jay's division to spread the risk with a partner. Also, Sheinberg was never really his own man with an even more cautious Wasserman constantly looking over his shoulder.

From Jay's perspective, MCA was at war with Disney, which meant taking chances pushing the design envelope further than any theme park had ever attempted. Everything was designed to not only win battles but also to win the total war.

In Sheinberg's mind, Jay's war meant that the budgets became collateral damage. Sheinberg was frustrated with cost overruns, and by July 1988 decided to lay down the law. He wanted Jay to agree not to build a new attraction until everything was fully designed and budgeted with fixed bids. He also did not want Jay to advertise, promote, or open something before it was "totally ready." Sheinberg deemed, "We will offer no attraction before its time."

Jay strongly opposed the new policies. He thought his boss was overreacting. Frequently, complex attractions did not run smoothly on opening day. One of the biggest challenges was they never built things twice. Everything was handcrafted. Every attraction required modifications after gaining operating experience. Jay was confident he had the right properties to work with, and when those attractions hit full stride the payoff would be extremely rewarding.

Another consideration was timing. Timing was everything. A firm deadline got people to do their superhuman best and not futz around with the smallest detail, shining it to perfection. If the creative team rushed for a summer opening and then had to delay because the attraction did not immediately achieve its entertainment potential, it would impair the park's marketing capabilities and have a significant impact on profits.

It is hard to get fixed bids because they were building something that had never been created before. Even when they did get fixed bids, Universal would frequently have to come up with additional money either because the vendor could not find the cash to correct a serious problem or they would blame the delays or changes on Jay's people. Jay wanted to set a target, do the best good faith estimating that could be done, and then rush to meet the deadline as best they could.

Building theme park attractions is not like other construction projects. Many of their vendors were relatively small. There were not many companies that could build one-of-a-kind attractions. When projects started to go over budget, they knew that MCA could sue them and put them out of business or pay for some compromise solution and complete the project.

Jay told Sheinberg that he sincerely believed that opening a show in an imperfect condition would not have a meaningful long-term negative reaction so long as they worked at a fast pace to finalize it. Unlike a movie, which must be judged on its individual merits, USF was appreciated as a total experience, with the multitude of elements leaving the visitor with an overall impression. Sheinberg relented, Jay was relieved, and business went on as usual.

## Enter the Rank Organisation

February 28, 1989, was an important day. Simultaneous press conferences were scheduled for Orlando and at the Palladium nightclub in New York to provide a sneak peek of the Florida park. Jay was nervous and told Sheinberg that he did not trust Drabinsky and that he was a "loose cannon who is only interested in promoting himself or helping Cineplex's financial image."

By early 1989, the house of cards that Drabinsky had built for himself was beginning to crash. Cineplex Odeon was struggling under a mountain of debt due to overexpansion. Jay's concern was Drabinsky using the opportunity to impress the financial community in light of Cineplex's problems. He knew Drabinsky did not care about USF.

On March 22, 1989, Drabinsky sold Cineplex Odeon's interest in USF to Rank of Britain for $150 million. Sheinberg said of Drabinsky, "Did it turn out to be more expensive than we thought? Obviously. Did it become too big for Cineplex? Yes." By the end of 1989, Wasserman and Sheinberg had soured on Drabinsky. They gave him an ultimatum to pay $1.2 billion for MCA's share in the movie chain or be fired. On December 14, 1989, Wasserman and Sheinberg won the battle and Drabinsky was out. However, Drabinsky continued to look for a white knight to bail him out of his theme park agreement. He found it in the name of the Rank Organisation. Rank was a small British art-house movie production company and the owner of casinos and betting shops in England. They owned the Hard Rock Café chain and had interests ranging from vacation resort properties to a partnership with Xerox. From MCA's point of view, the deal seemed good because Rank had better connections for European expansion.

To counteract this negative message, Jay insisted that Sheinberg represent MCA at all press events. "In short, USF represents the biggest project in our company's history, and the new MCA-Rank partnership is the biggest transaction we have ever entered into," Jay told his boss. "We have too much at stake to take a hands-off attitude and let persons with conflicting self-interests or little knowledge shape what is being presented to the public." In the end, the press conference was uneventful.

With Rank on board, Jay's team went back to ideas that were abandoned due to Cineplex Odeon's restrictive funding. MCA wanted to bring back the nighttime stunt show spectacular in the central lagoon. They wanted to have Tom Williams promoted, and Jeff McNair replaced. Jay also wanted approval on a proposal from Dan Slusser to invest in the expansion of the studio services. Slusser had been very successful in lining up productions, unlike his competitors over at Disney.

Over time, Rank would be no better than Cineplex Odeon. They had their financial problems. They enjoyed the prestige of ownership without contributing much. They were dreary corporate stereotypes with no creative strengths, and they put several of their executives in positions overseeing and commenting on Universal's creative efforts. They also insisted on using the Hard Rock Café brand for the restaurants and hotels in the Florida project, even though it was already losing its "flair." In addition to the Hard Rock Café, they also ran Lombards, the fine dining establishment in the park. Like Cineplex Odeon, they also wanted to modify the financial agreement so that they received a management fee. Jay declined their request.

More importantly, like Cineplex Odeon, their goal was to minimize their investment and pull the money out quickly. They were not in it to build something special. The Rank position was eventually purchased by the Blackstone Group, an investment company. Blackstone was willing to take a back seat and let Universal do what they did best. Eventually, the Blackstone Group's interest was purchased by Comcast, which now owns 100% of Universal Orlando as well as NBCUniversal. Jeff McNair continues in a management role at Universal Orlando with the title of managing director, negotiating with foreign governments for new parks and reporting directly to Universal Parks chairman and CEO Tom Williams.

In 2009, Drabinsky, along with Myron Gottlieb, were convicted and sentenced to prison for fraud and forgery. Drabinsky served 17 months in jail before being granted parole.

## Disney-MGM opens

On May 1, 1989, the Disney-MGM Studios theme park opened to the public. At the last minute, the name was changed from the Disney-MGM Studio Tour to the Disney-MGM theme park to strengthen the image of the tourist side of the park. The reality was that little production had been booked for the studio. All the action was taking place over at Universal. The cost of the 135-acre park had ballooned from an estimated $500 million to $550 million. Disney hoped that attendance would be between 3–5 million a year.

Publicly, Michael Eisner was proud of Disney's third gate in Florida. He felt like he had won the race and beat Universal. Terry Winnick visited the new park during their Cast Member Preview day. The first thing Winnick noticed was the small parking lot. Disney-MGM was the first of the Disney Florida parks where the on-property buses took priority over guests arriving by automobile. The locker facility was smaller than the other parks, leading Winnick to believe that Disney was expecting a relatively short length of stay.

Walking along Hollywood Boulevard, Winnick took note of the building façades. Some of the façades were duplicative of those Jay had selected so many years before. However, none were dressed, aged, "propped-out," or signed to represent actual "working" motion picture sets. There was theatrical lighting visible on the rooftops to try to add "authenticity," but the signing and graphics were also not authentic to Hollywood nor "motion-picture like."

Unlike Jay's goal of building a real working studio at Universal, it would be obvious to visitors that they were visiting a Disney theme park. Winnick felt that the Imagineers were not trying to achieve an accurate representation of any famous location from motion pictures or television. They were just attempting to create a caricature of the "real" Hollywood one might remember from films.

Then Winnick began to visit the attractions. Superstar Television was a copy of the original Screen Test Theatre at Universal Studios Hollywood (USH). Sponsored by Sony, it used electronic equipment clearly labeled JVC.

The big attraction was the Backstage Studio Tour. A copy of the Studio Tour in Hollywood, Disney used eleven six-car trams carrying 211 passengers. The first 30 minutes of the tour passes by studio production offices, the construction mill, and through an impressive wardrobe department. The trams then passed through a Residential Street. Winnick noticed that the guide was unaware of the one façade most guests might recognize from *Miami Vice*. The design of the sets and locations did not employ the "typical" studio-type construction techniques. For example, all four walls were present. The skin of the fourth wall was simply removed, exposing the structural elements. True exterior film sets would probably not even have the fourth wall. The structure looked fake.

From there, the trams passed through a New York/brown stone street and then entered Catastrophe Canyon. Winnick said of Catastrophe Canyon that it contained many of the same elements as the proposed Hollywood Boulevard attraction from the original Florida plans. That show planned on combining the technologies from Earthquake, the Flash Flood, and the new Universal Hellfighters pyrotechnic effects.

The second half of the tour took approximately one hour. No longer on the trams, guests walked through the facilities in groups of 250+. Winnick found himself following a group including Michael Eisner, Jeffrey Katzenberg, Frank Wells, Dick Nunis, and George Lucas. Nearby were staff carrying clipboards.

The show began with a segment featuring a miniature battleship similar to the one at Universal City; it was not operational during the preview. However, Winnick did enjoy the portion of the show that included the guests as participants in a sea battle with the result edited and broadcast to the audience. He felt it was well executed.

The Special Effects Laboratory was the next stop. Inside of a soundstage, guests could peer down onto a set dressed with props, electrical equipment, and other paraphernalia to make it "look" authentic. From there, the show was the same as the way Universal did it at the Special Effects Stage with Robert Wagner's film. At one point, the host turns to the audience and says, "Do you believe in ghosts? I do believe in ghosts. They are here." These were the same lines used during the Ghostbusters segment during the show at USH. Winnick was confused.

The next room was a blue-screen demonstration. Once more, the set was decorated to look "authentic," but Winnick was not buying it. The show was again similar to the demonstration at USH. From there, guests were escorted into Soundstage 1 down a long, dark corridor with a window along the left-hand side. This allowed viewing down into the actual production soundstages below. Inside of the largest soundstage on the Disney lot (15,000 square feet), Winnick saw the sets from *Superboy*. To his trained eye, he noticed that the sets had not been used for several days. With no action taking place below, guests stood and watched a three-minute video starring the members of *The Cosby Show*.

Inside of an empty Soundstage 2, the guide mentioned that they had completed filming a commercial in the space "just last week." From there, the group walked to the viewing platform above Soundstage 3. The soundstage was the home of the *New Mickey Mouse Club*, and an audition was taking place during the tour. Winnick chuckled during the video where Warren Beatty, dressed like Dick Tracy, discussed fog, the wind, rain, sound, and other elements that make filming on a soundstage effective. The production was shot on the Universal lot with Stage 19 clearly in the background.

In the Post Production Facility, Winnick was blown away. He thought the space was one of the most impressive studio buildings he had ever been in, complete with state-of-the-art equipment, first class décor, and many busy technicians. The Post Group, an outside post-production organization leasing space from Disney, operated the facility.

Once again, guests were asked to watch an entertaining two-minute video about a topic that was unrelated to the space they were standing in. Once again, the guide made no reference to what was happening in front of the guests on the other side of the glass. The tour ended in the Walt Disney Theater where guests watched a six-minute film that included clips from upcoming Disney productions. Winnick noted Michael Eisner wearing a Mickey Mouse watch hosted the film and Mickey Mouse was wearing a Michael Eisner watch.

From there, Winnick visited the Animation Department. Prominently featured was a display of Disney art. However, none of the pieces was labeled. A lost opportunity. The display was a prelude to a ten-minute film about the world of animation hosted by Robin Williams and Walter

Cronkite. Winnick enjoyed the movie. Guests exited into a working animation studio, although at the time, Winnick was not sure how "authentic" it was. The sound from the video monitors overhead was overlapping, and there was no direction on where to go next.

Having walked past the animation departments, the group of Disney executives, guests, and Winnick stepped into a small room containing a bank of television monitors and approximately twenty seats. The group was over 60 people, and many were forced to stand. Apparently, someone had miscalculated here, and Eisner, Nunis, and Lucas were deep in discussion about how they would modify this chamber without tearing down the entire building.

Winnick could not help but notice that the Monster Sound Theater Foley demonstration was exactly the one pitched to Eisner back when he was with Paramount. Superstar Television Theater was another copy, this time of USH's Screen Test Theatre.

Along with MCA's Jack McDaniel, Winnick was sitting in the tram behind Eisner and his entourage as they took their maiden voyage on The Great Movie Ride, an attraction on which they had bet the house. For Winnick, this was the only "set/show" facility that met Disney quality standards. The lobby was beautifully executed and most impressive.

The MCA men were not impressed with the audio-animatronics used during the Chicago "back alley" scene where the guide leaves the guests stranded. The slow speed of the ride vehicles made the escape from the back alley anti-climactic. They were amused that Disney would use a direct take-off of the Conan transformation to bring the guide back to life later in the tour.

Although some of the animated characters were unusually good likenesses of the celebrities and the sets were nice, overall Winnick was disappointed. He was not the only one. Like a memorable theater performance, Eisner stepped off the tram and perfectly pantomimed that moment of clarity (and despair) when a movie character realizes that he has been let down by his Imagineers. Having overheard Eisner and company during their walk, Winnick was confident that they were going to request many changes and much money would be spent making improvements before the park's grand opening.

As Winnick was walking out of the park, one youngster near him kept asking his mother where E.T. was. Of course, the answer was "E.T. is not here. He is coming to Orlando *later*." The Universal people felt Eisner's pain and then howled all the way back to their hotel.

Overall, it was evident that Disney had attempted to recreate the Universal experience in Hollywood in their style. They used script material, words, and techniques that Universal had been using for years. Although

Disney-MGM was a "theme park," not a "real working studio," Winnick was not sure that the public would be able to tell the difference.

The most identifiable difference between the Disney facility and what Universal was planning on building up the interstate was that in the Disney park the visitor, with a few exceptions, was a spectator. At Universal, the visitor would truly be a *participant*. Winnick predicted that once the word got out, this would give Universal the real edge.

## Orlando Magazine

For years, the group who designed and built the attractions for the tour was called Planning and Development. In 1989, Jay decided to honor them with a new name; Universal Creative. Consistent with the MCA culture, they were never exploited publicly like the Imagineers at Disney. Jay found many of the Disney guys to be one-dimensional. His men were resourceful. They were not spoiled. There was a different culture. No one thought outside the box like Universal Creative.

The department was lean so that Jay did not have to lay off people during slow periods. It was easier to staff up on consultants and work his small staff 24 hours a day during the busy times.

Nevertheless, Jay had enough after reading an article in the May edition of *Orlando Magazine* where Michael Eisner laid out his vision for the Disney-MGM Studios. Jay contacted the magazine and sat down with writer Edward L. Prizer over three days to tell his side of the story.

"MCA vs. Disney: The Inside Story of an Epic Confrontation" was published in September 1989 and begins with the author describing Jay as "a normally soft-spoken, exceedingly courteous gentleman, intellectual in appearance and manner. But he was in an aggressive mood when we sat down at the conference table."

Jay spoke plainly. "What do you think they would say if we were to build a Disneyland, simply copying their design and layout?" he asked. "Of course, we wouldn't call ourselves a Magic Kingdom or name our rides Big Thunder Mountain, Haunted Mansion, or Star Tours, but how difficult do you think it would be to change the name of the attractions while building essentially the same thing? That's exactly what these people did. They took our format, show content, sets, and configurations and put their name on it, modified slightly by inserting the MGM logo."

Jay declared, "By any other name, it is a rip-off. We know it, you know it and they know it. Why do you think they have concocted this elaborate story that they were only fulfilling their corporate destiny by implementing Walt's dream for a studio tour? That's one Disney fairy tale that won't play. This is one time the big lie, no matter how often repeated, won't work. If

Mr. Disney's plan represents, as they claim, a studio tour that's very close to what they built, let them make it public and compare it with ours."

Prizer had been reporting on the growth of Disney in central Florida for decades and recalled a time when he had talked with Card Walker, president of Walt Disney Productions, in 1974 at the Lake Buena Vista Club. At that point, Walker said there were no plans to take production away from Hollywood, but a studio tour as an attraction had been considered and subsequently tabled.

"After Walt's death, we decided it would be a fantastic thing to bring Hollywood to Florida," Dick Nunis told Prizer. "We tried the idea with Card Walker, but we couldn't get the studio executives to agree to it, so we decided not to do it. A few years later we tried it again with Ron Miller (who succeeded Walker as president), and again we decided not to do it."s

Jay dismissed all of that. "Don't you find it strange that Mr. Eisner now claims his Disney-MGM Studio Theme Park is very close to Walt Disney's original concept? Mr. Disney's concept for a studio tour had to be the best-kept secret in the world. Think about how much has been written about this visionary man and his ideas and not a word about a studio tour since 1947. How remarkable. But if Mr. Disney's long hidden plan for a studio tour is 'very close' to what Disney just opened, it's all the more remarkable in that it also appears to be usurped from our Hollywood tour and our 1981 Florida Plan."

Erwin Okun, senior vice president of Corporate Communications at Disney, did not help matters when he falsely claimed, "We had Walt's designs at the last annual meeting for anyone who wanted to see them. They're in color. Before he thought of Disneyland, he thought of the studio tour, to be located in Burbank. That was about 1950." The real history of Disneyland shows otherwise.

Jay claimed, "They have shamelessly usurped our attractions, shows, set streets, tram tour structure, and design as well as usurping liberally from our 1981 Florida studio plan which we presented to Paramount officials when Mr. Eisner was president in July of 1981 on a confidential basis." At the time, Eisner blamed the failure for a deal on Gulf and Western CEO Charles Bluhdorn, but Jay knew this was a fabrication.

"Your vision would have to be severely impaired not to see that the Disney-MGM Studio Tour represents at least 80 percent of what we showed them or what was copied from the Universal Tour in Hollywood," he told the magazine.

A defensive Okun told the press, "It would be natural to turn to the history of moviemaking for a studio tour. Things that would be familiar, recognizable to the general public. Generic things. The background of filmmaking itself became the creative source for our Imagineers. Many of our Imagineers came out of moviemaking themselves and had their knowledge and perspectives." Finally, he added another falsehood regarding the meeting at Universal: "Mr. Eisner was not present."

A defiant Jay told Prizer, "They did everything humanly possible to keep us from coming to Orlando. They have every right to go into the studio tour business. This is a free enterprise economy. But it does not give them the right to use our costly research and plans, then claim it was some long-hidden plan from Mr. Disney."

Bob Ward supported his boss's claims. Since Disney had copied the old plans, everything was scrapped, and Universal had to start all over. "Everything we were going to do in 1981 and everything we're now doing in the studio tour in Hollywood has either been eliminated or changed," Ward said.

For example, Universal dropped the stunt show because of the Indiana Jones Epic Stunt Theater. The Screen Test Theatre has been modified to an Ultimatte format with six different films to stand out from Disney's offerings. Murder She Wrote replaced the Sound Effect Theater because of Monster Sound Show.

Disney's Catastrophe Canyon forced Universal to abandon two different attractions including an earthquake experience and an oilfield explosion. Instead, Universal came up with an inside show where guests would encounter an earthquake while riding the BART in San Francisco. The inspiration for the BART sequence came from producer Jennings Lang. Another attraction, two theaters presenting the history of cinema, were crossed off the opening day offerings due to The Great Movie Ride.

*The Los Angeles Times* followed up with independent theme park designers to compare the plans for both parks, and many would only speak off the record. What they found were plans that were similar, and "two of them said that the similarities were 'too close for just coincidence' and 'extreme.'" Dave Schweninger, president of Sequoia Creative, did go on the record and said, "I can't deny they're very similar." However, he cautioned about any malicious behavior. He said, "People all over the country don't have a lot of facts and breadth (knowledge about the movie business) and what they perceive is the palm trees, the architecture, all those kinds of things. They know there are sound effects, and they want to see them [created]." When Jay Stein heard of Schweninger's comments, he countered, "They [Disney] could have done sound effects a million ways. There is nothing that is generic to a studio tour."

However, with challenges came opportunity. Disney opening first turned out to be an advantage. Jay saw what they were building, and he knew he could pick them off one by one. "I think they're very vulnerable," he said. "It IS a little like war. It means that when you invade, you make damn sure that your army is big enough and strong enough to win." He suggested that Disney was "offering their guests approximately one-third of what we're offering." He promised, "Across the board, we're going to deliver a more impressive entertainment experience. [Universal] needs to create and deliver an entertainment experience that is so different and superior that we can assure ourselves that we're going to capture a big enough market share to make this thing profitable."

Jay said, "Disney put trams in because we had trams, but there was no need for them." After all, the only reason they had a tram in Universal City was the hill. Florida was flat. Peter Alexander added, "Once we were no longer dealing with trams we got people involved in the action. We played with scenes with *you* as the actor." Bob Ward found another benefit. "Each experience was longer without the tram," he said. "We allowed four or five minutes for a ride. With the tram, it was two minutes."

## College Hill

Even while construction was under way in Florida, Jay was already thinking about the future. Over one Labor Day holiday weekend in the late 80s, Jay, Richard Swann, Swann's daughter, and her future husband went to the Thousand Islands in the St. Lawrence Seaway. One day they took a boat ride up the St. Lawrence to Kingston in Canada, a great, but small college town. They walked everywhere in the town, the college, and the taverns. Swann finally got bored and suggested they head back to their hotel across the St. Lawrence from Alexander Bay. Jay then told him to be patient, as he was getting ideas for a second gate. Jay's wheels were always turning.

To beat Disney, he knew that Universal had to offer all of the amenities of a full-service resort. On February 9, 1990, he unveiled his plans to Wasserman and Sheinberg. Two Rank executives were also present: Michael Gifford, managing director and group executive, and Terry North.

Jay and Bob Ward described the only resort of its kind in the world. The overall master plan called for a resort complex with a second theme park, up to seven themed hotels, a nighttime entertainment zone, and a retail, commercial corner all connected by a water taxi system. The resort would be compact and everything within easy walking distance unlike Disney, which is spread out. Jay said, "And we know, based on USF's success, that if you offer the public a superior product they will beat a path to your door. What we can offer that Disney can't is accessibility and convenience." The total cost of the project was expected to be $2 billion. If built, the resort would employee 8,325 full-time and 4,770 part-time people.

The success of Church Street Station in downtown Orlando and Pleasure Island at Walt Disney World demonstrated that there was a market for a nighttime entertainment zone. Jay felt Pleasure Island suffered from a fatal flaw. "A flaw that is inherent in the Disney manner in all of their activities: It is too cute, too Disney-ish, and too structured and antiseptic, and their pricing strategy has been a major turnoff with locals," he said. Universal could deliver an adult entertainment experience that had "true character and soul." He started to sketch out the ideas for the entertainment complex while his team was busy getting USF up and running.

The centerpiece of the expansion would be College Hill. Think *Animal House*. It will always be party time, whether it is a victory party or finals are over. Jay's concept was to create a college "commons," a fraternity/sorority row, and a near campus business street around and leading away from a lake. Fraternity/sorority row would house the better restaurants. There would be a commons or quad for outdoor entertainment purposes and a gym for large events.

College Hill would have a wide selection of one-of-a-kind fun places and immerse the guest in its party atmosphere; but, unlike the competition, Universal would feature the "star" appeal of Planet Hollywood and Jimmy Buffet's Margaritaville.

The business district was modeled after State Street in Madison, Telegraph Avenue in Berkeley, and the Westwood of old. Along the street would be famous bars, restaurants, and shops themed to various schools. The menus would reflect food indigenous to particular schools. Off the main street of the business district would be alleys with jazz and comedy clubs. Above the shops would be hotel accomodations.

Every night would be homecoming or some other high-energy event, with college bands playing, pep rallies, and fight songs, cheerleaders, and bonfires. "There will always be an excuse to party—whether it is football or basketball season or spring break," Jay suggested. The street entertainment would be first class. The project would benefit by proximity to the ever-expanding convention center, and marketing would target locals.

Just like the theme park, authenticity was critical. "In order to achieve this environmental realism ('earthiness,' if you will) and capture the operational spirit of 'college life,' we will need to have multiple, experienced, independent operators creating the necessary diversity," Jay said. "The collegiate business district we envision will certainly not be 'cute,' or sterile, or too clean not to feel real. It is like the difference between a set at Disney/MGM and a realistic street façade at USF—one is make believe, as it never was, and the other seems like the real thing."

## The International Drive Assocation

Leading up to the USF opening, Disney went all out to make life difficult for MCA. Disney put pressure on Mears Transportation to refuse to take people from their hotels to Universal. Mears was doing great business picking up visitors along International Drive and dropping them off at the big malls and the Disney parks. They had racks of brochures in hotel lobbies promoting possible destinations. Because of the pressure, they did not include Universal as a destination. When Jay learned of the Mears issue, his team made sure that Universal had brochures at every motel and hotel. They also concentrated on marketing to the growing timeshare market.

At the direction of USF, Swann organized a group called the International Drive Association consisting of International Drive hotel proprietors and merchants, Sea World, and Universal. The primary purpose was to improve traffic congestion on I-Drive and to keep it competitive with Disney.

The main debate was light rails or buses up and down I-Drive. The committee voted to create a taxing district for the purpose of buying and running gas-powered trollies up and down International Drive and over to USF. Dick Batchelor and his wife, Andrea Cudrea, an Orlando TV anchor, proposed the system. Other interests in the negotiations were Bill Davis, president of SeaWorld Orlando, Robert Earl of the Hard Rock chain, Orlando hotelier Harris Rosen, other hotels, and several other entities.

USF did not believe that a trolley would guarantee enough additional attendance to justify the extra tax to support the district. USF was not opposed to a light rail system so long as it directly served USF. Swann was instructed to get Universal's property out of the plan before the district was formed. The county agreed to eliminate the USF property from the district with USF agreeing to join the district if and when a light rail system was created with a stop on the USF property. That agreement has been lost in the bowels of local government.

Another hurdle was when Warner Bros. and Disney teamed up and refused to distribute films to theaters that showed non-theatrical commercials. At the time, theater chains began supplementing their revenues with product ads. Universal was going to take advantage of this trend. With this outlet closed off, Universal would have to increase its marketing budget by $1.5 million.

Disney's plans ultimately backfired. Because of their efforts, all they did was to embolden Sid Sheinberg and Lew Wasserman to go further with Jay's plans. MCA started to look at Disney's businesses to see if they were violating various laws. For example, was the four-day ticket or the Reedy Creek Improvement District, the public governmental body that oversees the Disney property, an anti-trust violation? Disney dropped the boycott.

## Tweak the Mouse

The man in charge of selling Universal Studios Florida to the world was David Weitzner. Weitzner was trying to extricate himself from the employ of Jerry Weintraub and the Weintraub Entertainment Group. He got a call from Jon Sheinberg, a friend and the son of Sid Sheinberg. Sheinberg told him that there was a top marketing job at Universal and asked if Weitzner was interested. He had worked at the studio twelve years before, and his friend Tom Pollock was running the film division. What could be better?

Instead of meeting with Pollock, Sid Sheinberg had Weitzner meet with Jay. Suddenly, Weitzner realized he was not interviewing for a job heading the marketing department at the film division but the Recreation Division. A day later he met with Jay again; they talked, or as Weitzner describes it, he *listened* for about an hour. Most of the conversation centered on Universal City. Jay liked that Weitzner came from the film-making side of the business, just like him. Then Jay suggested they take a short drive to MCA's Planning and Development offices on Lankershim Boulevard to look at some models and artists renderings of the Orlando park.

What Weitzner saw erased the slightest doubt about joining Jay and his team. He thought the elaborate presentation that the team had been using was the most amazing thing and a marketing executive's dream. He recalled Jay's smile, which seemed to say, "I told you so." Weitzner was named the president of Worldwide Marketing the next day.

One thing that made the transition smooth for Weitzner was his close and personal relationship with Steven Spielberg. They had worked together in the past when he was responsible for the marketing campaign for *E.T. the Extra-Terrestrial* (1982) During one brainstorming meeting with Weitzner, Sheinberg, and Jay, Spielberg suggested the phrase that bests defined the Universal experience: Ride the Movies. At Universal, the theatrical experience would be extended. Not only would visitors see the movie, but they would also become participants. It was a eureka moment.

Weitzner turned to Steve Hayman, Hal Kaufman, and Bruce Miller from the advertising firm Foote, Cone & Belding to develop the marketing plans. Kaufman, a copywriter, described the challenge of going against the strongest brand in the business. He said what Disney did well was selling the forest. If one of the Disney parks burnt down tomorrow, they would be able to advertise "come feel the warmth" and people would visit. Universal's strength was selling the trees; promoting one attraction at a time. Each attraction was marketed like the release of a major motion picture.

In preparation for a marketing presentation to MCA and Cineplex management before the opening of the Florida park, Jay told the team from Foote, Cone & Belding to lead the effort, and that the meeting participants did not know anything about marketing. He warned them they will be peppered with questions but whatever happened, Jay informed them that he did not want the participants to get a hit off his marketing team. He did not even want one to get out of the infield. One more thing: they were on their own. Jay put the fear of God into his marketing team just before they walked into the conference room. Jay did not want to change the marketing plans, and it was Foote, Cone & Belding's responsibility to sell it. Jay was proud of the ideas, and he did not want the others to screw it up.

On one side of the table were the top brass from MCA. On the other was the team from Cineplex Odeon. Questions came from the left and the right including Sheinberg asking why there was no advertising for Texas since he just had relatives move into Corpus Christie. In the end, the presentation was successful. Jay turned to Bruce Miller and with typical understated faint praise said, "You did okay."

After at least a dozen flights from Los Angeles to Orlando, all on Delta Airlines, which had the only two daily non-stop flights, Weitzner noticed that the Disney executives all sat on one side of first-class while the Universal executives sat on the other side. Both teams were trying to cast a wandering eye at what was on the competition's computer screens. This "us against them" attitude was fostered daily by Jay and to a lesser extent, Sid Sheinberg.

It was on one of these flights that Weitzner came up with a brilliant plan. He noticed that Delta had a monthly in-flight magazine called *Sky Magazine*. At the time, Delta was known as the "official airline of Walt Disney World." Weitzner saw the opportunity for a marketing home run and secretly and successfully negotiated an exclusive three-year agreement for thirty-six covers of the magazine. Later, Weitzner said he was sure the salesman who made the deal thought he had died and gone to media heaven until he found out the buyer was none other than Universal Studios.

A few weeks later, at one of the monthly Joint Venture board meetings in Orlando, Weitzner waited for just the right moment, suddenly stood up, and threw down on the table a mocked up copy of the first three-page gatefold with the rendering of the new theme park. Weitzner secretly had the Foote, Cone & Belding team mock up the advertisement. Not even Jay knew what was coming. The response was everything Weitzner hoped for.

When word got back to Michael Eisner, he was less than pleased. Prompted by Jay, the *Sky Magazine* ads allowed Universal to "tweak the mouse" monthly. After the first year, Wasserman called Weitzner into his office. He told the young executive to cancel the final two years of the contract. Wasserman felt that they had made their point.

Another marketing coup was the billboard campaign. The marketing team secured the best remaining advertisement sites along I-4 and other freeways in the Orlando and central Florida area, especially those roads leading from the airport. One of the things that puzzled Jay was that Disney did not do billboard advertising for their parks. At the very least, once they knew Universal was coming to Orlando; Disney could have acquired the best remaining billboard sites and preempted the marketing campaign.

Universal began to install incredible, one-of-a-kind, three-dimensional billboards with movement. Starting in 1988, central Florida got its first glimpse at the upcoming theme park wars when E.T.'s head and animated 30-foot long fingers cast in three-dimensional Plexiglas beckoned from a Florida interstate. The caption read, "Fly with me in 1990" and at night his eyes would light up. They called these "spectaculars," and they featured most of the attractions and shows for the yet-to-open Universal Studios Florida. Every few months they would introduce another one. Each billboard cost more than $25,000 each to build. People were so impressed; they would pull over to the side of the road and take photos. Since Universal had locked up the best locations, Disney could not fight back.

Jay had based his strategy on General James H. Doolittle's 1942 bombing raid on Tokyo just months after the attack on Pearl Harbor. The raid caused negligible material damage to Japan, but it succeeded in its goal of raising American morale and casting doubt in Japan on the ability of its military leaders to defend their home islands. He confessed that he might have overpaid to get some of these billboards, but they got the job done. Every time Michael Eisner drove from the airport to the Disney property, there was no way to avoid them. Disney knew Universal was coming, ready to fight, and fight hard. So successful were the billboards in capturing the public's attention and the amount of press throughout the country and the world, both Disney and Sea World would soon copy the concept.

Even the television advertising campaign got the Hollywood star treatment. Jay and David Weitzner reached out to Tom Pollock, chairperson of Universal's film division, who proposed they hire Richard Donner. Donner was an accomplished major film director with hits such as *Superman*, *The Goonies*, *Lethal Weapon*, and *Maverick*. He also had a background in television commercials. In turn, Donner hired Stephen Goldblatt, the cinematographer responsible for *Lethal Weapon* and *Batman Forever*. They hired the director for $1 million, and he was worth every penny.

When Steve Hayman and his team brought the commercials to Jay for his final review, Jay sat there impassively, then gave the team his highest compliment, "Not a bad piece of shit." He paused. "Of course, I gave you $3.5 million to shoot the goddamn thing."

Jay could be direct. During one marketing meeting Tom Lazansky handed Jay a videocassette of the Imagine Entertainment film *Cry Baby* with a commercial for the launch of the Florida park. After viewing the commercial,

Jay angrily turned to Lazansky and said, " I would just like to take that cassette and shove it up your ass." Sheepishly, Lazansky turned to copywriter Hal Kaufman and said, "I am glad we weren't presenting outdoors."

Many years later, Kaufman suggested that the campaign may have been a mistake. The idea of stressing the park's authentic movie-making roots may have worked in Hollywood, but in Florida people visit primarily to go to a theme park. The advertising campaign left an impression that the park was not for families with kids, but serious movie fans.

An additional source of revenue was sponsorship from some of America's biggest corporations. Walt Disney pioneered this concept for Disneyland. His successors took this idea to extreme lengths for EPCOT. Now, everybody did it.

Steve Lew was put in charge of this crucial and challenging task. Bruce Miller, with a Los Angeles advertising agency, and Mark H. McCormack, the founder of the International Management Group (IMG), assisted him. McCormack was a high-powered executive who patterned his life after Lew Wasserman. In fact, in his book *What they Don't Teach You at Harvard Business School: Notes from a Street-Smart Executive*, he states that fact right up front. In the case of a dispute between IMG and Universal that could not be resolved, it would be submitted to McCormack and Wasserman for resolution.

At a meeting with the Joint Venture team, Bruce Miller laid out the advertising plan for the launch of the park. He ran through the list of big names including AT&T, Pepsi, and so on. However, in typical Sheinberg backhanded fashion, he said, "Any schmuck can spend his own money to promote his product; the genius is in getting some other schmuck to spend his money to promote your product." Years later Miller found himself at a restaurant in New York when he came across Sheinberg and his wife, Lorraine Gary. He went up to reintroduce himself and related the story to Lorraine. She chuckled and said, "Yes, that sure sounds like Sid." Sponsorships became a significant revenue source totaling in the tens of millions of dollars.

For Jay, nothing was left to chance. He demanded final approval of all creative endeavors, from television and radio commercials to billboards, live show, attraction scripts, and even the music. He was willing to spend the dollars necessary (usually within ever-changing approved budget guidelines) to achieve the goals. Jay cared, and he wanted to *win*. Several years later he recalled, "We had to fight for every inch."

Looking for any opportunity, Jay recognized that 1990 would mark the 75th anniversary of Universal Studios. "From Carl Laemmle and the earliest stars, up to our present mega-hits, our company has a unique and distinguished history, and over the years has been a leading force in motion pictures, television, and music," Jay wrote to Sheinberg and Wasserman.

"Over the past three-quarters of a century, we've been associated with some of the best-known talent and the most famous of innovative movie and television products, winning our share of awards and public acclaim." He noted, "We should be proud of our heritage, and it was time to take a bow." This milestone was something that they could exploit.

There was talk at the studio of producing a television special to mark the occasion. Jay felt so strongly about the idea that he volunteered to have his division pay the $1.6 million production cost if the studio did not want to. Jay suggested a television special would allow viewers to "come away feeling entertained, enlightened, and in awe of the amazing depth and scope of our company."

He reminded his bosses that Disney goes "to great lengths to celebrate any trivial commemorative occasion. If we ever want to be thought of as a co-equal on a worldwide scale, we should let the world know of our long heritage and list of accomplishments, as we cannot expect the public to be aware of these things, especially internationally." Disney built a brand and Jay felt that Universal could do the same. However, Sid Sheinberg disagreed. Talk of a television special ceased in March 1990.

## Far More Ambitious

Jay was in Florida almost full time with his wife. During the final weeks before opening, all day long his staff was coming in reporting to Jay on the difficulties they were having meeting the opening deadline. However, all of them continued to assure him that either by computer or by hand everything would be working on opening day.

Shortly before the park had opened, Jay's team threw him a surprise party to commemorate his 30$^{th}$ anniversary working for MCA. The party took place on one of the soundstages. People from multiple divisions of MCA with whom he was close attended. Sid Sheinberg submitted a videotaped commentary as did Wasserman, Spielberg, Azoff, Weintraub, and others who could not attend. Milt Rosen, a comedic writer Jay and Tony Sauber knew, wrote some "roast" type comments for various people to share about Jay. It was an extremely enjoyable, drunken affair. The master of ceremonies for the roast portion was a very inebriated David Weitzner who, when introducing Sauber, said, "If Tony didn't exist, Jay Stein would have had to invent him."

David Weitzner had been responsible for many Hollywood premieres but nothing at the scale of the grand opening ceremonies for Universal Studios Florida. The gathering of stars was unprecedented. The marketing team turned to sponsor US Airways who lent them a 737. They also chartered approximately fifteen private jets for the celebrity "heavy hitters" who would refuse to fly with another star. The guests stayed at the exclusive Villas of Grand Cypress for a couple of days.

The story of Universal Studios Florida opening day has become legend. Many of the rides were not working, broke down frequently, or could only work with teams of people behind the "curtain" pulling the levers by hand. It was a 102-degree day, sweltering and raining. People were angry and stormed the gates. The park was giving free tickets left and right.

Why did it open on that day? Simple. In show business, the show always begins on time. The marketing department had to commit to advertising and the A-list celebrities needed to be booked in advance for the grand opening ceremony.

Jay told *Orlando Magazine*, "The day Sid and Lew said we'll go and we'll do it with Spielberg, all of us knew we'd have to create something far more spectacular than we'd ever planned. Far more ambitious. Far more costly. Far more sophisticated. It was the decision of this team that we would build something that has no parallel."

Jay knew he had to open when he did. He counted on memories being short, knowing any problems are forgotten after a year or two. Look at Disneyland. That opening day disaster was broadcast live on network television to the biggest audience ever, up to that time.

He believed things would have been worse if he had waited. P&D was always raising issues and making excuses, but nobody told Jay it could not be done. Jay learned in Hollywood that nothing ever worked right when it first opened. He also knew if you let a creative person wait until they thought they were ready, then nothing would ever be completed. Among the biggest fiascos, Jaws did not work on opening day and would never function properly. Things were so bad, Tom Williams shut down the ride shortly after the opening, and Jay contacted United Technologies, makers of military submarines, to consult on how to fix it.

Then there came pressure from Wasserman. If they had waited, they would have missed the summer season. This was the largest investment in MCA's history, and Wasserman was anxious to see the start of return on his investment. Jay accepted full responsibility for his decision to open and years later said, "You are going to have casualties when you go to war."

Even though Universal used the press to publicize the opening, when they stumbled, the press pounced and pounced hard. Still, it was worth it. What visitors found once they passed through the front gates was a Hollywood that never existed yet was always in their mind. The front lot section was based on Universal City before the MCA Tower was built. Jay personally picked out many of the buildings he wanted to reproduce while walking around the streets of Hollywood. He took photos and passed them along to his team.

For the New York section, they got permission to reproduce the famous façade of Tiffany & Company. Originally planned as a jewelry store, just before the park opened Tiffany rescinded their approval for the use of their name. It did not matter. Jay already had the iconic façade built and quickly had the name changed to I. Stein & Co., in honor of his brother Ira, who owned a jewelry store in Brentwood, California.

Jay's standards were high, and he joked that every building on the San Francisco pier "had the proper amount of bird shit." That was the level of detail that he was seeking. In tribute, the Universal Creative team placed Jay's face onto the archangel that overlooks Gramercy Park in the New York section. They even created a statue of Lew Wasserman where his head is affixed to Abraham Lincoln's body and his signature glasses are held in his hand behind his back. Nobody was brave enough to tell Wasserman.

The day after the grand opening ceremonies, Jay sat down with his marketing team to figure out what to do next. They talked about the negative press reaction; how some of the rides didn't operate as expected, or operate at all. They spoke of the great party and the positives that came from that.

Faithful to the spirit of the MCA culture, Jay never heard a negative word regarding opening day from Wasserman or Sheinberg. They did call every night to keep current on the problems and to listen to what Jay was doing to correct them. Nevertheless, Jay tried, learned his lessons, was fixing his mistakes, and was ready to move on to the next deal. That is the way you did it at MCA.

## Getting it Right

Just before the grand opening, Jay replaced Steve Lew by putting Tom Williams in charge of the park. Lew was a loyal and valuable employee, but Jay felt that Williams could better handle angry guests and a hostile press, and most importantly get things working.

Williams started as the assistant manager of the Village Sports store in Yosemite and almost lost a leg trying to fix a ski lift. He was as loyal as they came and performed beautifully. His leadership was exemplary, and Jay believes it was one of the best business decisions he ever made.

Barry Upson put together the team that built the park. Along with Lew and Williams, the other members of the team were Jack McDaniel, executive vice president, MCA Recreation Services; Bob Ward, vice president, Design and Planning; Peter Alexander, vice president, Shows and Special Effects; and Terry Winnick, vice president, Special Projects. Every one of them were prepared to roll up their sleeves and fix whatever needed fixing. They were rightfully proud of what they had done.

Along with the Universal Creative team were McDevitt and Street, Korte (St. Louis), Holder (San Francisco), and Mellon Stuart, who made up the construction team. Bill Moss, who was construction manager at Epcot Center, was in charge for MCA. The ride mechanisms were built by Switzerland's Intamin, Arrow of Salt Lake City, and Ride & Show of Los Angeles.

On January 2, 1991, Disney CEO Michael Eisner was spotted with his entourage touring Universal Studios Florida. Ron Bension said that Universal did not invite Disney people on their property but was happy to sell them a ticket. Although the battle between Universal and Disney was fierce and mostly at arm's length, the two companies did come together for common industry issues. The Universal team frequently visited Disney-MGM. Over time, they got to know some of the key people such as Bob Allan, the first general manager; Bob Small, the hotelier for Disney hotel operations; Ted Kaye; and Dick Nunis, a senior Disney executive who was deeply involved in regional tourism, political, and business gatherings. One of Jay's fondest memories was the sight of Nunis walking through the Universal park with his eyes bugging out of his head in awe.

Did USF make an impact at Disney? The park outperformed Disney-MGM in its first full year. USF drew 6 million visitors in a terrible tourism year. Eighty percent of guest surveys stated that Universal was better than Disney-MGM. The Hard Rock Café at USF became the most successful in the chain.

The management team at Disney was afraid that visitors would skip Epcot and drive down to Universal. The whole purpose of the Walt Disney World expansion was to keep people for an extra day or two. Instead of visiting Epcot, they would visit Universal. Although Disney would never admit it, Steve Lew said that the average stay in Orlando was about three days, plus or minus. Disney had three parks and thousands of hotel rooms. Universal took part of or all of one day, and the stay in Orlando eventually extended.

USF showed how Michael Eisner became his own worst enemy. Until Universal came along, Disney had the entire amusement park market to itself. Sea World, Cedar Point, and Knott's Berry Farm were minor players. Disney added and could modify their attractions at a leisurely pace. Universal was the startup that changed their way of doing business; the competition forced them to make multi-million dollar investments that required more thrills. They never had to go into the marketplace to find new characters. Now that is all they do. Universal created a very competitive market and forced them into it.

Once Michael Eisner announced that Disney was going to build a studio-based theme park with a back-lot tram tour in Florida, Universal had two choices. They could come up with something quick or sell off the Florida property and retreat to Hollywood. Although the studio and tour were not a high priority to Wasserman, it became one when Eisner decided to meddle. Phil Hettema said, "It's classic Jay in so many ways because, on the one hand, Jay's ambitions are why that park [Florida] exists. It was in his fierce competition with Disney that he was able to leverage brilliantly, because Michael Eisner announced they were going to do a studio tour when Universal had already talked about it."

Gary Goddard said, "[Eisner] wanted to block Universal. He thought if he could get a studio tour going first they wouldn't bother coming." Instead, he woke up a sleeping giant and unleashed a competitor that would force him and his successors to spend at a rate they did not have to. Everyone in Hollywood knew that Lew Wasserman was very competitive and usually won. It was time to teach the youngster over at Disney a lesson. MCA was now in it to win it. Jay said, "I had a passion, the energy, the concepts, the strategy, the perseverance, the guts, the commitment to get even for stealing my ideas and doing everything possible, using every dirty trick, to prevent our expansion in Florida."

When construction for USF finally started, Michael Eisner said, "I resigned myself to the fact that the prospect of an aggressive competitor was an incentive to redouble our own efforts and not take our success for granted." While Jay was expanding the parameters of the modern theme park, Eisner's greatest contribution to the Disney theme parks was raising the prices on a continuing basis.

Not long after the grand opening, Ron Bension asked Jay whether he could come to Florida to see if he could help. The attraction reliability was still terrible. The guests and press were still complaining. When Bension got there, he was depressed. The team was shell shocked, some were panicked, others war weary. Some had given up and were just going through the motions. Even though they were tirelessly working to solve problems, there seemed to be a lack of focus and priority. Everything was a priority, and that was the biggest problem.

First was to "download" with Jay. Bension could not imagine what Jay was going through personally, but he did see for the first time some resignation on his part. They talked about the team, and Jay was down on them. Knowing Jay as well as Bension did, he realized that Jay was contributing to the overall lack of productivity and motivation. Jay could be relentless and for guys in the trenches (and the team had been in the trenches for many months pre- and post-opening) Jay's management style could backfire. Jay wanted everything at once for all things. Bension saw people telling him what he wanted to hear rather than the truth. Telling Jay "no" is okay as long as you have a plan and are prepared with answers.

Jay asked Bension to look at the attractions and operations to see what he could do. He felt that he had the benefit of not being through the war of opening USF. The team needed someone to lead them, and Bension had the luxury of coming in with fresh eyes and some credibility. Maybe he could see things clearly.

Bension, who had been focused on Hollywood during the development of the Florida park, came up with a fresh idea. Bension suggested that the priority was to get the press off their back and stop guest complaints so they could buy some time to get things right. He suggested that they give every guest who came to the park a free ticket to return. Buy a ticket for today's visit and come back anytime for a second visit. There was no expiration date, and the tickets are still good today.

David Weitzner described the suggestion as being like the moment when the seas parted. What a crazy idea. It said, "We are sorry. See the park today and come back when everything is working properly."

Bension also suggested that they put signs in front of the ticket booths that explained what was not working and the free return ticket policy. Who could complain if you told them before they spent any money what they were in for and that they could come back free when things were working? It worked, the complaints stopped, and the press went away.

Next came the attractions. Focus, prioritize, and execute. Bension organized teams so that people had specific responsibilities and attractions to focus on. There were too many people doing everything. They triaged the problems and prioritized the repairs.

Bension felt that giving the team a new face to complain to would help, and it did. The biggest thing he could do was to keep Jay away from the team as much as possible. Bension became the conduit and reduced the number of people that interfaced with Jay. Jay was an acquired taste. Few people could succeed with him normally, let alone when things were going wrong.

## The Smoking Gun Memo

*If you can keep your head when all about you*
*Are losing theirs and blaming it on you,*
*Yours is the Earth and everything that's in it,*
*And—which is more—you'll be a Man, my son!*

—Rudyard Kipling

With the grand opening of Universal Studios Florida just weeks away, Jay was working what seemed like 23 hours days to get it ready for its debut. What nobody knew was he spent the other hour dedicated to the future.

In a landmark memo to Sid Sheinberg, dated April 19, 1990, Jay outlined a vision for urban destination resorts in Hollywood and Florida that would rival anything that Disney could offer. Remarkably, he told his boss, "Because of the priority of USF; our creative staff has not been at all involved—in fact, is unaware of—this presentation." The only people privy to this concept were Tony Sauber and the researcher Sauber had hired, John Beam. Jay spent hundreds of hours dictating his thoughts to Sauber. Sauber would organize Jay's thoughts and ultimately put together a description for a second theme park adjacent to USF.

"But read on and see if you share my dream." What Jay was proposing was striking. His vision included multi-day resorts on both coasts with two major gated attractions, an expanded CityWalk/Cineplex/Amphitheatre area, multiple hotels catering to tourists and convention visitors, a centralized conference facility, and an internal transportation system providing convenient on-site mobility. This is what Disney was doing in Florida, and it was what they were going to do in California.

At the time, Disney was considering second gates for California in the parking lot of Disneyland or on the waterfront at the Port of Long Beach on property they acquired when they purchased the Wrather Corporation. The Wrather deal was primarily a way for Disney to buy back the rights to create Disney-branded hotels on the West Coast. Along with the Disneyland Hotel, they got the historic *Queen Mary*, the *Spruce Goose*, and adjacent land.

"While they [Disney] may lack something in Public Relations sensitivity, I must salute their chutzpah and willingness to take the heat in demanding zoning changes and local, state and federal funding, as well as their pitting of Long Beach and Anaheim against each other, but this is exactly what proved successful in Europe with Spain and France," Jay wrote. "While they claim to be considering both locations, it is starting to seem likely that Long Beach may be a 'straw man' or a 'fall-back' position being used primarily to secure a better deal from Anaheim."

It did not matter to Jay whether Disney expanded in Anaheim or Long Beach. Jay had them beat when it came to location. "The need to refocus on the unique nature and potential of Universal City—it is arguably the only place in southern California, perhaps in the entire country, that can offer a centrally located, easily accessible destination resort in the middle of a major urban area," Jay told Sheinberg. "Its potential as such dwarfs any of the more prosaic uses of the property being considered."

The research showed that visitors to the southern California region typically stayed in Los Angeles County and traveled to Orange County. Jay wrote, "There is only one area in Los Angeles that has the potential to offer visitors a full entertainment package, consisting of several days of theme park attendance, hotels catering to families, restaurants, adequate/convenient/safe nighttime entertainment, and accessibility to the other areas of interest in Los Angeles—Hollywood, Beverly Hills, the beach: this is Universal City."

Moreover, there was simply not enough remaining land in the greater Los Angeles area to allow anyone else to compete with them. "If we create such a full-service resort environment, even Disney's very ambitious plans would not be enough to offset our location and population advantage," Jay said.

Now he just needed something to draw people to the property.

## The Next Franchise?

For Universal's second gate, Jay wanted to create a contrast to round out the demographic appeal of the resort. Cartoon World would be a fundamentally different theme park experience than USH and USF. Cartoon World would be a fantasy environment; whimsical, light-hearted, adventurous, and thrilling, depending on the characters.

"What we have now at USH/USF is unique because we have blended (in the case of USH) or constructed (USF) an authentic Hollywood studio environment," Jay told his boss. "A place where real pictures are made. It doesn't look like a theme park; all streets are sets, all of which are shootable; there is daily actual and simulated production taking place; there is a studio tour and numerous opportunities to observe the art of movie making; many of our shows demonstrate technical film making processes."

Jay wrote to Sheinberg, "It is my belief, my hypothesis, that if you build a second (or third or fourth) major, well-conceived park in a market which offers the right conditions (weather, favorable local demographics and tourist visitation, sufficient hotel rooms/convention facilities and transportation infrastructure), you can prosper. As the new park in town, you will compete with everyone, but it will be the lesser parks that will be hurt the most, and, in time, the 'universe' of visitors will grow (assuming the hotel rooms and other tourist-related infrastructure keep pace)."

Cartoon World had to be a world-class theme park of the same magnitude and quality as USF. Jay did not want a mini-park, which would be perceived as a "kiddie park." If that were the case, the competition would simply expand their child-friendly areas, and Universal would have lost the competitive edge.

The biggest challenge would be collecting the best intellectual properties to exploit. Universal already had a winning strategy. Led by attorney Tony Sauber, Universal had a long history of acquiring theme park rights to the most visible intellectual properties in the industry. Jay also wanted to get Spielberg, Sheinberg, and David Geffen involved in the acquisition of rights. When MCA acquired Geffen Records in 1990, manager and record mogul David Geffen became the largest stockholder in MCA. He owned more shares than Wasserman. He was also a fan and supporter of the theme parks. Jay's wish list of intellectual properties included Looney Tunes, DC Comics, Hanna-Barbara, King Features, UPA, Walter Lantz, Jay Ward, Peanuts, and Dr. Seuss. Cartoon World was a park concept that could be exported around the world with local favorites added to enhance the mix.

Jay proposed that the heart of the new park would be familiar cartoon characters from Warner Bros. He told Sheinberg, "It is my firm belief that a deal with Warner's offers us the best possibility to create a successful second gate and suggests that we should proceed with them in order to ensure the significant worldwide growth potential that an alliance with Warner's would afford Universal."

Although Warner Bros. had a relationship with Six Flags, Jay thought they would be better off with Universal. The appeal at Six Flags was thrills, and the cartoon characters were lost in the clutter. Jay knew that simple theming was not enough.

He thought Spielberg could be particularly useful getting the rights from Warner Bros. The director had already teamed up with the studio to direct *The Color Purple* and *Empire of the Sun*. Plus, his production house produced cartoons such as *Tiny Toon Adventures, Animaniacs,* and *Pinky and the Brain*. A partnership was an opportunity for both studios to benefit by enhancing the profiles of characters like Bugs Bunny, Batman, Superman, Daffy Duck, and hundreds of others.

Jay's other concern was strategic. He did not want to have Warner Bros. as a direct competitor. At the time, a 415-acre theme park called Warner Bros. Movie World was under construction adjacent to the existing Warner Roadshow Studio complex on the Gold Coast, Queensland, Australia. Movie World opened on June 3, 1991.

The park was the brainchild of C.V. Wood, whose credits include Disneyland, Six Flags Over Texas, and Freedomland USA. Modeled after the Universal Studio Tour in Hollywood, Movie World combined a working studio and a tourist attraction with motion simulators, slow boat rides, and roller coasters. Jay told Sheinberg, "C.V. Wood may be the key here as he was the moving force for Movie World in Australia, and it was his exposure to our early 1980's plans and financial projections that were the genesis of that park, including its name. Michael Eisner could take lessons from Mr. Wood."

Overall, Jay was not impressed with Movie World. It was not in the same class as Universal Studios. He called it a third-rate rip-off of USF and another cheap attempt to leverage Warner's classic characters for a quick buck in a backwater market. Looking at what Warner Bros. had done in Australia as well as the Six Flags parks, Jay argued that Warner's had not demonstrated the ability to handle the most beloved characters in the world with sensitivity and imagination, let alone exploit their full merchandising potential. They failed to protect their world-class characters with high quality theming and an original storyline, presented with the most innovative, high-tech delivery systems.

In a conversation with Steven Spielberg, Jay compared the park to the *Gong Show* with marginal entertainment values. He told the director, "It's like comparing an old Republic film with one of yours."

Jay's calculation was that Universal did not have enough cartoon characters to make his park a reality and Warner Bros. would be unlikely to license their characters or they would just build something on their own, like in Australia. He had 27 years experience running a high quality, world-class theme park. What Universal could offer Warner Bros. was "one element that neither Warners nor any other theme park operator in the world can bring to the table—the creativity of Steven Spielberg."

What would make Cartoon World unique? "In fact, there is nothing protectable about the basic premise or theme I am proposing (as we have learned with our movie-themed parks)," Jay wrote to Sheinberg. "I truly think that if we assemble a package of the best characters—as we now have at USF with E.T., Jaws, Ghostbusters, King Kong, etc.—any competitor would think twice about entering the marketplace (just as I feel that USF, if it had been open as presently constituted, would have stopped Disney from going forward)."

Cartoon World would become the primary park. Any new animated feature or television series properties developed or acquired by Universal would first be offered to Cartoon World. This would include non-animated features (if the assets originated or were initially popularized as a comic or cartoon property). Examples included Batman, the Muppets, and Roger Rabbit. Spielberg half-owned Roger Rabbit along with Disney, and Jay had big plans for the character.

Jay had done his homework. "Based on this background, I am now ready to answer the question you really asked: whether Cartoon World will compete with, i.e. cannibalize, USH (or USF)," Jay wrote to Sheinberg. "I feel that the answer is 'yes', but that the impact on either of our parks will be temporary only. Still, during its first year, we will be devoting a disproportionate amount of our marketing efforts to Cartoon World. It will be new and locals and repeat out-of-town visitors will want to try it; thus, it may have a temporary negative effect on either USH or USF." The experience at Disney had shown the effects were temporary. Cartoon World was themed differently than USF, skewed more toward family and children, and not directly competitive.

The plan was to open Cartoon World at Universal City in Hollywood first and then expand into Florida. Jay's reasoning was "the land presently 'exists,' and Warner Bros. would probably find this location more appealing. Their studio was a short drive away and could be seen from the hilltop Tour Center.

For decades, Jay had witnessed film and television production moving off the back lot and onto location or on a soundstage. His success depended on finding the balance between the tour, accommodating the production staff, and fending off Albert Dorskind's desire to build office buildings and shopping malls. With the shift in equilibrium, Jay knew it was either going to be him or Dorskind who controlled the land at Universal City.

Jay suggested to Sheinberg that the existing studio facilities could be reduced to a USF-like representation, keeping just enough for legitimacy. Actual studio operations would be relocated or contracted out from one or more of the other existing studios that could be leased or purchased. Jay predicted that Universal City land would prove too valuable to support the large space demands (and fluctuating economics) of a major working studio.

The strategy for the future of California was evident. Build CityWalk. Continue to enhance the tour with USF-quality attractions. Relocate some of the studio facilities to create the land for Cartoon World. Build new tourist facilities such as hotels, restaurants, entertainment facilities. Buy Lakeside Country Club and make it an amenity for the resort.

Jay offered to develop a section of Cartoon World for Sheinberg so he could "appreciate its content, theming and feel." He proposed to produce a video that would explain how Cartoon World would be significantly different in theme content or feel from any movie-oriented park (Universal, Disney-MGM, or Warner Bros.). The video would demonstrate why the park must be done as a major facility, and why it is the best, most lucrative, and most natural form of exploitation for the Warner Bros. characters. He proclaimed, "No one else, not Disney and not anyone else, can duplicate what we can do here or offset our advantage."

By November 1990, Jay had refined the Cartoon World concept and was ready to reveal more to Sheinberg. He was confident that a cartoon-based theme park had the strongest and broadest appeal of any theme park ever conceived. He believed "that the prevailing reason why people go to theme parks is because they want to share a quality leisure experience with friends or family." People go to parks for a shared experience.

He carefully studied Disneyland and the Magic Kingdom to figure out why they were so popular. His conclusion was they had a quality product that was a first of its kind. Disney defined the market. He felt that people go to the Disney parks "to relive their childhood and share that experience with their own children. Or, if on an adults-only visit, just pretend they are young again." Disney capitalized on being an institution. They had proprietary characters and much of the architecture and ambiance of the Disney parks are a re-creation of the childhood of its adult patrons.

Jay understood that Disneyland was a re-creation of the childhood and intellectual pursuits of Walt Disney himself, which corresponded with the imagined, internalized, Americana childhood that everyone liked to imagine they had, although in reality, few did. Jay felt the Disney parks gave people an opportunity to escape into the charms, adventure, and fantasy of childhood. He told Sheinberg, "Many parents of today regret not being able to have their children grow up in a less complicated world where right and wrong are clearly defined and innocence is a virtue."

Jay believed that Cartoon World would have the same type of appeal but would be more popular due to the selection of characters. He envisioned a park where guests could interact with Bugs Bunny, Daffy Duck, Superman, and Batman. The park would have a much wider demographic than Disney with characters which "are infinitely more adaptable to exciting, humorous attractions." Jay felt the Warner stable of characters were better known, more popular, and appealed to broader demographics. The park would "be offering the 'hottest' stars of our culture. Bugs Bunny, Superman, and Batman are of international stature." Furthermore, such a park would not cannibalize the current movie-based park.

Strategically, he wanted to name the park Warner's Cartoon World. Jay felt that this would be a clear message to the public about the park's identity just as Universal Studios Florida did for the movie-based park. He also thought this would flatter Warner Bros. and make it easier to strike a deal. Jay felt the park could attract more than 10 million visitors a year, but Jay had a plan and ranked the rides with JayBangs so that he could scale back and build a more modest seven-million-visitor park. He noted that "star" power was critical and a stable of the most popular characters would give us the greatest chance of attaining their goals. For example, Disney had made deals with MGM, Henson, and Lucas to find the next generation of intellectual properties. "I personally believe our best chance to achieve our maximum attendance potential is to make use of the Warner's characters and therefore, it follows that a Warner's deal gives us the best chance to succeed, preempt competition, and protect our ability to establish destination resorts in Florida, Europe, and Asia."

Up until now, Disneyland and the Magic Kingdom never had direct head-on competition, and so much of their park rests comfortably on older technology. Jay wanted to offer an entire park that represented the highest level of proven technology; something that Disney could not afford to match for the incremental gain it would give them. Jay told Sheinberg that with Warner's characters, Universal would "have obviously enhanced our defensive position on a worldwide basis."

To prepare, Jay meticulously studied every attraction at Disneyland and the Magic Kingdom. His goal was *not* to duplicate what Disney had with a different set of characters. His plan was to demonstrate to Sheinberg that MCA could obtain the star power to design its own unique attractions in entirely new settings and win at every level. He used the baseball analogy that they had the better players at every position.

Jay gathered a dream team of theme park designers including Phil Hettema, Gary Goddard, Norm Newberry, Peter Alexander, Bob Ward, Barry Upson, Dale Mason, and Steven Spielberg. They took up Jay's challenge to beat Disney at their own game, and they exploded with copious, wonderful ideas and architectural concepts. The enthusiasm was contagious.

Jay liked Phil Hettema. "He had balls," Jay once proclaimed. Hettema spoke his mind, made his point, was honest, and had depth. Jay also like Bob Ward. He felt he was like Hettema. He always gave 100% and told the truth. Barry Upson was the master planner and a damned good one. Jay felt Upson was not necessarily a creative person or a show guy, but he knew how to create a site plan so things made sense. For example, Upson was responsible for creating the canals that connect various amenities within the resort area. Within months, they had produced four books detailing ideas for the new park. Each book covered one of the lands.

Guests entered Cartoon World through Comic Strip Lane. At the time, comic strips were still popular and read by at least 50 percent of the audience. The comic section was the third most popular within a newspaper outranked only by the front page and sports. Comic-strip characters also represented $9 billion in merchandise sold in 1989.

Comic Strip Lane would be a "unique environment that seems to be lifted from the comics." Many of the characters would come from the Sunday funnies such as Blondie, Garfield, Dennis the Menace, Lil' Abner, and Daisy Mae. "Toon"-style transportation vehicles would escort guests toward the Central Plaza where they could watch A Night at the Opera, a live character, special-effects filled, nightly entertainment extravaganza.

Looney Tunes Land would be home to Bugs Bunny, Road Runner, Wile E. Coyote, Daffy Duck, Porky Pig, and other popular Looney Tunes characters. In 1991, *The Los Angeles Times* noted that the Looney Tunes classic cartoons were number one among Saturday morning cartoon programming for more than a decade. The show was the longest-running and most watched network animation series in history. According to Warner Bros., Bugs Bunny has starred in more programs, on more channels, and been number one in the ratings more often than any other character, real or animated, in the history of television.

Signature rides included Coyote Canyon, a looping steel coaster; Duck Dodgers and the Red Planet, a motion simulator ride; and Sylvester's Nine Lives Ride, an Omnimover-based ride with a scary theme. Others included a water ride called Wabbit Season, an interactive dark ride using an electric-powered coaster called the Acme Factory, and Martian Mayhem, which Jay described as "Peter Pan with arcade action."

There were plenty of shows including the Pepe Le Pew Revue, an audio-animatronics show; Prof. Bugs Bunny's Acme Looniversity, a 3D film with a live host; and Yosemite Sam Rides Again, a 360-degree film where visitors sit in two-person motion simulator seats. There was even a complement of smaller rides to round out the offerings such as Plucky Duck's Plane Ride, a regular flat ride; the Jet Pack Rocket Ride, a swing ride like the Swinger at Knott's Berry Farm; and Dizzy Devil's Tasmanian Twister, like the Tea Cups at Disneyland.

Phil Hettema recalled that the attractions developed for Looney Tunes Land were some of the best of his esteemed career. Jay agreed and suggested his ideas for Cartoon World were world class. He said Hettema was an extraordinary talent, and his thoughts and concepts were always original and often cutting edge.

The other must-see destination would be Superhero Island. Here, the heroes of the DC Comics like Superman, Batman, Wonder Woman, and many others would come to life. DC Comics was the industry leader in the 20- to 30-year-old group. Comic book sales were on the rise once again, and there was an explosion of new comic books stores. Jay hired Gary Goddard to develop this area.

Thrills would be at the center of attractions such as the Adventures of Superman, which placed the rider flat on their stomach as they went through the experience; the 3D motion simulator Justice League MindWarp; and the dual hanging Batwing JetCoaster. Other rides included the Joker's Wild motion simulator and Joker's Madhouse, a wild mouse coaster.

Superhero Island would feature incredible stunt and special effects shows like the Batman and Robin Live Action Spectacular and DeathTraps—The Super Illusion Spectacular, a live magic show. The Superhero Cadet Training Center would have been the updated version of Tom Sawyer Island and provide a role-playing area with interactive electronic exhibits.

Just to be safe, Jay also recommended that Universal make a deal with Marvel "to protect our flanks and add further depth to the park." Success would come from maintaining "a consistency of theme—we should be the place where they can 'ride the cartoons.'"

Set in a natural environment, An L.A. Cartoon Land would feature characters ranging from Popeye, Woody Woodpecker, and Mr. Magoo to the Jay Ward catalog of characters like Dudley Do-Right, Rocky, and Bullwinkle. There were plenty of ways to get wet on Popeye's Adventure, a shoot-the-chute boat ride with animatronics, special effects, and a dark ride section; Dudley Do-Right's Sawmill, a flume ride; and Bluto's Bilge-Rat Barges river rapids rafting ride.

Along with all of the water rides, visitors could enjoy Mr. Magoo's Bumper Cars and Casper's Haunted House dark ride. Visitors could also score points at Popeye's Dockside Arcade with interactive games found on a midway. Entertainment was available at the Rough House Café, a live musical show, and the Mighty Mouse Theater, a black-light puppet show with special effects.

The World of Dr. Seuss would cater to the young and old. The beloved characters would form the foundation of the park's Fantasyland. Jay told Sheinberg Dr. Seuss offered "the perfect collection of characters to appeal to young children and their parents, and the best I can think of to nullify Disney's character advantage in this important market segment." Dr. Seuss had multi-generational appeal since the first book was published in 1937. He felt that the Seuss characters would make a statement to the public that Universal was delivering "Disney-quality" offerings. "It is like getting the *Parents Magazine* 'Seal of Approval.'" Four of the ten all-time best-selling hardcover books were by Dr. Seuss. There were no Disney books in the top ten.

Getting the theme park rights would be a once-in-a-lifetime opportunity for Universal. Theodor Geisel, better known as Dr. Seuss, told his wife Audrey, "Never license my characters to anyone who would round the edges." She said what made the Seuss books so special was, "He never let the school system have it to be a primer. He said, 'That will kill it. They have to read it after the throes of the school day.'"

As the president of Dr. Seuss Enterprises and the Dr. Seuss Foundation, Audrey Geisel resisted commercialization, and for many years she refused any merchandising deals. At one point, even Steven Spielberg approached her, and she turned him down.

She only relented in 1991, when someone in the MCA publishing division arranged a meeting through her literary agent and her attorney, during which Ron Bension, Phil Hettema, and a couple of other creative types were successful in convincing her to consider signing over the theme park rights.

At this meeting, Mrs. Geisel "fell in love" with Bension. As the presentation was going on, she could not believe what she saw and continuously asked, "Can you really do that?" She was "sold" by Bension and Hettema. After that, Tony Sauber took over and made the deal, got the contract signed, and was the continuing interface with her, her agent, and her attorney on both legal/business and creative matters.

Interestingly, because of Geisel's satisfying relationship with Universal, including the fact that she was frequently consulted and approved all the details of Seuss Landing at Islands of Adventure, Sauber became the go-between to set up meetings that led to Universal doing the live-action *Grinch* and the *Cat in the Hat* movies.

The major attractions would be the Cat in the Hat dark ride, the If I Ran the Zoo water dark ride, the gas-powered Sylvester McMonkey's Driving Machines, and The Grinch's Sleigh Ride children's coaster.

Other proposed rides included the Caroseussel, a carousel with show elements; the Dumbo-like spinner Flying Pans; a small boat ride called One Fish, Two Fish; and another spinner based on The Thinks You Can Think. The children's play area would be themed after Oh, The Places You'll Go.

Entertainment offerings included live storytelling at the Storybook Theater and a 3D film based on Horton Hears a Who. The big show would have been the Dr. Seuss Circus, a live Cirque du Soleil-style show with live performers, audio-animatronics, and special effects.

Cartoon World would have revolutionized the theme park industry with an unmatchable stable of characters placed in a unique environment and supported with state of the art ride and show technology. With this package of world-class characters, Jay was confident that he could have crushed Disney's outdated technology.

So what happened? The deal came close, so very close, but the Warner Bros. executives wanted more than Jay could convince Sheinberg and Wasserman to pay.

In one corner were Jay, Ron Bension, and Skip Paul. In the other corner were Terry Semel and Bob Daly from Time Warner. They held the rights to DC Comics and Looney Tunes. MCA's first offer was a 6% royalty, while Warner countered with 10%. The negotiations dragged on for months. At one point, the two parties came within two points, with Warner down to 8% and MCA holding steady at 6%. Jay Stein and his team had put in so much work on developing concepts based on the Warner characters that he was pressing his bosses to agree to the 8%. He argued that the cost to MCA would be approximately $70,000 more per year than their current offer.

It seemed that every time the parties met, Semel would try to change the deal or decide he did not want to do it. Internally, this was creating frustration within the halls of MCA. They did not have approval on a second gate in Florida so they were spending lots of effort, manpower, and money on a park they possibly could not get the rights to and might not ever build. Tony Sauber was having success getting some of the tertiary rights deals done, but the park required the Warner Bros. characters in order to make it preemptive to a Disney counter attack.

Bension felt they would never get the rights, or it would be too costly. He also noticed that Jay was becoming disenchanted. It was a difficult couple of years. Bension had the utmost respect for Jay and wanted him to be happy and for things to go smoothly. However, the difficulties with Warner Bros. and the strain between Jay, Wasserman, and Sheinberg were taking a toll.

Sheinberg killed the deal and told Terry Semel, "We don't need your [expletive] characters." Although the difference seemed trivial, in Sheinberg's mind he had a number, and the final deal was too expensive. He did not want to set a precedent for the money necessary to secure a licensing deal.

For Jay, it was one of the worst business decisions MCA ever made. It came down to egos. He said that Sheinberg claiming that they did not need the Warner Bros. characters was shortsighted. Jay came too close to let this deal slip away. After all, Disney was spending large sums of money for the theme park rights from George Lucas properties including Star Wars and Indiana Jones.

Those facts did not matter. Within the culture at MCA, Sheinberg's decision made sense. MCA was always concerned most about the art of the deal; unfortunately even more so than the long-range potential of the combined entity. Making a great deal was always the key factor in any negotiation. MCA's heritage was as agents with a reputation of being demanding dealmakers. Wasserman was the very best. Sheinberg was cut from the same cloth but slightly more flexible and risk tolerant.

The two MCA leaders could not bring themselves to up the ante and were willing to walk away from something so grand, so potentially profitable, and bullet proof from the competition. Sheinberg had a figure in mind, and when it did not go his way, his ego prevented him from taking the risk. It was a once-in-a-lifetime opportunity to become the unequivocal leader in the world of theme parks. Egos forced short-term thinking and destroyed long-range planning.

Making a deal, building a park featuring Warner Bros. characters, marketing their characters, and enhancing their prestige in an entirely new venue might be distasteful to some rival Universal executives but only if they maintained a short-term view. If, however, they saw the project in a larger context, Jay knew instinctively that the Warner characters would give him the level of credibility and world-wide appeal that could ensure growth and expansion commensurate with Disney's success in the same market.

He figured that the cost differential between acquiring second-tier characters (with the required investment in marketing and promotion) and obtaining the rights to the Warner Bros. characters was minor when compared to the $1 billion cost of the second gate. It was miniscule when viewed as an incremental portion of the $3 billion total cost of the build out. Moreover, it would become infinitesimal when compared to the potential of their worldwide franchise. Bension said, "One gets what one pays for."

Second-tier, less known characters were expensive to market and promote, and required additional image building. Also, the parsing out of the rights over the years limited the potential for some of the properties.

Bension pointed to Hanna-Barbera. The deal had been good for the cartoon maker through licensing revenues but not so good for Universal. For example, Paramount's $50 million *Flintstones* movie translated into less-than-favorable merchandising rights. Paramount also prevented Universal from creating an attraction based on the movie.

Jay's frustration was also extended to the Warner Bros. executives, especially Semel and Daly. They failed to compromise, take a little less, and give their characters a home that they could be proud of, plus a never-ending stream of royalty payments that would have pleased even their most critical stockholders. Warner Bros. management said they were firm and knew what their characters were worth and declined to hold any more meetings. They were concerned that their characters would not be limited to Cartoon World but would find their way into the movie park even after Jay assured them that this would not happen. This was an egregious error, the direct result of corporate egotism.

Ultimately, Jay felt that the greatest impediment may have been Robert Pittman, an aggressive, young executive who supposedly could figure out what would appeal to young people. At the time, Warner Bros. owned the Six Flags chain of amusement parks. Pittman was put in charge in 1991. Six Flags was a poor investment, run poorly. For the most part, Six Flags would put character names on rides without any serious theming and have costumed characters walk around.

MCA recognized this existing relationship and was willing to allow them to continue the use of characters at the existing Six Flag parks to the extent they were then being used but did add limitations on the expansion of those uses. An ambitious Pittman convinced his bosses that Warner Bros. could do so much more with the characters and suggested that they not make a deal so that he could use them in building a theme park empire. Unfortunately, he did nothing and left the company. Warner Bros. sold Six Flags in 1995. Years later, Jay said that it becomes more evident, even today with new management, that Warner's has no clue how to exploit their characters in movies or in the theme parks. He added it is shameful that they are unable to leverage their world-class characters and their current management is no more talented than the people he was dealing with many years before.

Jay also felt that Steven Spielberg might have also played a factor during the negotiations. The director was supportive of Jay, but he had relationships with both MCA and Warner Bros. Cartoon World featured creative properties that were not his, so his input was limited. Also, the deal with Warner Bros. might have complicated his creative consultant royalty entitlements with MCA. If Spielberg raised even the slightest concern, Sheinberg would have taken any measure to protect their existing relationship.

Around November 1992, Spielberg became interested in bringing *Jurassic Park* to the theme parks. Jay could not agree more. He was looking for a perfect property to build a flume ride at USF. They did not have one, and with the Florida weather, a good super soaker made sense.

For Wasserman and Sheinberg, there was a standing rule: be nice to Steven and let him do whatever he wants. He was like the Hope Diamond and was shielded from everybody. They did not have much choice. Spielberg's production firm Amblin grossed $548.7 million, or 60% of Universal's movie revenues in 1993. Even the shouting matches that routinely took place during meetings were quelled while the director was in the room.

Jay wanted to put the ride in the movie-based parks. "Devoting a whole land to *Jurassic Park* is too much of the same thing," Jay told his boss. "If using *Jurassic Park* as the primary anchor element for the second gate is questionable now, it is less likely to make sense in 1998 when we open, and certainly not in 2008, ten years after we open." Sheinberg had other ideas.

He pointed to other popular franchises like *E.T.*, *Batman*, and *Back to the Future*, and noted they are ideal for one or two rides but not "thematic diversification" to carry 20% of an entire theme park. Jay said, "Constructing an entire land around *Jurassic Park* is neither technically nor economically feasible and would have limited entertainment value. Dinosaurs can be used two primary ways: to put the visitor in jeopardy or view them safely but as close as possible like on a safari."

Then Jay wrote to Spielberg, "I assume that the principal reason for this change of direction is your belief that *Jurassic Park* should play a major role in the second gate. Also, I understand that you believe that *Jurassic Park* when combined with a collection of second-tier properties (Hanna-Barbera, Marvel, Popeye and others), will eliminate the need for the Warner properties."

Jay argued, "While I have no doubt as to the success of the film, nor its longevity in other venues (like *E.T.*), I would first like to explain why I believe *Jurassic Park* is not appropriate as the principal theme for a second gate nor as a land within that attraction. Second, I firmly believe the greatest potential for success in Orlando and other markets would include a deal with Warner Bros., especially if we are to continue to grow and mature as a dominant player in the family entertainment theme-park business. Third, while second-tier families of characters could add significantly to the value of Cartoon World, these characters are less well known and would require substantial financial investment in marketing and promotion to increase the public's level of awareness."

The argument was simple: it was not good business for them to weaken their USF franchise by using movie properties in their cartoon theme park when the goal was to create a second gate attraction which served to complement USF rather than compete with it. It was important to protect Universal's existing movie theme-park franchise and use its second-gate attraction to compete with another Disney park.

In a memorandum to Spielberg, Jay said, "Hopefully, you'll agree that Sid must be disabused of the notion that *Jurassic Park* should become a separate land in the second gate." Jay said, "It is the quintessential embodiment of your "Ride the Movies" concept, rather than as a land in an adjacent park, where it might actually cannibalize USF."

*Jay, just prior to USF opening, posing with Jaws, 1990.*

*Jay and Steven Spielberg taking a publicity photo on the ET ride, 1990.*

*Barry Upson (back to the camera), Gary Goddard, Steven Spielberg, and Sid Sheinberg about to do the walkthrough of the Jurassic Park ride model.*

*Jay with partners at the pre-opening publicity event in New York City, with the Universal Studios Florida model in the background. The strained looks betray the strained relationships.*

*Jay, on a windy day, waiting for the stunt show facade to revolve and transform into the Universal Amphitheatre stage. (Note the sound wall: it failed, and the amphitheatre had to be enclosed.)*

*Sir Richard Attenborough, Gary Goddard, and Steven Spielberg at the main entrance to the set of Jurassic Park during the pre-show/queue video shoot.*

*Steve Lew congratulating Jay on opening day at Universal Studios Florida. Behind Lew is Rank Chairman Sir Patrick Meaney.*

*Jay, Steven Spielberg, and Lew Wasserman heading to their places for the opening day ceremony at Universal Studios Florida.*

*Jay, being congratulated by Lew and Edie Wasserman at opening night party.*

*Jay, in his office, photographed for the MCA annual report.*

*Jay, with the microphone and standing to the left of Steven Spielberg, for the dedication ceremonies at Universal Studios Florida.*

*Jay awaiting his call to the podium on opening day at Universal Studios Florida.*

*Jay being presented with an award on behalf of Universal Studios Hollywood in 1992 by Jean Firstenberg, director of the American Film Institute.*

*Jay and director John Landis on Universal Studio Florida's N.Y. Street themed as 1931 Chicago for the Disney movie Oscar. The N.Y. street at Disney-MGM Studios could not be used because it looked fake.*

Bob Ward, Jay Stein, Gary Goddard, and Harrison "Buzz" Price at IAAPA in 1999, the year that Jay was inducted into the IAAPA Hall of Fame.

Jay's return visit to Univeral Parks and Resorts after 25 years to celebrate his granddaughter's birthday. Current UPR chairman and CEO Tom Williams is seated to Jay's left. Jay requested that anyone still working who remembered him attend this luncheon. It was a grand, tearful reunion.

*Chapter 7*
# Universal Studios Hollywood

## 25 Years Too Early

Disney was not Jay's only competition. Throughout his career, one of his biggest obstacles had been Albert Dorskind and his successors in the battle for the highest and best use of Universal City's limited land.

In the world of real estate, some say that the secret to success is "location, location, location." Within southern California, Universal City was perfectly located. It was just over the hill from the Los Angeles basin and at the edge of the San Fernando Valley. It was immediately adjacent to one of the busiest freeways in Los Angeles. A developer could not ask for more.

Of course, the primary business at Universal City was still making entertainment. The front lot soundstages and the back lot were integral to that industry. The Studio Tour created a profitable secondary use. It is hard to imagine that anybody, other than Jay, ever expected that the tour business would become the economic equivalent of a blockbuster motion picture each and every year at a fraction of the cost and risk.

Albert Dorskind wanted to build more office buildings and a shopping center on the hilltop. He greatly admired what was happening at Century City, a large mixed-use development on the former 20th Century Fox back lot. Jay argued that a shopping center would take up a lot of land, and their visitors generate tiny incremental profit. Why trade profit dollars for rental income? A mall might draw luncheon business from the park, but that was all.

It was not as if the tour was getting a free ride from Dorskind's MCA development. In 1988, the tour began to pay an annual fee of $1.5 million for the lower-lot facilities that they used. Larry Spungin, who assisted and later succeeded Albert Dorskind, proposed to raise the price to $5 million annually. Bension protested and wrote, "If we were in a 'stand-alone' position and could act solely in our best interests, we would not tram visitors to the lower lot at all, but would expand on the top of the hill with a few soundstages and a 'walking tour' of the 'back lot' *ala* Florida. A set-up like Florida would clearly work, would be much more economical to operate, and would presumably not trigger any studio rent."

Another lost opportunity in Jay's mind was the hotels. He could not understand why Dorskind treated the hotels as arms-length rental operations that totally ignored the potential synergies. Disney recognized the benefit of integrated hotels. He told Dorskind, "There is probably no other place in the world that can offer an attractive, safe property of this size under single ownership, adjacent to a major freeway, in the heart of a major city." It was all about location.

Jay and Bension argued for two theme parks and some commercial elements blended in. They pointed to Disney's commitment to expand in Anaheim. They described a future where the movie studio's presence could become more compact, taking advantage of the trend of productions shooting on location or on a soundstage. Bension said, "We have a great story to tell—a way of revitalizing the tourist/convention business in Los Angeles, of promoting Hollywood, and a very attractive, non-polluting, high-tax and job-generating project." The weak economy at the time provided a perfect opportunity to take advantage of the regulatory hurdles. The only thing that could prevent the Studio Tour from growing was land. With Dorskind holding a different vision for Universal City and the keys, Jay and Bension needed to come up with a cunning plan. They did.

## Repositioning USH

Since its inception in 1964, the root of the Universal Studios Tour was, in essence, a glitzy "industrial tour." They even called themselves "The Tour." The back lot tram was the primary element; guests boarded as they walked through the turnstile, and at about two hours (with some breaks off the tram), it was the central feature of the guest's day.

The biggest constraint to growth at Universal Studios Hollywood was its being landlocked by steep topography, the Universal Amphitheatre, and CityWalk. There was not enough parking, and the trams limited the park's capacity. Management had to squeeze operation efficiency out of the system. Moreover, Jay and Bension were trying to change Universal's image locally from an every-couple-of-years "studio tour" visit to an annual-visit theme park like Disneyland.

Over the years, the tram ride was de-emphasized. As visitation to southern California leveled off, the park became more dependent upon locals. A successful locals business meant repeat visits. To gain more repeat visits, Jay had to offer something new that was exciting enough to compete with Disney and Magic Mountain (hence, the increased emphasis on "thrill"). He also had to de-emphasize the tram ride by making it shorter, by repositioning it as an option selected from among an extensive menu of choices, and by developing new attractions independent from the tram ride.

With Jay busy in Florida and Steve Lew spending more and more time there, Ron Bension became responsible for Universal Studios Hollywood. Although Bension was known as Mr. Operations, he enjoyed the creative process. Bension had gained valuable insights being on the execution side of a project. He was aware of what worked creatively and mechanically. He also witnessed the brilliant marketing campaigns that Jay spearheaded and learned a lot.

Bension was a good soldier but not afraid to speak his mind when he disagreed. Jay treated Bension and the Florida management the way Wasserman managed all of his division presidents; they were generals who were required to defend their territory to the death. That is how Bension approached his new position. That was the MCA way. With the Florida park under development, Jay started to treat Bension differently. Even Barry Upson noticed and mentioned it to Bension. Whatever it was, it gave Bension more confidence and ability to contribute.

The success of the theme park was finally influencing Wasserman's decisions related to real-estate development at Universal City. Larry Spungin and the Development Division did not welcome these changes. For decades, Dorskind had Wasserman's ear. They would do anything to limit or inhibit the tour's expansion and develop the real estate in Dorskind's "vision." Those in the Recreation Division saw them as the bad guys, not truthful, bullies when they could be, and disliked by Jay, Bension, and the rest of the team. The wars over parking, land use, power, and water consumption, rights of way, zoning—you name it—became legend between the two divisions.

Jay and Bension could sense the end was near for the Development Division. Over the next few years, they would prove themselves right. Sheinberg was not a fan and the decisions that Dorskind and his successors had made proved them to be poor long-term stewards of the property. They were unimaginative businessmen, duplicitous in their actions and words.

Bension was privy to some of the planning for Florida but surprisingly very little. In hindsight, that turned out to be a good thing. His relative independence forced his growth as a leader. With Jay's support but without his presence, Bension had to deal directly with Wasserman and Sheinberg and fight about land use with those running the studio, the amphitheatre, and MCA Development. All of these people represented Wasserman's pet projects.

## The Strike of 1988

Ron Bension and Dan Slusser frequently would spend time together and share war stories. With one in charge of the tour and the other in charge of the studio, it made sense. Out of these talks came a mutual respect and confidence. In 1988, this friendship would become critical when Bension decided to take on the Teamsters if he could not get them to receive straight-time pay for weekends. Bension felt it ridiculous that they got double time, but for years during negotiations, MCA always backed down.

To get his way, Bension had to hold tough and to prepare for a strike by the Teamsters. Along with Slusser's help and advice, Bension got all the managers together and created a plan to train as many tram drivers as possible. Bension put Felix Mussende in charge of all the details for the training and operations. Slusser praised the plan and felt that the drivers would ultimately cave.

Then, during the process, they started to realize that the special-effects technicians, maintenance, electrical, and other union members might also walk if the Teamsters decided to strike. Since these employees were frequently the only people who know how the attractions worked, Bension called on Lloyd Hamm and Russ Randall to put together a plan using outside vendors to keep the park running. During the summer of 1988, training began. Complicating matters was Wasserman's loyalty to the unions. He felt the actions of his company went against everything he stood for.

August 1, 1988, the start of the busiest week of the year, is when the Teamsters went on strike. The other unions honored the strike and did not cross the picket line. Management was ready. The attractions were up and running, and the first filled tram left, driven by Richard Annis, an operations supervisor. Things were going well until Mussende got a call that Annis' tram had jackknifed at the flood scene. Bension began to have doubts about their readiness. Thankfully, they got the tram straightened out, no one was hurt, and for the next week, the tour had never run smoother. As a testament to the USH management, to this day they are the only Hollywood studio to continue operations during a Teamster strike.

One of Jay's proudest moments was the 25th-anniversary celebration of the Studio Tour. *The Los Angeles Times* sent a supplement documenting the event to 1.1 million readers. In a memo to his staff on June 9, 1989, Jay reminded them that the tour had become the third largest visitor attraction in the United States. There were now over 2,000 employees serving up to 31,000 visitors per day. By 1989, more than 60 million guests had taken the tour.

He confessed to his team that when he started, he was a skeptic. He did not believe that the tour and production could co-exist. Nevertheless, they did, and the rest was history. Along the way, Universal adopted the tagline "We Say Hollywood to the World", and now they invite the public to "Ride the Movies."

To celebrate the changes, Jay proposed a name change from the Universal Studios Tour to Universal Studios Hollywood. Research showed that labeling the attraction as a "tour" was perceived as a negative to the local market. From a marketing point of view, adding the Hollywood tag to the name was a much better "sell" internationally, domestically, and locally. It would also help to distinguish the attraction from its Florida counterpart. And it induced Disney to capitalize on using the word Hollywood in a new motion picture division called Hollywood Pictures.

Bension's personality and business temperament were like his boss. Bension learned his craft just like Jay, by *doing*. He started work at MCA as a teenager, cleaning up the outdoor dining areas, and rose very rapidly through the supervisory ranks. He had little in the way of formal education, and having worked for only Jay, who in turn had only worked for Lew Wasserman, he was "rough"—a screamer and yeller in the MCA tradition.

At one point, Bension confided to Tony Sauber that he wanted to have a calmer rapport with co-workers than Jay had, and asked the attorney to tell him whenever he started acting "too much like Jay." Sauber had a chance to test this idea early on when he was in Bension's office during a speaker phone conversation with a department head who was getting screamed at. When Bension looked at Sauber, he stopped yelling, apologized, and agreed his advisor was right and thanked him.

Bension tried to experience everything firsthand, from planning, operations, marketing, and finance to how one creates a restaurant, a ride, or a store. Bension had good sense, was a good judge of people, and like Jay, he had what a bullshit detector. He could tell when people were trying to put something over on him, or were less sure of themselves than they tried to appear, even if it was an outside consultant giving him an opinion in the consultant's field of expertise. Bension, as well as Jay, had the insight to ask probing questions to pick holes in an expert's theories.

Bension's older brother Marc also worked his way up through the ranks of the tour, and by the 1980s was running the Universal Amphitheatre. There were natural areas of overlap and conflict between the tour and and the amphitheatre since the Music Group of MCA was now managing the amphitheatre.

Frustrated, Bension asked Sauber to draft a memo to Sheinberg, with a copy to Marc Bension, as to why the tour's interests should take priority in a particular area of conflict. Naturally, it was a persuasive memo, and Marc Bension immediately knew Sauber wrote it and called him to his office and asked if he would write his rebuttal, giving him the arguments to make. Therefore, anonymously, Sauber wrote two memos to Sheinberg, arguing both sides of an issue. Even today, Sauber does not think Ron ever realized he was the one to write the rebuttal to his memo.

A third Bension brother, Morris, also worked at the tour as a driver. He never wanted to do anything more. He was adamantly pro-labor and would try to enforce the Teamsters agreement to keep Ron from making changes in working conditions and, at times, filed grievances against Ron's actions.

John Pugh was hired to help find a solution for the design and project development side. Pugh had done work for Knott's Berry Farm. Bension began to develop a broad plan over the course of a week. If they could get people down to the soundstage area without using the trams, he could eliminate all but forty-five minutes of the tram tour. As a result, this would significantly increase capacity as well as reduce costs. Estimated savings would be $1 million a year. Another benefit of the move would be to free up space on the hilltop (where the tram boarding area had been) for attraction space. With shortened wait times, park sales would increase.

He and John Pugh put into motion the design and construction of the one-quarter mile Starway escalator system. Built at a cost of $18 million, the Starway opened on March 15, 1991, and connected the Entertainment Center to the new Studio Center on the lower lot. The new facility was so named because it was the actual center of the front lot.

Next came parking. The solution seemed obvious. Multi-story parking garages. Bension spotted a two-acre site adjacent to Fung Lums, a restaurant on a level below the Tour Center, and wondered if he could build that up to the level of the upper park area near the stunt show. The site was a rugged hillside that was used as a backdrop for the 1950s television show *Laramie*.

At the bottom of Laramie Canyon was an acre and a half of land. By building an inverted pyramid, they created 4.5-acres of new land on the top for the Entertainment Center and 20 acres of new parking that could hold 2,850 cars. The parking structure sat conveniently in the middle of the property, thereby avoiding conflicts with the neighbors. With the parking situation resolved, now the tour was ready to handle up to 5.5 million visitors per year. If Dorskind did not want to reallocate land for the tour, then Jay would just build his own.

What Bension was able to accomplish, despite considerable internal opposition, was remarkable. Building that escalator, getting the parking structures approved, expanding the Tour Center footprint, increasing the overall attendance capacity, and giving guests more reasons to spend longer periods of time in the park to enjoy their experience was a monumental achievement. The changes contributed hundreds of millions of dollars to the bottom line.

A month after Bension started working on the expansion plan he was ready to pitch the ideas to Jay. His ambitious plan would cost $300 million over five years and would transform Universal Studios Tour, the industrial tour, into Universal Studios Hollywood, a destination theme park. To accomplish this task, Bension had to rely on what he called the "B" team and $300 million. His division ran almost separately from the Florida effort. Most of Jay's top folks were on site in Florida.

By the fall of 1989, Bension and Jay were ready to reveal their expansion plans to Sheinberg. Bension was feeling confident after the blockbuster year

Universal Studios Hollywood just had. The Earthquake attraction boosted attendance 29.8% since it opened on March 18. USH would hit 5 million by the end of the year. Better still, profits were projected to increase by 73% over 1988. This while the rest of the industry was flat. USH has become the largest non-Disney themed attraction in the world.

Even with this good news, Bension cautioned his bosses. Sometimes, like in 1982, 1983, 1984, whatever you do is not enough. When tourists are not coming to southern California, they are not coming to USH. You do your best to attract locals, but the tour format was not conducive to frequent visits. He also learned that sometimes well-known intellectual properties were too limited in their demographic appeals, such as *Conan* and *Star Trek*.

Bension felt that USH could be as big a draw as Disneyland. The park needed more repeat business. Significant changes to the Studio Tour would be required. He told his bosses, "We feel that people will come back in greater frequency once they realize that the 2½-hour tram ride and long waits in the park are no longer required, once we have achieved a critical mass of entertainment elements so that visitors leave feeling they have spent a very full day and not seen everything, and once we have the appeal of new premiere attractions (E.T. and Back to the Future) to provide the impetus for a return visit."

In the meantime, Bension had to tread water until the big guns came online. That is why the park was opening an American Tail live musical show and an enlargement of the Western stunt show for 1990. Then attractions imported from Florida would come.

## Back to the Future

For 1991, it would be the year of Back to the Future. Jay's team had been developing the ride fashioned after the movie. They had been working with Greg MacGillivary, a large format (IMAX) filmmaker. Bension recalled that the original idea for Back to the Future was a "relatively simple travelogue concept and not a story-based film."

Jay called Dan Slusser to take a look at some of the footage. After a couple of hours in the screening room, Slusser's only thought was, "Where is the story?" Jay asked him if he could put a production team together and take over the project. Jay also said that Steven Spielberg was a creative consultant on the project and wanted input on who they hired to do the special effects. Slusser spoke with Spielberg, and he said he liked the people at Industrial Light and Magic (ILM), a company owned by George Lucas. Slusser said he would contact them, and they agreed to join.

Then Slusser asked Spielberg if he would be comfortable if he had Doug Trumbull make a presentation. Trumbull was the award-winning special-effects wizard behind such films as *2001: A Space Odyssey* (1968) and *Blade Runner* (1982), and directed *Brain Storm* (1983) and *Silent Running* (1971). He had worked on the very first motion simulator called Tour of the Universe at the CN Tower in Toronto. The Canadian attraction opened in 1985. Spielberg agreed. When Slusser contacted Trumbull, he gave him an outline of the project and told him that ILM was in the picture so he would have to hit the presentation out of the park. He did, and he got the job.

Slusser had put together a great team and produced what was, if not the very best, was *one* of the best theme park rides of all time. At an event one evening, Slusser boasted to director James Cameron that the Back to the Future attraction was the most expensive film in the history of the industry, not *Titanic*. Based on the $16 million cost to produce the four-and-a-half minute movie, Slusser was right.

Bension was ready to place Back to the Future on top of the new parking structure. The ride's capacity would be reduced from 1,920 guests per hour to 1,600 guests per hour by eliminating an entire lower level and six cars and saving $9.75 million.

E.T. would open six months later. Already designed, it would be a simple matter to reproduce the attraction in Los Angeles. USH needed more child-friendly attractions, and E.T. would be the perfect addition. Moreover, AT&T wanted to sponsor the attraction to the tune of $9 million. Down the road was the Terminator show, which was already under development.

Director James Cameron would play a significant role in bringing Terminator 2:3D to life. He liked what he saw during Gary Goddard's original storyboard presentation and began to make suggestions for the actor that portrayed the Terminator character made famous by Arnold Schwarzenegger. Ron Bension said, "We can't expect these actors who get paid $15 an hour to be Arnold!" Cameron replied, "That's funny. For a long time, we wondered if we could have Arnold be an actor."

Important to Jay, investment in USH meant funds would not be diverted to one of Albert Dorskind's shopping mall projects. He always believed it was dumb to have a free shopping mall when he could force people to buy inside the paid gate. Universal would only get approximately 6% of sales in the form of rent from retail activities outside the park, but such transactions would use up many tourist dollars. If those dollars were spent *in* the park on items with greater mark-up, much more money would flow to Universal's bottom line.

Sheinberg listened intently. A bit more cautious, he suggested they choose between Back to the Future or E.T. for USH to open in 1991. Bension argued for Back to the Future then E.T. in 1992 or 1993. It was agreed that the attraction could take over space where the prop warehouse was located. The future and long-subdued potential of USH was underway.

Another goal for the Hollywood expansion was to provide more offerings for children. One of the big hits at USF was the Funtastic World of Hanna-Barbera. In guest surveys, the ride ranked higher than E.T. in guest satisfaction. Jay told the press, "I can personally attest to the difficulty of achieving the 'breakthrough' process of combining 3D-like computer generated backgrounds with the two-dimensional characters." Jay said to Sid Sheinberg, "We have a sure winner with no negatives."

Expectations were high for a West Coast version since there was nothing like it at the park. Rumors in the press were rampant that the ride was going to debut soon. Jay knew it would be a big hit and wanted to increase the ride capacity from 960 guests per hour to over 1,400 guests per hour. To do this, he wanted to use the motion bases that were developed for Back to the Future. Faster moving lines meant happier guests.

Another reason he wanted to upgrade the ride for Hollywood was economics. Jay wrote to Sheinberg, "If we don't go ahead, having done the USF attraction, we are really approaching the unenviable position Disney is in with the Muppets—they have a huge investment they cannot fully capitalize on because their rights are limited to one coast (their Florida rights are also short term), and other parks can make a deal for the characters."

Timing was also critical. Jay and Bension wanted to open the attraction toward the end of 1992. As part of the original agreement, Hanna-Barbera needed to approve the opening date of a West Coast version. They refused.

At the time, the Great American Communications Company owned Hanna-Barbera. Carl H. Linder, who owned the company, was considering selling the animation studio and he did not want to change the deal because they were unbundling obligations. Jay's solution? Buy Hanna-Barbera.

Negotiations began in the summer of 1991. Linder was asking between $350–$400 million, but MCA was offering far less. Super agent Michael Ovitz was representing Hanna-Barbera. Rumors in the press suggested things were looking good. One hang-up was Hanna Barbera's distribution agreement with Worldvision Enterprises Inc. for more than 5,000 half-hour episodes of cartoons.

MCA was not the only suitor. The Walt Disney Company looked. So did as many as a dozen others, including Hallmark Cards and L'Oreal. Ultimately, the negotiations failed, and Turner Broadcasting Systems bought Hanna-Barbera for $320 million. The Jetsons, Yogi Bear, and the Flintstones would stay on the East Coast. Turner, in turn, was later bought by Warner Bros.

# CityWalk

Albert Dorskind was obsessed by Tivoli Gardens, and he tried for decades to bring something like that to Universal City. By January 1991, it looked like he was finally going to get the entertainment center and shopping mall he had wanted. The planning for CityWalk was finally coming together and opened in May 1993. Dorskind claimed the shopping mall project was driven by the need to create a dynamic path for people walking between the current studio tour, the Cineplex Odeon multiplex, and the Universal Amphitheatre.

Frequently, Dorskind's division would be at odds with Jay's Recreation Division on how best to use the land. Dorskind's lieutenant and hatchet man was Larry Spungin. Jay described Spungin as a sweaty-palmed lawyer who would never look you in the eye and a devious bureaucrat without a creative bone in his body whose specialty was drafting real estate leases, and he could never grasp the big picture. He protected Dorskind and Dorskind usually won because of his unusual relationship with Wasserman.

Over the years, development at Universal City had been piecemeal, and many master plans had come and gone. To make a statement, Dorskind and Spungin hired star architect John Jerde to come up with a blueprint for the hilltop. Jerde wanted to create what he called "a venue for human intercourse." As a result, the mall became a two-block-long "street" framed with juxtaposed façades, historic neon signs, towers, and billboards.

Jay's first impression was diplomatic. In a memo to Spungin, he said, "I feel that CityWalk is the right idea for our property and is long overdue. It is a concept I have advocated and endorsed for over 25 years, going back to the Counter Culture Complex."

He was not a fan of the entertainment mall project, but he recognized this is what his bosses wanted. He thought it was silly to trade 35% profits on food and merchandise for rental income of 6%.

Being Jay, he offered some advice. His concern was that the entertainment elements were not strong enough. The only real draws would be the MTV Complex with a record store and restaurant, the UCLA Extension Program, and restaurants like Gladstone's with their popular following. There was a need for additional elements of "excitement" to draw locals. After a review of the feasibility studies, he noticed that they overestimated the support of USH patrons. Jay believed once Back to the Future and E.T. opened, the typical guest would spend six hours within the park leaving very little time or money to wander around a shopping mall. He warned Spungin, "A 'unique' shopping center alone won't succeed—we need to rely on the strength of our entertainment package to establish our 'presence' and 'soul.'"

# Chapter 8
# Cartoon World

## Matsushita

In late 1989, Jay was summoned to Lew Wasserman's office. When he arrived, he saw all the other MCA divisional presidents waiting to go in. The topic of the meeting was a mystery to all of the participants. Sheinberg opened the door and asked everyone to come in and take a seat.

Wasserman spoke first. Matsushita Industrial Electric Co. was acquiring MCA. After a long series of negotiations, a purchase price of $6.59 billion was agreed upon, and the basic premise was that Wasserman and Sheinberg would continue to run the company and Matsushita would provide the capital for expansion and growth. It was viewed as a marriage of a hardware and a software company.

Wasserman told his men that Matsushita was the 12$^{th}$ largest company in the world, they had very deep pockets, and MCA needed their financial wherewithal to compete. Wasserman had high hopes. He insisted that the top management team would remain in place for several years to implement their grand plans. The only change was the current leadership would now report to Osaka. Wasserman expected the Japanese to be hands-off owners. Moreover, the Japanese would be paying $72 per share at a time when MCA was trading at $26 per share.

When he finished, Wasserman asked if there were any questions. Jay was stunned—and angry. He thought he was hallucinating and wanted to jump up and say, "This is a death trap! Don't do it!" When it was Jay's turn to speak, he said that he had been trying for almost twenty years negotiating with potential partners with land for a park in Japan. Jay recalled the times when he visited Japan seeking to work out a deal. Everybody would be smoking in the conference room. They would work out a deal and then the next day, as if nothing had been agreed upon, it would start over. Jay had learned that Japanese companies would never give you a yes or no. He argued that their business culture and operating methods would be anathema to the way that MCA did business. Jay felt that having Matsushita as a parent was going to be a disaster. Jay wanted to resign on the spot.

Wasserman listened to his team. Then he calmly responded. Nobody was going anywhere. Everyone would have to agree to finish out their employment contract. Anybody leaving the company would forego the balance of their vesting. They would get nothing if they left. For all of the men in the room, this meant seven-figure bonus payments. For Jay, it was a hard pill to swallow, but he agreed to finish out his contract as a consultant. He would never go to Osaka. Matsushita would take control of MCA in 1991.

How did Matsushita find out that MCA was for sale? Most scholars credit super agent and former Universal Studio tour guide Michael Ovitz for being the catalyst for the deal. However, it was a group led by Skip Paul and Frank Stanek who deserve the credit.

By the late 1980s, Lew Wasserman began considering the unthinkable, selling MCA. Wasserman recognized that the business was changing, and MCA needed more financial resources to compete. He had also survived a recent health scare. If the right suitor came along, someone who would give him the cash to do what he wanted, without interfering in the way he ran the business, maybe MCA could be for sale. Very few companies would qualify under Wasserman's list of expectations.

At the same time, a group was put together to shop for international locations for the Recreation Division. Jay had attempted to strike a deal in Japan but lacked the patience to work within the Japanese business culture. Skip Paul, Frank Stanek, and Biff Gale were assigned the task.

In a meeting in with executives from Matsushita, Paul began his pitch on the benefits of building a theme park in Osaka, Japan. He suggested that Osaka would be a perfect location. Matsushita was a major employer in the city; it would be an opportunity to replace the surrounding tank farms, ship-building yards, and warehouses with hotels and shopping districts.

Then something strange began to happen. All the Matsushita executives could talk about was everything but the theme park. The Matsushita executives asked questions about MCA's television and film production, their movie library, the record labels, as well as the theme parks.

Sony, their primary competitor, had recently bought Columbia Pictures. Whatever Sony did Matsushita was soon to follow. Sony sold Betamax videotape machines while Panasonic (a Matsushita brand) sold VHS tape machines. Japan had a strong currency; the United States provided a low tax rate, and Matsushita was a huge company with seemingly endless resources. It became quickly evident to Paul that Matsushita wanted to buy MCA.

When Paul returned to the United States, Wasserman and Sheinberg asked how the presentation went. What started out as a pitch for a deal at the corporate level to partner on a theme park soon evolved into the sale of the legendary entertainment company to Matsushita.

Six months later, Matsushita executives called Michael Ovitz for his help, since he facilitated the Columbia sale to Sony. What Ovitz did not know was that Paul and Stanek had already done the hard part. Despite that, Ovitz would once again take credit for his brilliant business acumen.

# Unquestioned Integrity

Shortly after learning that Matsushita was taking over, Jay asked Sheinberg if he could become a consultant and help whenever he was needed. Jay's only constraint was that he never wanted to go to Osaka, and he never did. He recommended Ron Bension to replace him as Recreation Group chairman and he immediately began to implement his priorities and strategies using the management skills he had acquired over his long tenure within the division.

For Jay, Bension was his first and only choice to succeed him. He was Jay's protégé. Jay appreciated the fact that, like himself, Bension learned the business from the ground up and worked his way to the top. Jay felt that Bension was smart, tenacious, personable, and a risk taker. He was also a solid businessman, a good soldier, honest, courageous, and had unquestioned integrity. On top of all that, Bension was a very creative guy.

Filling Jay's shoes was going to be a tough job. Fortunately, Bension's relationships with Wasserman and Sheinberg were strong. While Jay was focused on Orlando, Bension often had to go directly to Wasserman and Sheinberg. Then he would call Jay immediately afterward to complete the communication loop. Bension said each had their personality and management style, and each treated him fairly and with respect. He recalled that Wasserman was feared by many and respected by all. It was common for Wasserman to call whomever he wanted whenever he wanted. Bension quickly learned that the calls would be frequent, and Wasserman had usually known the answers to the questions he would ask. You had to be prepared or be slaughtered.

Bension was lucky to have the confidence of senior management. COO John Leisner and Dan Slusser advised him on how to deal with some of the politics. They taught him to stand up for what was right or at least what he thought was right. Due to this experience, Bension decided he would never go behind people's backs. A frontal assault would be his method of choice.

His hands-on experiences and up-through-the-ranks ascendency served him well with his relationship with the front line employees throughout his career. He never lost his appreciation for the hard work that goes into making for an hourly wage. During his tenure at Universal, the trust with hardcore union employees lasted until his final days. He always knew he could reach out to them and get answers or favors done.

Bension turned to his management staff and had every department head teach him their responsibilities. It was an incredible experience, and the overview gave him a broader and more detailed view of the business and the ability to know as much, or in some cases, more than the people in those departments did.

As a consultant, Jay gained a unique perspective on the organization he built. Trying to find opportunities to keep himself busy without getting in Bension's way, he looked at the advertising campaigns produced by Disney and Universal. He concluded that Universal needed to step up on out-of-market advertising. The recommendation represented a significant change for Universal to do heavy advertising (especially television) in markets far from Los Angeles and Orlando—in the markets where the tourists come from. It was very expensive since only a small number of people seeing the commercials would be coming to Los Angeles or Orlando.

However, Universal could no longer ride on Disney's coattails but had to take the offensive and start their own out-of-the-market campaign. If not, Universal would continue to lose market share. Jay said, "The public has been brainwashed into thinking Disney is better—and once that perception becomes accepted, we will be in serious trouble." He recommended a $10 million investment and projected that it would increase attendance by as much as 300,000 people, which would represent a 5% growth over the previous year. Jay said, "Let's go mouse hunting again."

## A Change of Pace

In fall of 1990, after USF had opened, Jay moved back to Los Angeles. He gave up his office in the executive tower and moved into a suite of rooms in the producer's building. Tony Sauber relocated with him.

Jay's heart was no longer in his work due to the sale to Matshuista. He knew he was on a sinking ship and had lost the fire-in-the-belly attitude that got him this far in his career. So he started by working only a few days a week. Many of those were short days now that he was renting a beautiful house on the water just south of Santa Barbara from actor Kevin Costner, who was his neighbor and became his fishing buddy. Still, when the creative muses hit, he would call Sauber and describe concepts for new attractions.

One of those attractions was a concept for USH based on the successful movie *Backdraft*, directed by Ron Howard. Bension sent Sauber to New York with Hettema and another creative person to present the concept to Ron Howard and secure his approval. Sauber said, "Howard was like a kid—genuinely excited that we could create these searing fires and then put them out in an instant." He fully approved and even was willing to appear in a short introductory film.

At about this time there was a deadly fire at a "fun house" attraction in New Jersey and corporate executives were sent to jail for their negligence. This frightened Lew Wasserman and he directly entrusted Sauber to do whatever was necessary to make sure there was no chance whatsoever of a catastrophe at the Backdraft show.

In reality, the show was safe, despite a finale of a raging inferno—the fires used were gas, with instantaneous cut-off switches, plus there was nothing on the stage that could burn—the gas was just burning in the air. However, to satisfy Wasserman, Sauber hired three different types of fire experts and had them each write reports at three various stages of completion, including when everything was ready to open. Somehow, even with the usual inclination of consultants to "hedge" their opinions, on each level, from each consultant, they got definite opinions that the show was safe.

About three months after Backdraft opened, Sauber was in Bension's office on a high floor of the executive office building, with a good view of the soundstage that housed Backdraft. Over the two-way radio comes word that "Backdraft was on fire." Sauber ran to the window and was yelling, "That's impossible, impossible, it can't catch on fire." Nevertheless, he was wrong. Flames were shooting up out of the roof of the soundstage. The media, with their helicopters, were covering it within a few minutes. It turned out the fire had nothing to do with the show. A worker was repairing the air conditioning unit on the roof, and he set some of the insulation on fire. The show was not affected, but the fire got a lot of media coverage.

The final project that Jay worked on before retiring was a park well ahead of its time. Sports World would place guests right in the middle of their favorite sport. Imagine riding a horse in the Kentucky Derby, pinch hitting against some of the best pitchers in the Major Leagues, throwing a touchdown pass in the Super Bowl, making the winning basket or free throw in the NBA finals, shooting the winning slap shot, playing goalie in the Stanley Cup finals, or executing golf shots on the world's best courses against the best pro golfers. How about kicking or defending the winning goal in the World Cup Soccer finals, playing tennis against the best pros at Wimbledon, or performing in the Olympics in snowboarding. Other ideas included competing in NASCAR, Formula 1, or Moto Cross. Jay even considered bull or bronc riding, sky diving, and mountain climbing. He outlined plans for water skiing, performing individual track and field events, or surfing the biggest waves. He even had boxing with points being scored without actual contact. All of the major sports would be represented.

Two significant hurdles faced this project. First, acquiring the rights to the various sporting leagues and star players would be tough, but doable, by giving a percentage of the gross to each sports' safety program or retired players in need. Second, the available technologies to make the experiences real were not available at the time. Virtual reality opens the door. All of Jay's notes went into a briefcase never to be seen again.

When Bension wanted Jay's input, he would try to arrange a meeting back in Universal City. Bension wanted Jay's advice, and Jay wanted to be consulted and give advice. The problem was, on weekdays it might take him a 2-hour drive each way to get to the studio, and there were too many people involved to bring the studio to Jay. Occasionally, Phil Hettema would drive out to show Jay something and pick his brain.

Because of time factors, Jay did not want to attend morning meetings, at least before 10:00 a.m. or 11:00 a.m., but Bension and the others had full-time jobs, and it was hard to schedule their creative meetings around Jay's schedule. Both felt the other was slighting them. Bension asked Sauber to try to broker a mutually satisfactory plan, but it never materialized. Jay had given his heart and soul to MCA. Blood, sweat, and gusto. It was time for him to bow out. However, Jay had one more trick up his sleeve.

## There Was Only One Boss

On January 6, 1993, MCA quietly announced that Jay Stein would be resigning as chairman and chief executive of the MCA Recreation Services Group and as vice president of MCA. His longtime protégé Ron Bension would be taking over. The stated reason for Jay's departure was "personal and charitable pursuits." He was only 55 years old and had worked at the company since 1959. Jay had dedicated his life to building MCA's Recreation Services Group since he took over in 1967.

In show business, going out on top is a rare feat. Jay was proud that he had created a template that was successful, something that had legs, and something that could be exported overseas. Jay's theme parks would become his legacy and entertain millions for years to come.

Before the public announcement, he wrote a note to Steven Spielberg. He wanted to assure the director that he would still be involved as a consultant to see the Cartoon World project through and to assist in the foreign expansion. Not long after Spielberg got the note, he called Jay and revealed that he had learned of the retirement from Sheinberg. Spielberg said, "You're too young to retire. Why now?" Jay explained that his reasons would be explained in the press release. Speilberg would have none of it. He told Jay he had *already* read the press release and wanted to know the real reasons.

Jay told the director that he had spent 33 years at MCA and he was burnt out and it was time for him to step down. He was not going too far as he had agreed to work the remaining two years of his contract as a consultant. He assured Spielberg that the Recreation Division was in good hands with Ron Bension at the helm. Jay had complete confidence in Bension's ability. Jay had left Bension a blueprint for future expansion and an outline for a second gate.

"Why don't you just take a leave of absence and see how you feel after being away for a while," Spielberg suggested. No. Jay told him there was more to it and a short break would not change his mind. Jay then disclosed his warnings to Wasserman and Sheinberg about the sale, his frustrations working with the Japanese, and his belief that their culture and operating methods would be anathema to them. The sale was going to turn out to be a disaster and Jay did not want to be on the ship when it hit the iceberg. Although Speilberg disagreed with Jay's assessment of Matsushita, he wished Jay good luck and hoped that he would change his mind.

Reactions from Jay's colleagues were immediate.

Steve Lew said, "Through the years, most [of Jay's] efforts were successful no matter whether it was a free-standing restaurant design and menu, a theme park ride or show, the layout of a theme park, the look of a building façade, and on and on. Truly remarkable. In some cases, meetings led to raised voices, threats, emotional outbursts, and hurt feelings. He knew the end game, and when the yelling, screaming, and emotion was over with, the subject of the next meeting began as if the just-concluded drama had not occurred, and we moved on. Today, my respect for and trust in him has not wavered, and we have developed a solid and mutually trusting long-term relationship and friendship. We live a few minutes from one another and get together often."

Terry Winnick said, "There was only one boss, Jay. It was tough to hand over the keys to Ron [Bension]." Peter Alexander said, "He was a very good executive. He was actually good at motivating people to work for him. We all did the best work we ever did working for Jay Stein because he was so demanding. He was so difficult to work for, but he drove us."

Gary Goddard admired Stein. He said, "There was Walt Disney but after Walt Disney, it was Jay Stein and his building of the parks into something new and different. He knew instantly what it was that would set Universal apart. Real water, real fire, real pyros, in-your-face and putting people in the middle of the action. Something Disney didn't do and really because of their audience base, couldn't do." He added, "He was in the game to win—and he (we) had to do it for a fraction of what Disney was doing it for—and yet—we had to compete. Guys like me need guys like Jay for great things to happen."

Phil Hettema was blunt, "Jay was a true P.T. Barnum. He didn't have a lot of budgets to add things to the tour, so he always designed things by making the commercial in his mind first. The additions often did not live up to the hype, but it pumped people through the gates." He added, "I really do think Jay Stein, as colorful and as challenging of a guy, was a visionary.

He wasn't just being competitive; it was that he really had a vision. The fact that this vision was so not of the traditional Disney mold is exactly what set Universal apart."

Richard Swann said that Jay was to USF what Walt Disney and his brother were to Disney. Jay was the Disney package wrapped in one skin. He was very creative, understood the current culture knowing what the public wanted, and understood equally the business side of the business.

In 1999, Jay was inducted into the International Association of Amusement Parks and Attractions (IAAPA) Hall of Fame.

## Go-No Go

Approval for a second gate landed in the lap of Sid Sheinberg. On January 25, 1993, Sheinberg, Skip Paul, and Ron Bension met to discuss the matter. They sat in Sheinberg's office for what seemed like the umpteenth time requesting funding and approval to proceed.

For the park to open on schedule in early 1998, Barry Upson needed a commitment by March 1. Upson's team had developed the concept to the 70% level. They had assumed they were building a seven-million-visitor park at a cost of $1 billion. They were prepared to switch out Dr. Seuss for Spielberg's *Tiny Toons* or Hanna-Barbera characters.

In typical Sheinberg fashion, he would not say yes, while the entire time being supportive of the concept and rationale. Bension distinctly remembered that last meeting when Sheinberg virtually went through all of the reasons they should do the project, repeating almost word for word the numerous memos he had sent regarding the project, and it seemed like the meeting was ending without a definitive decision. Bension finally asked, "Does that mean yes?" Sheinberg said it did. However, he never said, "Yes." That was just the way he worked.

The March deadline passed, and Jay immediately fired off a memo to Sheinberg. He wanted his former boss and now client to reopen the negotiations with Warner Bros. "Let me digress for just one moment and correct something you said. You said: 'no less an expert than Jay Stein said it couldn't be done' (i.e., create the second gate without Warner characters). That sentence is essentially correct but for one word. What I would say and have stated in the past was that it 'shouldn't be done.'" He argued, "The theme of Cartoon World has the strongest and the broadest appeal of any theme park ever built. It is very difficult—tantamount to impossible—for a theme park to turn characters into 'stars.' By affiliating with Warner, we are keeping them from competing with us and despoiling foreign markets."

Jay reminded Sheinberg, "Disney will stop at nothing to protect themselves. How long would it take Eisner and Wells to figure out that the only way to nullify our penetration is to build a directly competitive cartoon-oriented park on their property and to populate it with Warner's characters (with whom they might make a major alliance, as distasteful as they might find us). While USF competes with Disney-MGM, Cartoon World would aim at the Magic Kingdom and EPCOT. Just like how Disney was strengthened by MGM, Universal would be stronger with Warner. A unique theme is necessary for success. The most successful parks are those with a very clear theme." As a bonus, Universal would get the first pick of any Warner movies for the film-based theme parks.

The final lobbying effort did not work. By November 1993, the tentative name for the second gate was Universal's Islands of Adventure—Home of Jurassic Park. While Cartoon World was developed around the Warner Bros. characters, once that possibility evaporated, Jeff McNair suggested a "Legends" theme, which Bension determined had potential.

On December 15, 1993, the go-no go decision was made, and Cartoon World featuring the Warner Bros. characters was officially shelved. Despite this decision, the idea itself never died, and close to 50% of Islands of Adventures came to be based on Cartoon World characters.

## Chapter 9
# That's a Wrap

## Whispers in the Dark

Unfortunately, shortly after their purchase of MCA, Matsushita fell on some hard times financially and did not have the capital to support MCA's planned acquisitions of Virgin Records and CBS Records or build a Universal Studios theme park in Japan. These events resulted in a culture clash that led to Matsushita selling to Seagram.

In April 1995, Seagram Company Ltd. acquired 80 percent of MCA from Matsushita for $5.7 billion. The company had no direct show business experience but its ambitious chief executive, Edgar M. Bronfman Jr., longed to be a major player in the entertainment industry, as evidenced in his families' early investment in the Cineplex Odeon chain. Earlier in his career, Bronfman Jr. produced the 1981 film *The Border* with Jack Nicholson and wrote a couple of songs including "Whispers in the Dark."

To buy the entertainment giant, Bronfman Jr. sold off 156 million shares of chemical and oil giant DuPont for $8.8 billion. At the time, the income from DuPont accounted for 70% of Seagram's earnings.

For many at MCA, the acquisition seemed like the end was near to the frustrating times working for the Japanese. Sheinberg took Dan Slusser to a meeting with Bronfman Jr. right after the sale, and he was impressed. For the next few months, he became Bronfman Jr.'s biggest fan and spoke out publicly to praise his new boss at employee meetings and management retreats.

The expansion in Florida was already green lit, and Bronfman Jr. used it as one of the shining assets he was buying. Even before the deal was closed, he boasted that he had big plans for Florida and Osaka. He sent Bension and his team to travel the country doing presentations for bankers and the Seagram family.

Now that Cartoon World would not be using the Warner Bros. characters, it fell on Tony Sauber's lap to find replacements. These included an exclusive agreement for the utilization of all of the Marvel characters on the East Coast, all of the comic-strip characters controlled by King Features or Tribune Media Services, all of the Jay Ward characters, and all of the Dr. Seuss characters. Other characters or properties were "one or two offs," such as Beetlejuice and many individual comic-strip characters such as Cathy, Lil' Abner, and Momma, to which they had just the rights to minor uses and use in advertising. In the majority of cases, it was Sauber who made the initial approach to the rights holder, usually with a cold call.

While the plans for the park were still in flux, Sauber would attend all of the creative meetings so he could advise whether MCA had the rights for whatever attraction was under discussion. If they did not, they would ask the attorney if he could acquire them. One of the "lands" of IOA, the Lost Continent, featured all generic characters, and Sauber enjoyed referring to it as "Public Domain Land."

When he did make a deal, it was his responsibility to ensure the uses being contemplated were consistent with the contract and the owner's feelings about how their property should be utilized. It was his job to sell the owners on what they could do for their property, take the owners to see presentations and secure creative approvals, and keep them informed of what was happening. As IOA got closer to the opening, these tasks were becoming very time-consuming. At that point, Sauber was the only one still at Universal who had the contacts with these owners, and he felt it was a pleasant job showing them around and entertaining them.

As the months went by, new people joined MCA. First, it was Ron Meyers and then Howard Weitzman followed by Sandy Climan. Weitzman was best known to the public as the attorney who told OJ Simpson to talk to the police. Bruce Hack took over as CFO, backing himself up with Brian Mulligan. It was not clear from the beginning just who was doing what. They all had executive vice president status, and each one believed he was in charge.

There were some disturbing trends. Bronfman Sr. put Wasserman on the Seagram's Board. Wasserman purchased 10,000 shares of the Seagram Company. When he returned from the first board meeting, Dan Slusser asked him how the meeting went. He said, "Edgar Sr. spoke; we listened."

Wasserman got a new job title as chairman emeritus, and he had an office on the 15th floor and a contract for the remainder of his life. He had built a great company and wanted to be helpful. However, no one wanted his input.

Soon after the purchase, the old team from MCA noticed that things were changing and not necessarily for the better. Bronfman Jr. threw a big party for Lew Wasserman's 80th birthday on the Phantom Stage (Stage 28). Invitations were sent to all the Hollywood elite as well as the MCA senior management.

The party was held inside one of Universal's giant soundstages. When the time came for Bronfman Jr. to step up to the microphone, he took a couple of minutes to praise the entertainment legend, presented him a scale model of the MCA tower, and told the audience that the "Black Tower" would be changed to the Lew Wasserman Building.

Then he spent another fifteen minutes talking about his father. Bension was in the audience and found this insulting and disrespectful to Wasserman. Here was Bronfman Jr. taking this moment to thank his father for buying him a new toy. Bension left the party very upset.

The next day, in print, Edgar Jr. berated the building as "so non-Hollywood." Wasserman spent the next few years having lunch with long-time MCA personnel. A few were still employed, and many had left voluntarily or were asked to leave.

The lack of respect extended into the work environment. Although Bronfman Jr. could be pleasant, Bension never knew where he stood. After one meeting, Bension returned to his office and told his team, "Boys, things are going to change around here. This is a family business; what is *sound* business is secondary."

Bronfman Jr. hired attorney Howard Weitzman and Sandy Climan to oversee the theme parks. The weekend before their start, there was a leadership meeting at Bronfman's house with Bension and some Seagram folks to go over "strategy."

On Sunday morning, Bronfman Jr. called Dan Slusser and said: "I've just retained Rem Koolhaas. He will be here on Monday to look around to give us some ideas about what improvements we can make." Slusser asked what areas he should show Koolhaas and Bronfman said whatever he wanted to see.

Koolhaas was a world famous Dutch architect. He was planning enhancements to the studio and business center districts with additional soundstages, post-production studios, and office space. Many of those elements would be placed near Lankershim Boulevard. Also part of the master plan were a lake, as many as eight hotels, a new circulation system, and a heliport. The entire property was subject to a Hollywood makeover. The good news was Bill DeCinces (the studio manager and a licensed architect) was ecstatic.

An hour later, Slusser got a call from Weitzman and was told that he would head up the master plan effort and that he [Weitzman] had already talked to Koolhaas. The call was the first time that Weitzman and Slusser had ever spoken. Koolhaas submitted some plans (which Slusser never saw) and a bill in the multiple $100,000 range. By 1997, his plan was dead.

The Recreation Division was spending more money than most of the other divisions combined and their profitability and contribution to the bottom line was substantial. During the quarterly reviews when Bension and his staff would discuss their business plans, Weitzman, Meyer, and

Climan would doze off. When Frank Biondi attended the meetings, he would sit back and read *Cable Today* the entire time. Bension felt the only one paying attention was the CFO, Bruce Hack. Bension felt this was a company in big trouble. Sheinberg was also unimpressed. He said, "I think the ultimate 'fire-ee' will be Edgar [Bronfman Jr.]. There comes a time when there's nobody else to blame."

By mid-November 1995, Dan Slusser had enough. He sent his first letter of resignation to Weitzman and Meyer. The next day Weitzman contacted Slusser and asked to have dinner. They met at the Bistro Gardens, and Weitzman asked Slusser to stay. He was told that he was a vital part of the team. He was offered a six-figure salary increase and a promise of a significant year-end bonus. Slusser said that it was not about the money, but he felt it did not register. He accepted the offer and decided to try to make it work.

A short time later, Weitzman told him to work with Jonathan Waxman of Ark Consulting to remodel the commissary. Slusser pointed out that the commissary had been remodeled a couple of years earlier, and if we had that kind of money to spend, there were some places where it would be far more productive. Weitzman said, "Get used to the new way, it's not about money."

He was right. For a company in debt, money was being wasted on all sorts of projects. For example, Slusser's team broke through the 14$^{th}$ floor to provide for a circular staircase to the 15th floor so the key executives did not have to wait for the elevator. They were required to work with Juan Montoya, Edgar Bronfman Jr.'s wife's decorator on the top three floors. Montoya was one of the most cooperative and considerate decorators Slusser had ever worked with.

Unfortunately, he had never decorated an office environment where the requirements of the job dictate the layout, and the furnishings must serve the employee. Most of the furniture did not fit and had to be modified. The cabinets were hung too high to be reached by the employees. The holes in the paneling had to be repaired. The desks and chairs were of residential construction, not commercial grade. All of the furniture had to be braced or rebuilt. Most of the items were ordered late and had long lead times. Some of the electrical outlets and telephone boxes had to be relocated at the last minute in executive offices because the placement of the furniture, directed by the designer, was inconsistent with the wishes of the executives assigned to the offices. In the end, Slusser just rejected any further change requests by both designers and started moving people into their offices and dealing with their needs so that they could function.

They added personal bathrooms, with showers, to four offices on the 14$^{th}$ floor, and two on the 15$^{th}$ and 16$^{th}$ floors, so the key executives did not have to walk twenty feet to the restroom on the floor. They demolished the 16th floor that had been Jules Stein's office facing the street and the board room facing the studio. Then they built a new board room facing Lankershim Blvd. and a new office for Bronfman Jr. so he could see the studio out of his window. The project, once completed, cost over $10 million. That was more than the expense of the tower when it was originally built.

Then the finger pointing started. Fortunately, Slusser's staff always kept detailed records of all studio construction projects and all of his memos to Weitzman about the designers' changes and cost overruns. He had written numerous memos to Weitzman about Ron Meyers's decorator Naomi Leff, who was rude, disorganized, and had little regard for anyone and no regard for their money. Change orders were frequent. They had to pull up the tile in Bronfman's bathroom to put down marble. They had to remove the paneling on his office walls after it was finished. The entertainment center was modified three times.

Then came the issue of home screening rooms. Weitzman told Slusser that all of the new executive vice presidents were talking about building screen rooms at their homes. He asked what the policy was. Was there a cap on how much they could spend? Slusser replied that Wasserman and Sheinberg both had screening rooms at home, and they paid for them out of their own pockets. In fact, he had just finished installing a system in Sheinberg's beach house. Slusser also mentioned that producer Tom Pollock made a deal with Sheinberg to take a salary reduction until his was paid for. He reminded Weitzman that these projects were expensive because it was necessary to build a room inside a room so that people could not hear the theater in every other room. His response was, "That's not going to fly." Slusser never heard any more.

During another meeting, Weitzman told Slusser that he had been sitting down with some people and was going to start to bring them on the lot so he would need to have space for them. Hosting production companies were par for the course, so Slusser asked for an idea of the people Weitzman was talking with. Weitzman said, "Penny Marshall, Danny DeVito, and I just made a deal with Cristina Ferrare. She was going to do a new audience show here for the tourists on the hill." Puzzled, Slusser asked if Universal Television was distributing the show. Weitzman said no, the Family Channel was. Ferrare's husband was Tony Thomopoulos, CEO of Family Channel.

Slusser asked Weitzman if he had talked to Bension about this. He said no and then wondered why. Slusser reminded him that the Recreation Division would have to bear the cost of construction and the show since the studio did not do tourist attractions. That was Bension's area. Weitzman ordered Slusser to tell Bension what he was going to do with Ferrare and how much it will help attract visitors.

The next day, Slusser talked with Bension and shared what he knew. Bension said to tell Weitzman no, that is not the type of show that would appeal to the majority of the theme park visitors, and the exposure on the Family Channel would do nothing for attendance.

Slusser told Bension he suspected that this was Weitzman's idea because he represented her previous husband, John DeLorean. However, he was not sure who might be blessing it. Slusser suggested to Bension that he have Molly Miles put together a presentation on the demographics to prove that this is not the target market for tour visitors, and as such, not a good use of his resources, and *that* should put it to bed.

Miles made a persuasive case that the Family Channel audience was not the theme park's target audience. After Miles had left the room, Weitzman said they were already committed, so, "Let's get started." Slusser returned to the nagging question of who would pay for the production. "If it is not the tour or the studio, what are my options? Your overhead account?" Weitzman said, "Let's go."

They built a set on the edge of the tour so there could be a tram drop-off point for the audience. After construction, Brian Mulligan called Slusser, yelling, "Why did you charge the cost of that show to Howard's [Weitzman's] overhead?" Slusser barked back, "Because he told me to and there was no place else for it to go." The show ran for four years.

Around March 1996, just as it started to look like things were settling down, and the reckless spending was ending, Slusser received a call from Bronfman Jr. They had hired Frank Biondi Jr. as chairman, and they needed to relocate him and his secretary from Viacom in New York to the MCA office in New York for a couple of months until they could be moved to Universal City.

Slusser flew to New York to meet with Frank and his secretary. After touring the offices on Park Avenue, which were decorated with Jules Stein antiques, he got a list of the moves they wanted, the wall changes, and the new furniture. Then Slusser contacted Bronfman Jr. and told him how much the changes would cost. He reminded his boss that Biondi Jr. was only going to be there for less than 90 days, and he would be traveling to the West Coast most of the time. Bronfman Jr. said we needed to make our new chairman comfortable.

A few weeks later Biondi Jr. called Slusser and said he was going to be on the West Coast for a few days and needed to do an uplink broadcast for a talk he was giving on high-definition television. It was originally going to be uplinked from CBS in New York. Universal Studios did not have the broadcast capabilities that CBS did. After Slusser had priced it out, he told him they could save tens of thousands of dollars if he flew back to New York a day early. Despite that advice his answer was, "Let's do it here."

The frugal MCA guys were stunned. However, they did as they were told. Slusser stayed on the set with Dick Stump and Lou Wolf. They looked at each other in amazement. What Bondi Jr. knew about HDTV was less than most 8$^{th}$-grade students already know, and they paid an ungodly sum to share it with a group of people who understood HDTV thoroughly.

Shortly after that, the real estate liquidation started. Slusser and his team consisting of real estate attorney Jerry Blair and studio manager Bill DeCinces were told to start selling the New York office, the apartment in the Sherry Netherlands, the two apartments in Trump Tower, the Stein flat in London, and the music company offices in Piccadilly Square. Sid Sheinberg and Steven Spielberg bought the Trump Tower apartments. Slusser made a few profitable rental deals on the Sherry apartments with producer Joel Silver.

The properties went fast, but it was like watching MCA history disappear. Jules Stein, Wasserman, and many world-famous celebrities had stayed in the MCA flat in London. Slusser was the last one there and spent the night reading the guest book. It had the signatures of many famous people. He is proud to say he was the last person to sign that guest book. He brought it home and gave it to Mike Samuel, corporate secretary for the archives. Its current whereabouts are unknown.

Unfortunately, as fast as they were generating capital money, back at the studio Bronfman Jr. and his leadership team were spending it faster. The re-engineering was taking a human toll. The severance packages were great and good people were leaving the company at a rapid pace.

In spring of 1996, Bension and Glenn Gumpel came to Tony Sauber to inform him that they were hiring someone else to take over his principal duties. They asked if he would be willing to stay with the company at the same compensation. Although at first it came as a shock, to Sauber it made sense. Bension was staffing up with his set of lieutenants, generally younger, hard-driving, high-tech people, and Sauber had long said he would be retiring at the start of 2000.

The sharp, young entertainment lawyer that Bension and Gumpel hired was a good fit for his superiors but did not treat Sauber with the respect he felt he deserved. The new hire expected the veteran to "jump" when he was asked to do something. Sauber was looking forward to retirement. Then, the new attorney left the company after only one year.

## Exit Bension

Weitzman was spreading his wings. He was trying to touch everything. Some within the company fretted that Weitzman thought he was much smarter than everyone else was. Then Weitzman started pushing for control of the Recreation Division and that pitted him against Ron Bension.

Dan Slusser had an office nearby Bension, and the two men would often talk. Slusser thought that Bension was a bright, young, hard charging, and accomplished executive who had studied under Jay, and Bension was not giving any quarter. Slusser advised patience, but that was not Bension's strong suit.

Bension knew his days were numbered. He recognized that Weitzman was a terrible business person on most occasions and a bad guy always. The only thing Bension cared about was what his division was doing. He was totally committed to the $4 billion in projects they were actively building and the team of people he had brought together. He resigned himself to keeping the team focused, and if and when he left, he would walk out with a check, his integrity, and never look back.

One Monday, Weitzman asked Bension to join him for dinner at Dan Tana's in West Hollywood. Weitzman wanted to "clear the air and develop a better working relationship." Bension's dislike for the man was well known, and he knew that Weitzman was frustrated that Bension did not report directly to him.

Unbeknownst to Bension, Weitzman also invited Glenn Gumpel. They were having drinks when Weitzman began pitching that they were a team and that Bension needed to join in. He said they all loved the veteran MCA man, and he could be a real asset as part of the "team."

Weitzman was offering to help. Bension told him no, that he did not think he needed the help. He told them that he and Sandy Climan were not smart businesspeople and knew nothing about themed entertainment.

Then Weitzman got up to go the bathroom. Gumpel yelled at Bension, "You can't do that; you can't say those things to him. He is trying to help you." Bension told Gumpel, "Yes, I can, and I just did. Weitzman wants my job or for me to be his boy, neither of which are going to happen."

Weitzman returned and more sternly told Bension how important it was for him to get in line with the "team." Bension replied, "If being on the team means I have to agree with you, you can go fuck yourself." They never did get to their entrees.

What Bension was not taking into consideration was that Ron Meyer was letting Weitzman do whatever he wished, and Bronfman Jr. was oblivious as to what was going on. When Bension had enough, he gave Bronfman Jr. an ultimatum. That strategy did not go well.

On November 6, 1996, Ron Meyer, MCA president and CEO, announced a management shakeup in its theme park division that included the departure of Ron Bension. He would not elaborate on the reasons for Bension's resignation, saying that a replacement would be chosen shortly. Bension lasted 18 months with Seagram. By the time he left MCA at the end of 1996, the steel had risen from the ground at IOA and the foundations were being poured in Osaka. It would be left to others to see those projects through to their completion.

Weitzman told members of his staff that the reason that Bension had to go was that he was tired of being like the circus owner's son who wanted to have a say in running things but had to sneak under the tent because of the MCA veteran.

Jay felt that firing Ron Bension was one of the biggest mistakes in the Recreation Division's history. "I just had too much Jay Stein in me," Bension once said. Although Jay retired because he did not think he could work for Matsushita, he felt that Seagram was worse. He could never imagine a more incompetent, inept, wasteful, extravagant, miscast group of untalented prima donnas who systematically emasculated a great company.

Bronfman and the ill-suited team he hired took a proven, well-managed company and allowed key executives to be fired (Ron Bension being the most noteworthy), or let them leave and replaced them with overpaid, new, greedy, spoiled, arrogant, reckless spending, narcissistic wannabes who almost destroyed the company.

That started the internal discussions about what to do now about a replacement. Weitzman indicated he could keep doing what he was doing and absorb the theme parks at the same time. Slusser thought that was a crazy idea, knowing it was an all-consuming job and required full-time dedication if it was going to continue to grow. He suggested Tom Williams.

Meyers told Slusser that he thought that Williams would not want to leave Florida. Slusser knew that Williams was a MCA man and would do whatever was required. Even if he did not want to move back to Los Angeles, Florida was going to be the flagship of the theme parks, and Williams could run the operations from there.

Instead, Weitzman hired Cathy Nichols, a consultant from McKinsey & Company, to run the division. She was essentially a numbers analyst with no experience or even interest in theme parks. Nichols never walked through the parks to observe how things were being run and had no interest in participating in the creative process. On her occasional trips into one of the parks for some specific reason, she would step over rather than pick up trash. By the fall of 1999, she was gone, and Tom Williams became president of the division.

Meanwhile, Slusser was getting more and more frustrated. His constant run-ins with Weitzman and the lack of involvement from Meyers, Bronfman Jr., and Biondi were too much. Now 58 years old, he began to reflect on how many good people had left, how many amateurs were running the show, and how much money had been wasted. Although he had three years left on a five-year employment contract, he dusted off his resignation letter and submitted it. He was gone by mid-January 1997. He urged his bosses to give Jim Watters his old job as he was the only chance they had of continuing to move forward. Weitzman said he wanted to interview other people.

Bronfman's plans for Orlando were becoming grander and more ambitious. He wanted to buy more land. Land meant more theme parks, hotels, shops, and restaurants. On January 26, 1998, Universal entered negotiations to purchase 2,000 acres from Lockheed Martin. The site would allow for eastward expansion adjacent to the convention center. Another thing he wanted (because Disney had one) was a water park. Later in 1998 he purchased Wet n' Wild, an existing Orlando attraction.

Shortly before the grand opening of IOA, a reporter from the *Orlando Sentinel* asked someone at USF to put them in touch with a person who could describe the origins of IOA. Sauber was asked and authorized to speak on behalf of the company. The article that subsequently appeared on May 21, 1999, correctly quoted Sauber about Jay's prolonged flash of creativity in May and June 1990 and described Ron Bension's ability to fine-tune the attractions and secure key rights.

However, Seagram owned Universal by that time, and the Seagram executives were apparently outraged at the obvious implication that Seagram had nothing to contribute to the park's creativity. A high-ranking executive criticized Sauber for putting such emphasis on Jay and Bension. Sauber did not care about the criticism. He was near retirement and wanted to make sure the record was correct.

In January 2000, Tony Sauber retired. He realized after Bension's firing that he was the only person left with both institutional memory and the necessary connections with all the rights holders involved in IOA. That is why the Seagram upper management urged him to stay. By 1998, they allowed him to work half time or less at full salary and benefits until 2000. Sauber could not have been happier. It was a great transition to retirement, and he could spend his last few years being the "expert" who could help out, advise, and sometimes mentor others. His job was to do mainly the "soft work" of keeping the rights holders happy, all while working three days a week, about 5 hours a day, except when traveling. His retirement party on January 6, 2000, was an exceptionally fancy affair. At the party, he was subject to a roster of humorous testimonial speakers, including Jay and Bension. Sauber thought it not a bad way to celebrate his 59th birthday. A week later, another retirement party was held for him in Orlando.

Universal's Islands of Adventure may have been a creative success, but it was a marketing disaster. From a marketing perspective, the only thing Universal did was confuse the consumer. When the Florida project was first announced, it was known as Universal City Florida. Then in November 1997, that name was shortened to Universal Florida. To launch the newly expanded resort, Edgar Bronfman Jr. came up with the name Universal Studios Escape.

Starting March 26, 1998, Universal Florida was no longer. The name was part of a much bigger plan to establish Universal as a brand equal to Disney. He said, "We're a little edgier. What is Disney? Disney is family, it's fun, it's warm, it's safe. We're not." Bronfman said Universal was "based on energy, exhilaration, excitement. And that means we're going to skew to a slightly older audience. North of 8, north of 9— that's who we're going after, plus parents." He believed Universal could "be leveraged into a brand if you can identify what it means and then take that meaning and generate revenue across new businesses."

Bronfman Jr. felt that many would want to escape from Disney's family-friendly resort for something a bit edgier. The plan was to focus advertising dollars on the Florida market with the hope that people who were visiting Walt Disney World would stay an extra day or two. A $60 million advertising plan was launched, and another $100 million of advertising was spent in conjunction with Universal marketing partners, such as Coca-Cola and Dodge.

Then Bronfman Jr. hired Elaine Garafolo to market the expansion. Conventional wisdom would suggest that Universal should have been talking about a brand-new theme park with cutting-edge rides, immersive theming, and popular characters. Instead, she focused on trying to sell the entire resort, as her boss wanted. The result was confusion. The park got lost.

A perplexed Michael Eisner said of Universal's marketing approach, "So far, their strategy—and I'm not giving away a strategy that's a secret—they don't spend a dollar marketing outside of Orlando, they're only going to cannibalize their own park." Eisner was right. Universal's marketing plan was flawed, and the park got off to a very slow start. First-year attendance was only 3.4 million, well below expectations. Ron Meyer tried to put a positive spin on it and said, "We just want them for two days instead of one. The good news for us is that we don't need a big piece of Disney. We just need a shave."

Jay was not invited to the grand opening.

Universal did not fare well under Bronfman Jr.'s leadership. He lost a fortune of his family's money, and was fleeced by Barry Diller, Vivendi, and most of his Hollywood peers. Bronfman Jr. did hire some good people such as Doug Morris. Nevertheless, many of his other executives turned out to be disasters. Sandy Climan, Dick Costolo, and Frank Biondi lasted only a few months after Bension left. They were not smart, totally fish out of water with no business acumen, and were so preoccupied with politics and "what would Edgar do or think" that they could not make a decision. When they did make decisions, they were solely based on politics and even then, they would attempt to build deniability around their involvement. Compared to the culture at MCA that Bension grew up with, it was no wonder he felt a sense of release. Ron Meyer, with his excellent interpersonal skills, is still there. Things did not turn out so well for Weitzman. Not long after Bension's exit, Weitzman was fired for lying to Bronfman, Jr. about a deal with Kodak.

Today, in charge of the incredibly successful Universal parks, are people that were hired by Jay and Bension. Tom Williams, who successfully charted the unsteady course of multiple owners over the past couple of decades, led the division into the powerhouse it is today. For a company that has changed corporate ownership five times since Wasserman sold MCA to Matsushita, it is an incredible record. Jay said, "Tom Williams is the right man to be in charge."

Bension hired Larry Kurzweil in 1996 to run CityWalk, and he became USH President in 2000 when Tom Williams moved up the corporate ladder. Bension also rehired Glenn Gumpel, who has built Universal Studios Japan into a multibillion-dollar property of its own.

# Epilogue

Ever since Jay took over the Studio Tour in 1967, he wanted to prove that Universal could compete with Disney at every level despite overwhelming odds and obstacles, both external and internal. It took twenty years to get Universal Studios Florida open, but when it did, Jay knew he had created a template that would not only succeed in Hollywood and Orlando but could go on to dominate the worldwide market for movie theme parks. His follow-up, the unrealized Cartoon World, could have been the biggest thing since Disneyland.

For Jay, the whole experience felt like war. It was just he and a small band of loyal troops against a formidable foe. He would never have the manpower or the resources of his enemy, so he had to be more strategic. To achieve total victory, Jay would have to learn who were his allies, who were his enemies, and who needed to be manipulated. There was no other option. Like his hero, General George Patton, said, "In case of doubt, attack."

The birth, survival, and eventual metamorphosis of Universal is an amazing story of sheer ambition, audacity, inspiration, innovation, and a mind-boggling combination of advances and reversals, creativity and commercialism, which is full of canny business strategy occasionally leavened with just plain dumb luck, both good and bad. It is a fascinating and complex David and Goliath story.

Jay spent over twenty years trying, persuading, creating, cajoling, strategizing, demanding, fighting, presenting, defending, justifying, collaborating, photographing, spying, sketching, motivating, demonstrating, convincing, compromising, manipulating, and persevering to make Universal credible and the fierce competitor it is today. USF would never exist without Jay's total belief and commitment that they could succeed.

Carl Laemmle lost control of Universal City in the late 1930s, and it was not until MCA purchased the property and the studio in the late 1950s and early 1960s that stability reigned. That all changed in 1990 when MCA went from Matsushita (electronics) to Seagram's (liquor) to Vivendi (water and sewers) to General Electric (pretty much everything), and then Comcast in 2009. General Electric was looking for the exit and found a willing partner in Comcast. In December 2009, a new partnership was formed to control NBC Universal. In a deal valued at $30 billion, Comcast would own 51% of the company, and General Electric would own the remaining 49%. The transaction was not simple. First, General Electric needed to buy out Vivendi's 20% share for $5.8 billion. Then the deal required passing muster with federal regulators, which it did. In February 2013, Comcast bought the remaining shares from General Electric.

Then came Comcast's January 2014 announcement to stock analysts in Las Vegas. For theme park fans, it must have sounded like they hit the jackpot. "We're doubling down on theme parks," according to Comcast's Brian Roberts. Steve Burke said, "We think there is a lot of 'there' there in the theme-park business for many years to come and that we have a low market share—and only one way to go." Although many market analysts expected Comcast to shed the theme park division as General Electric had been considering, Burke's experienced eye recognized that the business was an untapped growth engine. He knew that theme parks were one of the few areas of stable entertainment industry growth outside of cable television.

Burke pledged to invest at least $500 million per year in new attractions and upgrades to the North American parks in perpetuity. The goal was to open a new attraction every year at both Universal parks. Universal was going full steam ahead. Jay said, "Put your money on him [Burke]. He is one of the few people who understands the value of a one-of-a-kind, bigger-than-life attraction. It may cost a lot of money, but it is going to pay off."

Throughout all of the changes, under the leadership of Tom Williams, the theme parks were the only MCA division to survive and thrive. In 2016, the parks are expected to generate over $2 billion in profits. Universal opened its sixth hotel in Orlando. They now have 5,200 rooms with an annual occupancy rate of over 90%. There are more hotels on the way. Universal is also building a theme park in Beijing. Williams told Tony Sauber, "We have our hands full, but we're having a ball."

In 2015, Williams entered the International Association of Amusement Parks and Attractions (IAAPA) Hall of Fame.

Universal Studios Hollywood, Universal Studios Florida, and Islands of Adventure are the foundation, in fact, the entirety of what Comcast is now spending billions on to expand. After years of neglect and limited reinvestment from previous owners, they discovered with Harry Potter that the themed destination business requires creativity and reinvestment. Big bets on great products have always paid off. From single rides like Back to the Future, Earthquake, and Jurassic Park, to new parks across the globe, if you have spent the money and develop best-in-class attractions and environments, and then execute, your investment will pay off handsomely. Williams deserves credit for implementing what Jay considered his vision for expansion and growth. Jay has been the first to admit that he could not succeed in such a changing environment.

On June 22, 2016, Comcast announced a new five-year plan for the development of Universal City. The plan will reorient many of its soundstage production facilities to the east near its back lot, as it makes way for additional space to expand its theme park. Driving these changes is the recognition that much of the on-the-lot production has shifted to a mix of scripted television, live-audience shows, sitcoms, and new media projects, and as feature films migrate to other states and countries offering generous incentives. More importantly, the theme parks generate more profits than the movies or television. After 25 years, reality has caught up with Jay's vision.

Theme parks are like movies. They have a finite life. What may be a hit today is forgotten tomorrow. Sure, there are some blockbusters with a long life and multiple sequels, but those are rare. Nothing lasts forever. You need to reinvest. Recreate. Find the right characters, supply the correct number of JayBangs, and sell it to the world in a creative way. If you can reuse the basic mechanism, all the better. That is the Universal difference. That is Jay Stein.

# Appendix

These were the key executives at MCA Recreation Services and at Universal Studios Florida (Operations and Planning & Development) as of April 19, 1989:

## MCA Recreation Services Divisional Executives

- *Jay Stein*, Chairman and CEO.
- *Ron Bension*, President and COO.
- *Jack McDaniel*, Executive Vice President. Duties: Broad executive responsibility for the entire Recreation Services Group. Oversees a variety of special projects for Universal Studios Florida (USF) and in his absence is authorized to act upon Jay's behalf.
- *David Weitzner*, President, World-Wide Marketing. Duties: Coordination of the activities of all marketing departments (including USF) within the Recreation Services Group.
- *Barry Upson*, Executive Vice President, P & D. Duties: Responsible for the activities of the Planning & Development teams in both Los Angeles and Florida. From time-to-time he is called upon to critique the development and progress of the European and Japanese projects.
- *Bernie Fisher*, Executive Vice President. Duties: Preparation and review of all financial analyses for entities within the Recreation Services Group. He also devotes a substantial amount of his time to the business analysis of foreign project endeavors.
- *Tony Sauber*, Vice President, Business and Legal Affairs. Duties: As the senior legal counsel for the Recreation Services Group, he is responsible for the review and execution of all contractual documents.
- *Warren Holcomb*, Vice President, Administration. Duties: Responsibilities include the negotiation and administration of all organized labor agreements to which the Los Angeles and Yosemite operations are signatory. He is also responsible for the establishment of personnel policies and wage and salary administration for the entire group including USF.

## Universal Studios Florida, Operations

- *Steve Lew*, President. Duties: Primary focus during pre-opening phase of the USF project is the solicitation and execution of corporate sponsorship agreements. He is also the primary contact and liaison for projects in all state, local and community matters.
- *Tom Williams*, Executive Vice President, Operations. Duties: Management of all USF operating departments. Specific duties include the maintenance of the USF pre-opening budget as well as the negotiation of all concessionaire agreements.
- *Gary Faulkner*, Vice President and CFO. Duties: Responsibilities include the financial management of all matters pertaining to the USF project excluding capital expenditures. Also responsible for the preparation of all financial proformas as well as the interface with a consortion of banks in the transmittal of progress reports and draw down of construction loans.
- *Bob Reitman*, Executive Vice President, Marketing. Duties: Day-to-day administration of the USF marketing group.
- *Rick Larson*, Vice President, Administration. Duties: Administration of the Human Resources department. He is also responsible for the legal affairs and purchasing functions.

## Universal Studios Florida, Planning & Development

- *Mike Bartlett*, Senior Vice President, Planning & Development. Duties: Responsibilities include the management and supervision of all Planning & Development personnel assigned to the USF project.
- *David Milhausen*, Vice President, Finance and Administration. Duties: Preparation and maintenance of all USF capital project budget.
- *Bill Moss*, Vice President, Construction. Duties: Negotiation of all capital construction agreements. Also responsible for the supervision and coordination of all on-site construction related activities.
- *Peter Alexander*, Vice President, Show Development. Duties: Responsible for the creative development of all shows and attractions within the USF program.
- *Keith James*, Vice President, Production. Duties: Negotiation of all show and ride vendor contracts. Supervision of all personnel charged with the responsibility of installing show and ride components.
- *Bob Ward*, Vice President, Design. Duties: Responsible for the exterior visual development of USF including all architectural design, site planning, and area development.

- *Terry Winnick*, Vice President, Special Projects. Duties: Coordinating the interface between P & D and Operations. Also assigned to a variety of special projects such as the development of programs and events in support of the USF marketing effort.

*Jay, in 2016, long mellowed and retired.*

# Acknowledgments

It was not my intention to write this book. I was working on a book about Walt Disney's Mineral King when Jay Stein contacted me shortly after the release of *Universal vs. Disney: The Unofficial Guide*. While researching that book, I tried to contact Jay but he was considered such a recluse, nobody ever expected him to participate. Moreover, they were right. Then I got his email. We talked. I was hooked. I pushed the Walt book to the side and dived deep into the world of MCA. Throughout the book I use the familiar "Jay" versus his full name. As you will see, the whole Stein name thing plays a part in the story and I just wanted to make my life a lot easier.

Thank you, Jay. And to Connie, his wonderful wife. This book is dedicated to you.

Tony Sauber is a remarkable man. How he put up with Jay for so many years just boggles my mind. Without Tony, this book would not have been possible.

Robert Finkelstein. Nice foreword. I am honored.

I am indebted to Leslie Haber. She took on the challenge of editing this book and I cannot overstate how much I needed her help.

Some of the best moments came from the testimony from Jay's peers. I hope I got it right. Thank you Ron Bension, Gary Goddard, Steve Hayman, Hal Kaufman, Allan Keen, Steve Lew, Jack McDaniel, Bruce Miller, Ron Miller, Skip Paul, Dan Slusser, Richard Swann, Barry Upson, Cliff Walker, Peter Alexander, Phil Hettema, Bob Ward, David Weitzner, Tom Williams, and Terry Winnick. There are more. And I thank them as well.

Writing books is not my full-time job. So I would like to thank all of those who have been inconvenienced in any way as I put this ship into the bottle. Thelma Herrea, Jim Korkis, Jeff Kurtti, Michelle McCarty, Bob McLain, Benny Boo O'Malley, Katherine Padilla, Todd Reagan, Dennis Ritchey, Greg Fisher, and tram loads of others.

# About the Author

Sam Gennawey is a prolific author and Disney historian, a contributor to *Planning Los Angeles* and other books, as well as a columnist for the popular MiceChat website.

His unique point of view built on his passion for history, his professional training as an urban planner, and his obsession with theme parks has brought speaking invitations from Walt Disney Imagineering, the Walt Disney Family Museum, Disney Creative, the American Planning Association, the California Preservation Foundation, the California League of Cities, and many Disneyana clubs, libraries and podcasts.

He is currently a senior associate at the planning firm of KPA.

## Other Books by Sam Gennawey

*Walt Disney and the Promise of Progress City, 2$^{nd}$ ed.* (2015)

*Universal vs. Disney: The Unofficial Guide to American Theme Parks' Greatest Rivalry* (2014)

*The Disneyland Story: The Unofficial Guide to the Evolution of Walt Disney's Dream* (2013)

# More Books from Theme Park Press

Theme Park Press is the largest independent publisher of Disney, Disney-related, and general interest theme park books in the world, with dozens of new releases each year.

Our authors include Disney historians like Jim Korkis and Didier Ghez, Disney animators and artists like Mel Shaw and Eric Larson, and such Disney notables as Van France, Tom Nabbe, and Bill "Sully" Sullivan, as well as many promising first-time authors.

We're always looking for new talent.

In March 2016, we published our 100th title. For a complete catalog, including book descriptions and excerpts, please visit:

**ThemeParkPress.com**

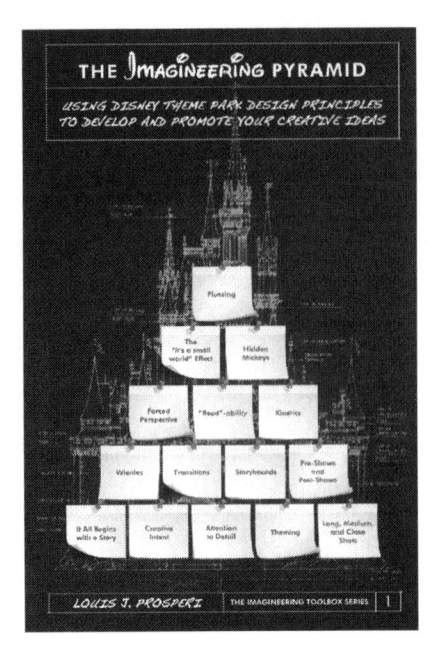

## Learn from the Disney Imagineers

Creativity. Innovation. Success. That's Disney Imagineering. It was the Imagineers who brought Walt Disney's dreams to life. Now *you* can tap into the principles of Imagineering to make *your* personal and professional dreams come true.

themeparkpress.com/books/imagineering-pyramid.htm

## The Secrets of Disney's Success

Disney's former director of Corporate Synergy, Lorraine Santoli, gives a first-person, behind-the-scenes account of how she and her colleagues spearheaded Disney's financial and cultural recovery during the Michael Eisner and Frank Wells era.

themeparkpress.com/books/disney-marketing-machine.htm

## Counting Pixie Dust

How much pixie dust is there at Walt Disney World, anyway? Can you count it? Nope. But there are many things at Disney World you *can* count, and Tony Caselnova has counted and measured and calculated and quantified them all.

themeparkpress.com/books/disney-numbers.htm

## Walt Disney and the Pursuit of Progress

Walt Disney is well-known for animation, theme parks, and Mickey Mouse. But his real passion was technology, and how he could use it to shape a better, prosperous, peaceful future for everyone.

themeparkpress.com/books/great-big-beautiful-tomorrow.htm

## Delivering Disney Magic

From his start as a submarine captain in Disneyland during the summer of 1967, until his final years with Disney as a vice president of Imagineering, Chuck Shields discovered the methods behind the magic. In his long-awaited book, he tells you how to put those methods to work for your organization.

themeparkpress.com/books/disney-apprentice.htm

## A Year in the Life of Disneyland

And what a year! In 1955, Walt Disney's dream of a theme park, the first of its kind in the world, came true. Disney historian Jim Korkis' entertaining tale of an American pop culture icon is power-packed with details, and the most thorough account of Disneyland's early days ever published.

themeparkpress.com/books/disneyland-1955.htm

Printed in Great Britain
by Amazon